Pocket Professional Guide

Guide to

More Th
Essential-to-Know Species

Robert G. Sprackland, Ph.D.

Dedication

For Family who helped make so much of this book possible:
Tina Gardner, M.D., Joseph Gardner, and nephews Jake Gardner and Luke
Gardner, for bringing the love and devotion of Natural History into a fourth
generation; and To my most faithful and longtime friend, King.
May he rest in peace.

Guide to Lizards
Project Team
Editor: Tom Mazorlig
Design: Angela Stanford
Indexer: Elizabeth Walker

T.F.H. Publications, Inc.
One TFH Plaza
Third and Union Avenues
Neptune City, NJ 07753

T.F.H. Publications
President/CEO: Glen S. Axelrod
Executive Vice President: Mark E.
Johnson
Publisher: Christopher T. Reggio
Production Manager: Kathy Bontz

Printed and bound in China

07 08 09 10 11 1 3 5 7 9 8 6 4 2
Library of Congress Cataloging-in-Publication Data
Sprackland, Robert G.
  Guide to lizards : more than 300 essential-to-know species / Robert G. Sprackland.
    p. cm.
  Includes bibliographical references and index.
  ISBN 978-0-7938-1276-9 (alk. paper)
  1. Lizards--Guidebooks. 2. Lizards--Encyclopedias. 3. Lizards--Identification. I. Title.
  QL666.L2S73 2010
  597.95--dc22
                        2009054161

This book has been published with the intent to provide accurate and authoritative
information in regard to the subject matter within. While every reasonable precaution
has been taken in preparation of this book, the author and publisher expressly disclaim
responsibility for any errors, omissions, or adverse effects arising from the use or appli-
cation of the information contained herein. The techniques and suggestions are used at
the reader's discretion and are not to be considered a substitute for veterinary care. If
you suspect a medical problem consult your veterinarian.

The Leader In Responsible Animal Care For Over 50 Years!®
www.tfh.com

Table of Contents

Introduction

young white-throated monitor (*Varanus albigularis*)

This book is intended to address two audiences interested in the extraordinary animals known as lizards. These are the ecotourists who venture off the beaten track and expect more from a holiday than lying about poolside sipping piña coladas, and the professional and amateur herpetocultural communities who are interested in thumbnail species sketches. Both audiences represent rapidly growing and financially powerful interests. According to the International Ecotourism Society, some 20 to 40 percent of all tourism is ecotourism, defined as "responsible travel to natural areas that conserves the environment and sustains the well-being of local people." For 1994, that amounted to $166 billion spent by people getting back to nature; by 2012 it is expected to reach $473 billion. That segment of the business is growing rapidly, accounting for a 10 to 30 percent rise in travel dollars per year (depending on the region), and presently accounts for about 25 percent of total tourism dollars, according to The International Ecotourism Society. Perhaps as twenty-first century First World people become more enmeshed in longer work weeks, struggling to survive against the inane "24/7" concept, the allure of nature and perceived pristine habitats in the Third World is drawing them as tourists in ever

Many popular tourist destinations are home to spectacular lizards, including the Caribbean Islands. Here, travelers can see the impressive rock iguanas.

greater numbers. In 2008, for example, about 922 million tourists were international travelers.

Similarly, while much of the pet and animal market has been a flat line for the past several years, herpetoculture—the keeping of live reptiles and amphibians in terraria—has continued to grow. Though exact figures are not available, a consensus from three industry sources points to an American herpetocultural community equivalent to the population of the greater New York metropolitan area.

For travelers seeking to observe birds, mammals, or fishes, there is a wealth of pocket guidebooks from which to choose. Even many insect groups and marine invertebrates are well represented, but there are few general guides to lizards. This is remarkable—my personal bias fueled by lifelong fascination for the subject aside—when we consider the truly vast array of lizards on our small blue planet.

THE WORLD OF LIZARDS

As a group, lizards represent over 4,000 described species, and some 20 to 40 new species are named each year. They are the largest and most diverse group of land vertebrates at the ordinal level (that is, a group equal in rank to turtles, crocodiles, or rodents) and range in size from tiny geckos that could completely curl up on my thumbnail to 10-foot (3 m) giants. Some lizards have sticky toe pads and can easily climb glass or run across ceilings, while others run across the water. There are lizards with limbs longer than their bodies, lizards with comically tiny legs, and lizards with no legs at all. Some have large lidless eyes, some have fleshy turret-like eyelids, and others are eyeless. There are delicate butterfly-like gliders and adept swimmers, some with tiny blunt tongues and some with tongues longer than their body. They are found in deserts and forests, on mountains and seashores, in pristine wilderness and human trash heaps. They may live for a year or for decades, mate with many partners each season or live monogamously for life. Some are mute and some have voices. So varied are these reptiles that it is only with considerable difficulty that we herpetologists even attempt to define the group.

There are far too many species and varieties of lizards to include any but a small fraction in this book, and a complete account would no longer qualify as a "pocket guide"! Nevertheless, I have included about a tenth of the known species in this book, and they have been chosen to provide a sampling of species most likely or easily encountered by ecotourists, along with some notable rarities for which herpetologists are eager to get new information, and a variety of species commonly kept by zoos and private herpetoculturists. The literature and websites listed in the back of this book can lead you to additional information, and each was selected based on its accuracy and reputation.

If you are new to bush walking in search of lizards, start by moving slowly and scan the environment carefully. While many lizards will permit a close enough approach that you can take a decent photograph, you have to see them first, and lizard camouflage is quite effective. Once you get the hang of it, you may become hooked on lizard-watching, but then, as D. H. Lawrence once wrote, if men were as much men as lizards are lizards, they would certainly be worth watching.

Enjoy!

USING THIS GUIDE

Species Arrangement

Ecotourists, like lizards, are likely to turn up almost anywhere. Only Antarctica will lack the reptiles. Consequently, this book was prepared so it would be useful to the traveler who will, over time, visit more than one foreign land. For terrarium keepers, too, clustering species

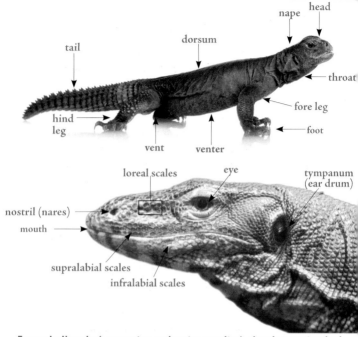

Example lizards (uromastyx and water monitor) showing anatomical terms used when discussing lizards.

by their distribution will provide a bit of additional insight into the species that may occur together naturally in the wild and, perhaps, in captivity as well. Therefore the species in this book are grouped among 10 geographic areas, making it easier for herpetologists, naturalists, travelers, and ecotourists to use. The regions, and their color-coded page headers, are:

1. North America, covering Canada and the United States (dark red)
2. Caribbean Islands (purple)
3. Mexico and Central America (dark green)
4. South America and the Galapagos (light yellow)
5. New Guinea, New Zealand, and Oceania (orange)
6. Australia (reddish brown)
7. Southeast and Eastern Asia (tan)
8. Southern Asia and the Middle East (brown)
9a. Continental Africa (green)

9b. Madagascar and Indian Ocean Islands (green)
10. Europe and Northern Asia (dark blue)

Within each geographical section, the lizards are arranged alphabetically by their scientific names. Some species occur in more than one region but are listed only in the region where they are most widespread. If you are in eastern Indonesia, for example, you may need to check both the New Guinea, New Zealand and Oceania *and* the Southeast and eastern Asia sections to identify a given species. On the last page of each section, there is a list of species that occur in that region but that are discussed in another section of this book. The list gives both the lizard and the region in which you will find that lizard's entry.

Species Entries

The entry for each species is organized in the following sections: scientific name, common name, family, length, habitat and range, natural history, care, and terrarium suitability index. The content of the sections are explained on the next few pages.

Scientific Name

All living things are assigned a scientific name when biologists formally describe them. For animals, the name must consist of a capitalized genus name and a never-capitalized trivial name. Together, both words compose the species name. For example, we humans are *Homo sapiens,* where *Homo* comes from the Greek word meaning "human" and *sapiens* is the Latin word for "wise." Most scientific names derive from actual words; they may come from any language but must be written in a Latinized form. Note also that a scientific name must also appear in italics or be underlined when in print. Examples of correctly written scientific names are: *Tyrannosaurus rex, Crotaphytus collaris, Phrynosoma douglassi,* and *Shinisaurus crocodilurus.* Each of those strange words means something. However, sometimes a taxonomist—the scientist who describes and names species—will make up a word that has no meaning whatsoever. One of the worst offenders was a taxonomist who lived in the middle to late nineteenth century and who was in a position to name scores of new species. His name was John Edward Gray, and as keeper of zoology at the British Museum of Natural History (now the Natural History Museum, London), he named many species of fishes, amphibians, reptiles, birds, and mammals. Among the names he bestowed that have no meaning in any language are some well-known skinks, including *Corucia*, *Egernia*, and *Tiliqua*. We may only imagine that he liked the sounds of the meaningless names.

In some cases, a scientific name will have a third part, such as in *Crotaphytus collaris baileyi*. This is the subspecific name, indicating that the animal in question belongs to one of the subspecies of the main species. Subspecies are assigned when there is a specific population of a species has some traits that set it apart from the rest of the species but this population is not so different that calling it a full species is warranted. The criteria for deciding if a subspecies is distinct enough to be called a full species are variable, and the status of subspecies often is controverisal.

A complete scientific name also includes the name or names of the scientists who described the animal, plus the year that the description was first published. These additional pieces of the name are never italicized. For an example, we'll use the Seram monitor: *Varanus ceramboensis* Philipp, Böhme, and Ziegler, 1999. In this example, the Seram monitor was described by three scientists (Kai Philipp, Wolfgang Böhme, and Thomas Ziegler) in a scientific journal in 1999. Sometimes, though, a describer's name and date appear in parentheses, as in *Varanus beccarii* (Doria, 1874). In this case, Count Doria named the lizard *Monitor beccarii* in 1874, but a later revising scientist placed the lizard into the genus *Varanus*. Because Doria was the first to describe the species, his name and publication date remain, but because the lizard is now in a different genus from the one in which it was first assigned, the describer's name and date are put in parentheses. Among the best known of the herpetologists are Europe's George Boulenger, John Gray, François Daudin, the Dumérils (father and son), Albert Günther, and Robert Mertens. Famous American describers include Spencer Baird, Charles Girard, Edward Hallowell, Leonard Stejneger, Edward Taylor, and Edward Cope.

The business of assigning—and in many cases altering—scientific names is the job of taxonomists. As new data become available, or as scientists with greater knowledge revise descriptions made by amateurs or people with limited information about a group, names may change. Though scientific names were intended to give stability to naming, many species are given many names before a "final" name sticks.

The third word in a scientific name indicates the subspecies, as in *Crotaphytus collaris baileyi,* **the western collared lizard. This one is performing a defensive display.**

Common Name

Common, or vernacular, names are those used by the non-scientist when talking about an animal. In this book, the common names given will generally be the English version of a name. Naturally, the common name given to an animal will be different in different languages. The animal called Komodo dragon by Americans is known locally on Komodo as the ora; the Mexican beaded lizard is known locally as *escorpión*, and so on.

Family

This section lists the taxonomic family in which the lizard resides. Taxonomic families are groups of genera (plural of genus) that are closely related. For example, collared lizards (genus *Crotaphytus*) and their closest relatives, the leopard lizards (genus *Gambelia*), are both united within the family Crotaphytidae. Some well-known lizard families include Agamidae (agamas), Chamaeleonidae (chameleons), Eublepharidae (eyelid geckos), Gekkonidae (true geckos), Iguanidae (iguanas), Lacertidae (true lizards), Phrynosomatidae (fence, spiny, and horned lizards), Polychrotidae (anoles), Scincidae (skinks), Teiidae (tegus and whiptails), and Varanidae (monitors). The number and status of lizard families is not settled, but current taxonomy generally recognizes about 40 families of lizards.

Family names always end with -idae. The nontechnical way to indicate a family is to use -id as a suffix, such as in iguanid, gekkonid,

Herpetologists measure lizards from snout to vent because many lizards lose their tails to predators and the tails may or may not regenerate. Here is a crested gecko with its freshly dropped tail.

and varanid. Formal family names are always capitalized; nontechnical names are not. The same rule applies to subfamilies, except that the suffix is -inae, as in Gekkoninae. The nontechnical form for a subfamily uses -ine as the suffix: gekkonines.

Length

The lengths of lizards are given in two numbers in this text. Because many lizards may lose their tails to predators or accidents, the standard measurement used by herpetologists is the snout-vent length (SVL), from the snout tip to the vent (cloaca, the shared opening for the reproductive, urinary, and digestive systems). Many species, though, tend to retain their tails, and intact tails can greatly increase the perceived length of the animal. Thus for each species I offer a maximum adult length, both as an SVL and a total length (TL) with an intact original tail. Measurements are given in inches, with millimeters in parentheses.

Habitat and Range

A general range map would be of limited use to a casual explorer, so I have included data that narrows down the places where you would be most likely to encounter a given species. For example, a lizard in the Southern Asia and Middle East section may be restricted to southern India, and then only in lowland swamps. The visitor to Iran should not, then, expect to see that south Asian species in Iran.

Natural History

Brief notes are given regarding distinctive characteristics or behaviors for each species, along with information that may help locate or identify specimens.

Care

Because many readers will also be herpetologists or herpetoculturists, basic information is given on the proper care of each lizard species in captivity. In most cases I give temperature ranges at which the lizards thrive, but readers should note that maximum temperatures are generally higher than should be used in all but very large terraria or should be restricted to a small basking area. If you are keeping lizards in captivity, their ability to withstand high temperatures must be offset by a simple way to escape to cooler areas. In this section, UV light and full-spectrum lighting refer to artificial lights that provide lizards with ultraviolet B waves, which are important for calcium metabolism. Be aware that many species are protected by local, national, and international laws. Before acquiring any lizard, reseach any applicable ordinances and stay within the confines of the law.

Terrarium Suitability Index

This is a numeric scale that indicates suitability of each species for captivity. Factors that are considered include disposition, hardiness, and breeding potential. More specifically, each lizard species is rated on a scale of 1 to 5, from most to least suitable for general captive conditions, as follows:

1: Beginner's level species that are easy to care for, are easy to breed, and resist illnesses.

2: Good animals for moderately experienced keepers; likely to breed and accept a variety of foods.

3: Moderately hardy and tend to feed after a brief settling-in period. May require a specialized diet, but readily eat if that item is provided. Generally unlikely to breed given present husbandry knowledge.

4: Suitable only for veteran and successful keepers with facilities and resources needed to help assure success.

5: Extremely difficult to maintain, unsuitable for captivity, or critically endangered in the wild. These animals may refuse to feed, become highly susceptible to diseases, or show aggressiveness that could be injurious to the animals, handlers, or both.

North America

Covering Canada and the United States

desert spiny lizard
(*Sceloporus magister*)

North America is a remnant of the prehistoric supercontinent Laurasia and thus shares many similar species of plants and animals with Eurasia. The continent is home to thirteen native families of lizards, representing amphisbaenids, iguanines (representing four families), geckonids, eublepharids, scincids, teiids, xantusiids, anguids, anniellids, and helodermatids. The most frequently encountered species are anoles, fence lizards, collared lizards, and racerunners/whiptails. But despite its great size, most of North America lies in the temperate zone and is not particularly good lizard-watching country. However, the number of represented families is high, and some places are lizard watchers' paradises. Lizards are most likely to be encountered between late April or early May through late September except in Florida, where they are active the year around. Look for them near cover, on tree trunks, rocky outcrops, and under shrub branches and fallen logs. They are also commonly found under rocks and wooden, metal, or plastic debris, or in excavated burrows or loose sand. Expect to spot lizards on hot (over 85° F [29°C]) bright days.

Anniella pulchra Gray, 1852
California Legless Lizard

Family: Anniellidae.
Length: SVL: 3.8 in. (96.5 mm). TL: 8.75 in. (222 mm.).
Habitat and Range: Coastal California from the Pajaro River south to northeastern Baja. Limited to loose, slightly moist sands and soils, from beaches to pine forests.
Natural History: Generally active within 1 to 5 inches (2.5-12.7 cm) of the surface of the soil, where it forages for small arthropods, including springtails, ants, and other such prey. Most often encountered under low brush, where they may bask or lie just beneath the surface. Legless lizards are live-bearing species, producing one to three young in late summer. A black subspecies, *Anniella pulchra nigra* Fischer, 1884, is found in Monterrey County and along Moro Bay. It may represent a distinct species.
Care: Very hardy, though rarely seen because they are almost always buried in the soil. Provide loose sand, a shallow water dish, and some bark or broad-leafed plant. Keep soil slightly moist, but never damp. Prefers low temperatures, from 65° to 73° F (16° to 23° C). Feed small mealworms, young crickets, and small worms.
Terrarium Suitability: 3

Anolis carolinensis Cuvier, 1817
Green Anole

Family: Polychrotidae.
Length: SVL: 2.25 in. (60 mm). TL: 5.5 in. (140 mm).
Habitat and Range: Most of the southeastern United States, from central North Carolina to Florida, and west to central Texas. Found in wooded areas on shrubs and trees but also locally common around houses and other human dwellings.
Natural History: The only anole native to the United States (though several species have been introduced), this species was also long known as the American chameleon because it changes color from green to brown. Males have a large red dewlap (fan of skin on the throat), used in displays to attract mates or warn off other males. Though the green anole is an iguanine lizard, its toes have sticky pads similar to those of geckos.
Care: Green anoles can be good beginner's lizards, but only if given proper care. Provide a roomy terrarium (a 10-gallon [37.9-l] aquarium—minimum—for a trio of one male and two females) with plenty of branches or plants for climbing and perching. Gently spray plants daily, as these lizards rarely drink from a dish. Provide small crickets, mealworms, wax worms, and other soft-bodied insects on a daily basis. Keep terrarium warm, between 68° and 88° F (20° and 31° C). Full-spectrum lighting is recommended.
Terrarium Suitability: 1

Anolis sagrei Duméril and Bibron, 1837
Brown Anole/Bahaman Anole

Family: Polychrotidae.
Length: SVL: 2 in. (51 mm). TL: 5 in. (121 mm)
Habitat and Range: Widely distributed throughout Central and northern South America, the islands of the Caribbean, and southern Florida, where it was introduced by human activity.
Natural History: Very similar to the green anole, with which it seems to be successfully competing in southern Florida. Brown anoles have limited color-changing abilities, ranging from dark to pale chocolate-brown. The dewlap (fan of skin on the throat) is orange-red with a bright yellow edge and is comparatively smaller than that of the green anole. Active only during the day, it is most often seen on tree trunks and low woody shrubs.
Care: A good beginner's lizard. Provide a roomy terrarium (a 10-gallon [37.9-l] aquarium for a trio of one male and two females) with plenty of branches or plants for climbing and perching. Gently spray plants daily, as these lizards rarely drink from a dish. Provide small crickets, mealworms, wax worms, and other soft-bodied insects on a daily basis. Keep terrarium warm, between 72° and 92° F (22° and 34° C). Provide this species with full-spectrum lighting..
Terrarium Suitability: 1

Aspidoscelis sexlineatus (Linnaeus, 1758)
Six-Lined Racerunner

Family: Teiidae.

Length: SVL: 3.5 in. (89 mm). TL: 10.6 in (270 mm).

Habitat and Range: Maryland south to Florida, west to eastern New Mexico, Colorado, and southeastern Wyoming. Follows the Mississippi River north into Wisconsin.

Natural History: This is a colorful, swift-moving grassland lizard that can be found in fields, prairies, and deserts. The name "racerunner" refers to their remarkable speed—they are arguably the fastest-running lizards in North America. The body typically has a greenish tint, especially on the sides, and six pale lines running the length of the body. The tail is extremely long and fragile. Note that this species was formerly placed in the genus *Cnemidophorus*.

Care: Six-lined racerunners can be kept in terraria suitable for brown and green anoles so long as there is plenty of floor space. They do best if there is a variety of low cover in the form of plants, branches, and large leaves. They will accept crickets, grasshoppers, mealworms, and fruit flies. Provide a daily light water misting. Keep terrarium warm by day (85° to 101° F [29° to 38° C]) and allow it to cool to about 70° F (21° C) at night. Full-spectrum lighting is recommended.

Terrarium Suitability: 2

Aspidoscelis tigris (Baird and Girard, 1852)
Western Whiptail/Tiger Whiptail

Family: Teiidae.

Length: SVL: 4.5 in (113 mm). TL: 9.6 in. (244 mm).

Habitat and Range: Found through much of eastern Oregon, southern Idaho, California, Nevada, Utah, Arizona, southern New Mexico, western Texas; its most southerly range extends into the Baja Peninsula and northern Mexico.

Natural History: Several subspecies are recognized, but all western whiptails have a tan body with dark spots, bands, or bars that produce a tiger-like effect. They prefer open habitats in desert and short grass areas but occasionally stray along creek sides and arroyos. They move about in a nervous manner, making short jerky bursts as they hunt small insects and spiders as prey. This species was formerly placed in the genus *Cnemidophorus*.

Care: This species requires considerable room, for it runs swiftly as it forages during the day. Provide a desert terrarium, with several inches (8 cm or so) of loose, slightly moist sand, large rocks, and bark pieces that provide cover. House males separately. Keep terrarium warm by day (85° to 101° F [29° to 38° C]), and avoid large temperature drops at night. Provide a daily diet of crickets and other small live insects. Full spectrum lighting is recommended.

Terrarium Suitability: 2

Here are six more of the many other North American Whiptails.

Aspidoscelis exsanguis
(Lowe, 1956)

Chihuahuan Spotted Whiptail
SVL: 4 in. (102 mm).

Aspidoscelis gularis
(Baird and Girard, 1852)

Texas Spotted Whiptail
SVL: 4.2 in. (107 mm).

Aspidoscelis inornata
(Baird, 1858)

Little Striped Whiptail
SVL: 3.4 in. (86 mm)

Aspidoscelis septemvittata
(Cope, 1892)

Plateau Spotted Whiptail
SVL: 4 in. (102 mm).

Aspidoscelis tesselata
(Say,1823)

Common Checkered Whiptail
SVL: 4.2 (107 mm).

Aspidoscelis velox
(Springer, 1928)

Plateau Striped Whiptail
SVL: 3.4 in. (86 mm).

21

Callisaurus draconoides Blainville, 1835
Zebra-Tailed Lizard

Family: Phrynosomatidae.
Length: SVL: 4 in. (102 mm). TL: 6.2 in. (157mm).
Habitat and Range: Generally found on flat desert with some rock and low shrub cover. Found in Nevada, southern and western Arizona, the southeastern quarter of California, Baja California, and the Mexican coast south to Sinaloa.
Natural History: A beautifully colored lizard with an unusual escape behavior. When chased, it curls the tail forward over the back— resembling a scorpion—and as it runs the black bars under the tail create an optical illusion. The lizard is very difficult to visually follow as a result. This species is often seen when being looked for under boards and other flat debris, but it is otherwise likely to be buried in the sand during the day.
Care: Provide zebra-tailed lizards with plenty of floor space and several inches (8 cm or so) of loose sand into which they will burrow. They require a variety of insects in the diet, including crickets, grasshoppers, small beetles, mealworms, and fruit flies. Provide a light water misting twice weekly. Keep terrarium warm by day (85° to 100° F [29° to 38° C]) and allow it to cool to about 70° F (21° C) at night. Provide about 12 hours of full-spectrum lighting daily.
Terrarium Suitability: 2

Coleonyx reticulatus Davis and Dixon, 1958
Big Bend Banded Gecko

Family: Eublepharidae.
Length: SVL: 3.3 in. (84 mm). TL: 7 in. (178 mm).
Habitat and Range: Restricted to the Big Bend region of Texas, with small isolated populations in northern Mexico.
Natural History: Little is known of this species, as it is nocturnal, secretive, and has a very limited range. It differs from other Texas-dwelling banded geckos in having enlarged raised scales intermixed among the tiny granular scales, similar to the condition seen in the popular pet the leopard gecko (see Region 8: Southern Asia and Middle East). The eyelids are moveable, there are no sticky pads on the toes, and the tail is cylindrical and fragile.
Care: Presumably, Big Bend banded geckos can be cared for in the same way as other American banded geckos (see C. *variegatus* in this section) However, they are both rare and protected by law, so it is unlikely they will be kept except by licensed researchers or zoos.
Terrarium Suitability: 4

Coleonyx switaki (**Murphy, 1974**)
Barefoot Gecko

Family: Eublepharidae.
Length: SVL: 3.3 in. (84 mm). TL: 8.5 in. (216 mm).
Habitat and Range: Extreme south-central California south into Baja, along the eastern coast. Found in rocky areas with plenty of cover.
Natural History: This is a rare and rarely seen gecko. Like other members of the genus *Coleonyx*, barefoot geckos have no sticky toe pads and possess moveable eyelids. The tail is cylindrical and can be waved when the gecko is threatened or disturbed. Excess fat is stored in the tail to help get the lizards through periods when insects are not available. The pattern consists of a light brown or tan background with symmetrically arranged small spots—not bands—on the back. Like the Big Bend gecko, this species has larger raised scales intermixed with the small granular scales.
Care: As per other banded geckos, this species does well in a terrarium that provides humid hiding places, loose soil, and a red bulb. Best kept with its own species, and only a single male per enclosure.
Terrarium Suitability: 4

Coleonyx variegatus (Baird, 1859)
Western Banded Gecko

Family: Eublepharidae.
Length: SVL: 3 in. (76.2 mm). TL: 7.5 in. (190.5 mm).
Habitat and Range: Dry sandy habitats of the southwestern United States and northwestern Mexico.
Natural History: This wide-ranging species is often mistakenly identified as a young Gila monster because of the banded pattern and short stout tail. They may squeak when handled or alarmed. Banded geckos are most likely to be encountered on or along roads in the evening, drawn by the heat of the pavement. They feed on a variety small arthropods and hide in burrows or plants during the day. Males have a pair of tiny spurs on each side of the tail near the hips.
Care: Banded geckos are American relatives of the Asiatic leopard geckos (see Region 8: Southern Asia and Middle East), and care is similar. Give geckos a place where they may hide during the day and a red heat bulb in place of a regular heat lamp—red light does not seem to disturb nocturnal animals. Temperatures should range from 76° to 84°F (24° to 29°C) Banded geckos will drink from a shallow dish and need to be fed small insects three to five times per week. Best housed with their own kind, or with similarly sized diurnal species such as fence lizards. Do not house two males in the same enclosure.
Terrarium Suitability: 1

Cophosaurus texanus (Troschel, 1850)
Greater Earless Lizard

Family: Phrynosomatidae.
Length: SVL: 3 in. (76.2 mm). TL: 7.5 in. (190.5 mm)
Habitat and Range: Found in deserts and flat shrub country in the southeastern quarter of Arizona, lowland New Mexico, much of Texas, and adjacent northern Mexico.
Natural History: This small, swift-running lizard is one of North America's most colorful species. The back is sandy gray, with greenish or yellow coloring on the rear half of the body. Males of this species are distinguished from the similar zebra-tailed lizard in having two long black crescent marks nearer the hip; in the zebra-tailed lizard the bars are nearer the front limbs. Additionally, greater earless lizards lack an external ear opening, though they do, in fact, have ears.
Care: Greater earless lizards are an active species and require a large terrarium with plenty of flat floor space. These lizards like it hot, between 90° and 115° F (32 to 46° C) during the day and as low as 70° F (21° C) at night. Provide daily access to full-spectrum lighting. When overheated, greater earless lizards dive into the sand, so provide several inches (8 cm or so) of slightly moist substrate in the cage. These lizards need daily feedings of small soft-bodied insects such as wingless fruit flies, ants, termites, young mealworms, and week-old crickets.
Terrarium Suitability: 2

Crotaphytus bicinctores Smith and Tanner, 1972
Great Basin Collared Lizard

Family: Crotaphytidae.
Length: SVL: 4.3 in. (114 mm). TL: 10 in. 254 mm)
Habitat and Range: Deserts and dry areas of southern California and western Arizona, north into Nevada, Idaho, and eastern Oregon.
Natural History: This western species is distinguished by the olive green body with thin light brown crossbands. Males are more intensely colored and have black belly patches near the groin. Like other collared lizards, this species has two characteristic velvety black collars around the neck, each separated by an unmarked white band. These lizards are active during the morning and late afternoon, avoiding the most intense heat of the day. Look for them in rocky desert arroyos and valleys.
Care: These lizards need a large terrarium with rocks to serve as both basking sites and refuge. Keep the air temperature high, from 90° to 115° F (32° to 46° C) during the day, and humidity between 40 and (rarely) 70 percent. Provide feedings of large insects such as grasshoppers, crickets, small beetles, and moths five times per week. Do not house with smaller lizards, even of their own kind, and do not house more than one male per enclosure. Provide 10 to 14 hours of full-spectrum lighting.
Terrarium Suitability: 1

female

male

Crotaphytus collaris (Say, 1823)
Eastern Collared Lizard

Family: Crotaphytidae.
Length: SVL: 4.5 in. (144 mm). TL: 14 in. (356 mm).
Habitat and Range: Most of Kansas and central Missouri south through northwestern Arkansas, most of Oklahoma, and central Texas. Found in open prairie and scrub desert in areas where hills are covered in rocks.
Natural History: Eastern collared lizards are among North America's largest and most conspicuous lizards. The body of males is green, and the head is brown, without distinct spots or markings. Females are brown, with dark and light speckling on the back. Both sexes have the pair of black collars. They are easily observed as they bask on rocks and lunge in pursuit of grasshoppers, flies, and other insects. If surprised in the open, they can run on just the hind limbs at considerable speed. Collared lizards cannot voluntarily drop the tail; if lost, the tail does not regrow. Mating takes place in May and June, and hatchlings emerge in late July through early September. Gravid females develop bright orange spots along the sides.
Care: These are very hardy and active display animals, though their relatively short life span of three to five years is a limit on their suitability. Care is as for *Crotaphytus bicinctores*.
Terrarium Suitability: 2

Crotaphytus nebrius **Axtell and Montanucci, 1977**
New Mexico Collared Lizard/Sonoran Collared Lizard

Family: Crotaphytidae.
Length: SVL: 4.5 in. (144 mm). TL: 14 in. (356 mm).
Habitat and Range: Occurs in deserts of southwestern New Mexico and much of Sonora, Mexico.
Natural History: This species possesses the distinct pair of black collars, but unlike most other collared lizards it lacks any green coloring on the body. New Mexican collared lizards are tan or light brown with an irregular mottling of darker gray and brown mixed with larger light spots on the body. The head is shorter and more blunt than that of the western collared lizard (a subspecies of the eastern collared lizard, *C. collaris baileyi*, found in some of the same areas as this species). Though harmless, collared lizards are able to bite hard enough to break skin and draw blood.
Care: Care is as for *Crotaphytus bicinctores*.
Terrarium Suitability: 2

Crotaphytus reticulatus Baird, 1858
Reticulate Collared Lizard

Family: Crotaphytidae.
Length: SVL: 5.5 in. (140 mm). TL: 14 in. (356 mm)
Habitat and Range: Restricted to rocky arroyos and canyons in the Big Bend region of Texas and adjacent Mexico.
Natural History: This species is poorly known, occurring as it does within a limited area. It is a beautiful lizard, with a less distinct collar than in other *Crotaphytus* and no trace of green coloring. The head is brown with indistinct darker marbling. The body is pale brown and cream, with distinct black spots forming the netlike dorsal pattern. Like other collared lizards, this species is found where there are plenty of rocks and boulders to serve as lookout sites and basking places, and they can run very swiftly on the hind limbs.
Care: Very rarely encountered in captivity, but care is the same as that for *Crotaphytus bicinctores*.
Terrarium Suitability: 3

Dipsosaurus dorsalis (Baird and Girard, 1852)
Desert Iguana

Family: Iguanidae.
Length: SVL: 6 in. (152 mm). TL: 15 in. (381 mm).
Habitat and Range: A resident of dry, sandy habitat from southern Nevada south through Arizona, southeastern California, and into Baja and northwestern Mexico.
Natural History: This is one of North America's largest lizards and, like the chuckwalla, is also a plant-eater. It also feeds on small arthropods and its own droppings, presumably when other food is scarce. Desert iguanas are characterized by the low crest of enlarged scales running down the center of the back, and a small, rounded head. This is perhaps the most heat-tolerant lizard in North America, being active at temperatures at which other lizards seek cover.
Care: Provide them with a staple diet of diced fruits (especially berries and cactus fruit), fresh leafy greens, dandelions, and an occasional offering of mealworms and wax worm—wash all produce well to remove possible pesticides or herbicides. Give the terrarium a substrate of 3 to 5 inches (76 to 127 mm) of loose sand and provide a combination of large rocks and plants. Keep the terrarium warm during the day, at 90° to 115° F (32° to 46° C) and room temperature at night. Each day provide 10 to 14 hours of full-spectrum lighting.
Terrarium Suitability: 2

Elgaria coerulea (Wiegmann, 1828)
Northern Alligator Lizard

Family: Anguidae.

Length: SVL: 5.8 in. (147 mm). TL: 14 in. (354 mm).

Habitat and Range: Southern British Columbia into northern Idaho and northwestern Montana, and south along the coastal range to eastern and western California (absent from central California). Isolated populations occur in western Nevada and southwestern Oregon. Lives in grassy woodlands where humidity is above 70 percent and there is plenty of shade.

Natural History: These lizards receive their name from its large rectangular scales, which vaguely resemble those of alligators. Alligator lizards are diurnal insect hunters most typically found in flat areas where low plants and considerable open field of vision are possible. They often shelter in mammal burrows. These large lizards have strong jaws and can give a painful nip. This species produces 2 to 15 live young. Northern alligator lizards were long placed in the genus *Gerrhonotus*.

Care: Alligator lizards require shelter such as bark strips or small logs, with a soil mixture as substrate. Provide various insects twice weekly. Keep the terrarium between 72° and 90° F (22° and 32° C). Humidity should stay between 70 and 85 percent. Full-spectrum lighting is recommended.

Terrarium Suitability: 1

Elgaria multicarinata (Blainville, 1835)
Southern Alligator Lizard

Family: Anguidae.
Length: SVL: 7 in. (178 mm). TL: 14.7 in. (373 mm).
Habitat and Range: South central Washington and north central Oregon south along the coastal mountain ranges into California (except the Central Valley) and into the northwestern third of Baja, Mexico. This species is found in drier habitats than its northern cousin, favoring dry grasslands, sparsely planted fields, chaparral, and pine forests.
Natural History: Similar in appearance to the northern alligator lizard, from which it is distinguished by a distinct pattern of irregular dark crossbands on the back that become black and white parallel bands on the sides. Because of its large size and strong jaws, southern alligator lizards can feed on a wide variety of live foods, ranging from insects, spiders (including black widows), and scorpions to other lizards, small snakes, and small mammals. Their shiny scales and tiny legs often lead casual observers to mistake alligator lizards for snakes. Formerly placed in the genus *Gerrhonotus*.
Care: Care as for northern alligator lizards, except keep air temperature warmer and feed daily. Provide a large dish for water; this species often soaks in water prior to shedding. Be careful when handling, as the bite may draw blood.
Terrarium Suitability: 1

Gambelia silus (Stejneger, 1890)
Blunt-Nosed Leopard Lizard

Family: Crotaphytidae.
Length: SVL: 5.8 in. (147 mm). TL: 14 in. (365 mm).
Habitat and Range: This endangered species is found in California's Central Valley, but agricultural use of natural habitat has reduced populations considerably. They now dwell in alkaline flat desert areas.
Natural History: These lizards are sit-and-wait predators, generally lying in wait for prey while concealed under low-growing shrubs. When insects or smaller lizards are spotted, the leopard lizard dashes out to ambush the prey. Differs from the long-nosed leopard lizard in having a striped, versus spotted, pattern on the throat.
Care: Blunt-nosed leopard lizards are strictly protected by law and are rarely encountered in captivity. They should be housed in large terraria with plenty of floor space and a few large rocks and low plants. Give the lizards a deep sand substrate. They should only be housed with their own species, with no more than one adult male per enclosure. Offer daily feedings of insects and supplement occasionally with pink mice, small live lizards, and washed dandelion flowers. Keep the air temperature high, from 90° to 115° F (32° to 46° C) during the day, and humidity between 40 and 70 percent. Requires daily access to 10 to 14 hours of full-spectrum lighting..
Terrarium Suitability: 3

Gambelia wislizeni (Baird and Girard, 1852)
Long-Nosed Leopard Lizard

Family: Crotaphytidae.
Length: SVL: 4.3 in. (114 mm). TL: 10 in. (254 mm)
Habitat and Range: Found in arid, open, flat desert where low growth vegetation offers some shelter. Ranges from extreme southwest Idaho through Nevada into south-central California east to eastern Arizona and into northern Mexico.
Natural History: A pugnacious and active predator found in flat desert habitats where low-growing plants are abundant. This lizard's prey consists largely of smaller lizards—such as side-blotched and horned lizards—and large insects. Long-nosed leopard lizards are active when temperatures are high; leopard lizards are able to run swiftly in pursuit of prey and to avoid predators. Gravid females display bright orange spots on their sides and belly.
Care: The care for this lizard is identical to that of the blunt-nosed leopard lizard. Long-nosed leopard lizards may be housed with other lizards of similar or slightly larger size, including collared lizards, desert iguanas, and chuckwallas. Offer daily feedings of insects, and supplement occasionally with pink mice, small live lizards, and washed dandelion flowers.
Terrarium Suitability: 2

Gonatodes fuscus (Hallowell, 1855)
Yellow-Headed Gecko

Family: Sphaerodactylidae.

Length: SVL: 1.4 in. (36 mm). TL 3.5 in. (89 mm).

Habitat and Range: This small species is found on Key West, Florida, several Caribbean islands, and Central America from Honduras to Panama.

Natural History: These small secretive lizards are active mainly at early dusk and early evening. Though they lack the sticky toe pads of many other gecko species, they are adept climbers, often found on walls, fences, and low shrubs. Males are slate gray to greenish with yellow heads; females are mottled gray and brown.

Care: These lizards are hardy, but they require daily feedings of wingless fruit flies, week-old crickets, or other tiny insects. Provide a soil substrate with leaf litter and spray lightly each afternoon. An under-terrarium heat tape is recommended; do not use heat rocks or heat lamps. Because of the small size of yellow-headed geckos, it is extremely difficult to handle them without causing injury.

Terrarium Suitability: 2

Heloderma suspectum Cope, 1869
Gila Monster
Venomous

Family: Helodermatidae.
Length: SVL: 14 in. (356 mm). TL: 24.5 in. (622 mm).
Habitat and Range: Confined to Arizona, small parts of adjacent states, and extreme northwestern Mexico. Found in arid habitats where plant life is plentiful.
Natural History: This is the region's largest lizard, and its only venomous lizard. This slow-moving lizard is active mainly at twilight and dawn. It feeds on eggs, young birds, and rodents. The tail is used to store reserves of fat. The venom is injected along grooves in the teeth of the lower jaw; it is neurotoxic in nature. Though bites are excruciatingly painful, there have been fewer than 20 human fatalities recorded over the past 150 years. No matter how "cute" or slow they may appear, *do not attempt to handle a Gila monster without proper training.*
Care: Gila monsters are fairly hardy to maintain in captivity, but they are only for experienced keepers and zoos. Provide these lizards with a deep substrate of loose, slightly damp sand or soil, and provide some hide boxes. Keep the terrarium at 90° to 115° F (32° to 46° C) during the day, and room temperature at night. Feed a variety of boiled eggs (with shells), freshly killed rodents, and large insects.
Terrarium Suitability: 4

Ophisaurus ventralis (Linnaeus, 1766)
Eastern Glass Lizard

Family: Anguidae.

Length: SVL: 12 in. (305 mm). TL: 43 in. (1,092 mm).

Habitat and Range: Coastal grasslands and moist open forests from North Carolina to the Florida Keys, and west to southern Mississippi and extreme southeastern Louisiana.

Natural History: This is one of four North American glass lizards—all legless—so called because the long fragile tail is easily broken off, even if a potential attacker does not touch the lizard. Though the tail will regenerate, the old tail cannot be rejoined to the lizard—despite common myth. Unlike other American legless lizards, this species lacks any distinct pattern or conspicuous markings. Older adults may appear green, with yellowish bellies. Though legless, these lizards have functional eyelids, exposed ear openings, and a short, broad tongue, all features that distinguish them from snakes.

Care: These large lizards do well if given a large enough terrarium. Provide a layer of soil and leaf or pine litter as substrate and a hollow log for refuge. Eastern glass lizards generally prefer shaded areas where air temperature is high (80° to 92° F [27° to 32° C]). Offer a varied diet that includes small diced fruits, snails, slugs, large insects, and pink mice.

Terrarium Suitability: 2

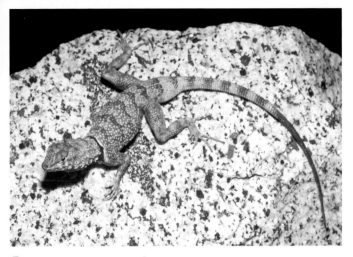

Petrosaurus mearnsi (Stejneger, 1894)
Banded Rock Lizard

Family: Phrynosomatidae.
Length: SVL: 4.2 in. (107 mm). TL: 9.45 in. (240 mm).
Habitat and Range: Inhabits boulder-strewn areas in south-central California and adjacent northern Baja California, Mexico.
Natural History: This is a streamlined and active lizard that resembles a large side-blotched lizard but has a single black neck collar with a white posterior border. The body is gray or olive with broad brown crossbands on which there are tiny white specks. The tail is gray and banded with darker gray. These lizards are active on hot days and spend much of the time actively hunting small insects, including flies and bees.
Care: These lizards need a large terrarium with plenty of large rocks that individual lizards will claim as personal territory. As residents of especially dry and hot deserts, they require little water, deriving most of their water from metabolism of foods. Give these lizards a variety of soft-bodied insects including fruit flies, flies, bees, ants, termites, crickets, and small beetles. Keep the terrarium warm during the day, at 90° to 115° F (32° to 46° C) with 10 to 14 hours of UV light, and at room temperature at night. You may safely house this species with western skinks, western fence lizards, horned lizards, and desert iguanas.
Terrarium Suitability: 2

Phrynosoma cornutum (Harlan, 1825)
Texas Horned Lizard

Family: Phrynosomatidae.
Length: SVL: 5 in. (127 mm). TL: 5.25 in. (133.4 mm)
Habitat and Range: Kansas south through Texas and much of New Mexico, south into the northeastern third of Mexico.
Natural History: Horned lizards are arguably the most unusual and distinctive North American reptiles. The round flat body makes them resemble toads more than lizards, hence the common but incorrect use of the name "horned toads" for them. The Texas horned lizard has some of the largest coronal (head) spines of the many species of *Phrynosoma*. The short stubby tail is not capable of being dropped or re-grown. Texas horned lizards like hot, sunny days, when they will take up a position along an ant trail and eat several hundred insects over a few hours.
Care: The problem in keeping horned lizards lies primarily in their need for live ants as a food source. A typical daily feeding may include 500 to 1,200 ants, which is difficult to provide in captivity. Keep daytime temperatures at 90° to 115° F (33° to 46° C) with 10 to 14 hours of UV light, and at room temperature at night. Though the lizards will accept small mealworms and young crickets, reports of successful husbandry using these substitutes are varied.
Terrarium Suitability: 4

At least four species of horned lizards defend themselves against predators by squirting blood from their eyes. The blood may project several feet (about 1.5 m). Chemicals in the blood are distasteful to some mammalian predators, notably to coyotes and felines. This defense does not seem to be effective against bird or reptile predators. Here, *P. cornutum* has recently performed this behavior, as evidenced by the blood on its face.

Phrynosoma coronatum (Blainville, 1835)
Coastal Horned Lizard

Family: Phrynosomatidae.
Length: SVL: 4.5 in. (114.3 mm). TL: 6.8 in. (172 mm)
Habitat and Range: The western half of California from Shasta south to La Paz in southern Baja California. Found in many different habitats from desert to sandy pine forest to grasslands.
Natural History: This large and distinctive horned lizard has the two central head horns larger than the rest. This is a giant among horned lizards, not easily confused with other local species. As anteaters, coastal horned lizards spend considerable time in the sun picking off ants from trails. The coastal and Texas horned lizards are two of several horned lizards that squirt blood from the corners of the eyes when threatened; along with startling the predator, canines and felines find it distasteful. Despite the horns and blood-squirting, horned lizards are easy prey for birds, mammals, larger lizards, and some snakes.
Care: See the Texas horned lizard (*P. cornutum*) for care details. Specimens of *P. coronatum* are just as difficult to keep. They have been successfully maintained and bred if kept in outdoor enclosures within their natural habitat.
Terrarium Suitability: 4

Plestiodon anthracinus (**Baird 1849**)
Coal Skink

Family: Scincidae
Length: SVL: 3.5 in. (88.5 mm). TL: 7.2 in. (183 mm).
Habitat and Range: Much of the eastern portion of the United States, from Maryland south to central Florida, and west to western Louisiana and southeastern Nebraska.
Natural History: Coal skinks are creatures of the leaf litter, hollow and fallen logs, and spaces under boards and flat rocks. They are bronze above, with chocolate brown flanks. Males may have copper or orange heads, especially in spring, and juveniles of both sexes have bright blue tails. They are active during the day, when they forage tirelessly for small insects and spiders.
Care: Terrarium animals require a slightly moist soil substrate and plenty of cover. Use live plants and mosses that will help retain humidity above 75 percent. Provide a flat shallow bowl of drinking water in which the skinks may also soak. Use indirect lighting to keep the terrarium between 68° and 86° F (20° and 30° C). Provide a few hours of UV lighting daily. Feed them gut-loaded small insects twice daily. Females may lay eggs communally. These hatch in four to five weeks, and the young should be fed wingless fruitflies, day-old crickets, springtails, and similar small fare.
Terrarium Suitability: 2

Plestiodon fasciatus (Linnaeus, 1758)
Five-Lined Skink

Family: Scincidae.

Length: SVL: 3.5 in. (86 mm). TL: 8.5 in. (216 mm).

Habitat and Range: Moist forests and shaded grasslands of most of the eastern half of the United States south of Iowa, New York, and New England. Ranges into New York along the Hudson River and extends south to Florida and west to Oklahoma and eastern Texas.

Natural History: This is a beautiful glossy-black lizard with five light eggshell-white lines running from the nape to the hips. In juveniles and adult females, the tail is brilliant cobalt blue, which possibly serves as a distraction when this skink is threatened by predators; the tail is very easily dropped but will re-grow sans blue coloration. Five-lined skinks are swift ground predators found foraging under leaf litter, loose bark, and fallen logs. They often will be basking on top of logs or rocks, but they dart away at any sign of a threat.

Care: These lizards are best housed only with their own kind, as they are very likely to drop their tails if disturbed by other species. They need a large quantity of small live foods, ranging from wingless fruit flies to young crickets to small red worms. Keep the terrarium warm but not hot, and maintain humidity at 70 to 100 percent. Do not handle these delicate and nervous lizards.

Terrarium Suitability: 2

Plestiodon obsoletus (Baird and Girard, 1852)
Great Plains Skink

Family: Scinicidae.
Length: SVL: 5.5 in. (143 mm). TL: 14 in. (350 mm).
Habitat and Range: A prairie resident found from southwestern Nebraska through most of Kansas south into northern Mexico and west into central Arizona.
Natural History: This is a conspicuous skink, with a black body on which each scale has a golden center. The resulting pattern makes the lizard appear made of metal. Young and females have bright blue tails (less intense in adults). Young are also black with reddish-orange spots on the head and neck. Great Plains skinks are pugnacious lizards capable of giving a painful bite that may draw blood. They are found in grasslands and take refuge beneath boulders and fallen logs, or in mammal burrows. They are active during the day, especially when temperatures are high.
Care: This is a hardy species that has been bred in captivity. Because they are aggressive, they are best housed with their own kind. Provide individual hiding places and several inches (about 8 cm) of soil into which skinks may dig. Feed these skinks a variety of live foods along with occasional offerings of fruit and edible flowers, such as dandelions and clover.
Terrarium Suitability: 1

Plestiodon septentrionalis (Baird 1858)
Prairie Skink

Family: Scincidae.
Length: SVL: 3.5 in. (88.5 mm). TL: 8.8 in. (223.5 mm).
Habitat and Range: A patchy distribution from southern Manitoba south to coastal Texas.
Natural History: Prairie skinks are handsome lizards with smooth shiny scales, and several stripes that extend from the side of the head down the body and tail. The stripes are dark brown, tan, bronze, and yellowish. The lower jaws and throat of breeding males may be coral pink. The tail of juveniles is pale blue. Prairie skinks are found in semi-arid regions where there is gravel or dry soil. If disturbed while foraging, these extremely quick lizards can dash to cover and seemingly disappear. They are excellent burrowers and are often underground. Males are territorial, especially during breeding season.
Care: Terrarium animals require a slightly moist soil substrate and plenty of cover. Use live plants to help retain humidity above 75 percent. Provide drinking water at all times. Use indirect lighting to keep the terrarium between 68° and 86° F (20° and 30° C). Provide a few hours of UV lighting daily. Feed them gut-loaded small insects twice daily, and supplement with diced fruits and small berries weekly. Females may lay eggs communally. These hatch in four to five weeks.
Terrarium Suitability: 2

Plestiodon skiltonianus (Gray, 1852)
Western Skink

Family: Scincidae
Length: SVL: 3 in. (81 mm). TL: 6.25 in. (158.75 mm)
Habitat and Range: Grasslands and open woodlands habitats from southern British Columbia through eastern Washington and Idaho south to Nevada and Utah and west to coastal and mountain California into Baja California.
Natural History: This beautiful elongated skink is common in a variety of habitats, from grassy lawns to prairie to high desert. Western skinks are active foragers that move in long swift bursts. The blue tail—brighter in juveniles than adults—is retained throughout life in both sexes. Look for them among leaf litter, in grassy areas where sunlight and shade are mixed, and near ponds.
Care: Western skinks do well in a terrarium that provides a soft, moist substrate and some sheets of bark. Live plants help maintain adequate humidity levels (70 to 85 percent). Keep the terrarium warm, but avoid direct exposure to heat lights—skinks may bask for short periods, but they do better if extremes in temperature are avoided. Skinks can be safely housed with other species from the same range, including fence lizards and other similar-sized skinks. Give western skinks five weekly feedings of small live insects and provide light mistings of water three times per week.
Terrarium Suitability: 1

Rhineura floridana (Baird, 1858)
Florida Worm Lizard

Family: Rhineuridae.

Length: SVL: 11.25 in. (286 mm)

Habitat and Range: A resident of loose, loamy soils and rotting logs in central Florida.

Natural History: Worm lizards are easily distinguished from snakes and all other legless lizards by their scales. The body is covered by hard shiny scales that form distinct annuli, or rings, giving them an earthworm-like appearance. This species is limbless and lacks visible eyes and ear openings, and the tail is only a very short projection beyond the cloaca. Even their status as lizards has been debated over the past century. Generally, worm lizards are grouped as a distinct suborder called Amphisbaenia, equal to snakes and lizards, but recent work has again placed all three groups within "lizards." Florida worm lizards are pale pink and spend most of their time burrowing in loose, slightly moist soils or in rotting logs where humidity levels are high. Foods include worms as well as springtails and other small, soft-bodied insects.

Care: There is virtually no information about the captive care of this species.

Terrarium Suitability: 5

Sauromalus ater Duméril, 1856
Chuckwalla

Family: Iguanidae.
Length: SVL: 9 in. (229 mm). TL: 18 in. (458 mm).
Habitat and Range: Deserts of extreme northern Mexico into New Mexico and Arizona west to parts of California and Nevada.
Natural History: This is North America's second largest native lizard and, like the largest (the Gila monster), is restricted to a small range in the deserts. Chuckwallas are long-lived herbivores that feed on cactus fruits, flowers, grasses, and insects. The tail is relatively short and blunt it does not drop off if seized. When threatened, chuckwallas dive into rocky crevices and swell themselves with air, making extraction difficult.
Care: Chuckwallas are big territorial lizards best housed in large terraria with only one male per enclosure. Provide 3 to 5 inches (76 to 127 mm) of loose sandy substrate and provide large rocks and plants such as cactus or low-growing shrubs, which you will need to replace as your chuckwalla grazes on them. Keep the terrarium warm during the day, at 90° to 115° F (33° to 46° C) and room temperature at night. Provide 10 to 12 hours of full-spectrum lighting daily. This species is compatible with desert iguanas, collared lizards, and leopard lizards.
Terrarium Suitability: 3

Sceloporus jarrovii Cope, 1875
Mountain Spiny Lizard

Family: Phrynosomatidae.
Length: SVL: 4.2 in. (107 mm). TL: 8.9 in. (225 mm).
Habitat and Range: Mountains above the 5,000-foot (1,524 m) mark of extreme southeastern Arizona, southwestern New Mexico, and Mexico to Veracruz. Found in a variety of habitats, but always where there are basking sites that allow access to some sun exposure.
Natural History: A beautiful metallic blue lizard with large keeled scales and a broad black neck collar with a white posterior border. As a resident of mountainous regions, these lizards thrive at lower ambient temperatures than many other native reptiles, being active when air temperatures are as low as 58° F (14.4 ° C). Cold individuals are almost uniformly gray. Males have bright blue belly and throat coloring. They feed on a variety of small arthropods and give birth to two to four live young.
Care: This is a moderately active lizard that does best in a large terrarium. Provide rocks, loamy substrate, and some upright logs or woody plants. Keep temperature between 72° and 86° F (22° and 30° C), but keep cooler--45° to 50° F (7° to 10° C)--during the winter. Provide 10 to 14 hours of full-spectrum lighting daily. Best housed with only its own species.
Terrarium Suitability: 2

Sceloporus magister **Hallowell, 1854**
Desert Spiny Lizard

Family: Phrynosomatidae.
Length: SVL: 5.6 in. (142 mm). TL: 12 in. (306 mm)
Habitat and Range: Most of the Sonora Desert, from Arizona and Utah south into northern Sinaloa and southwest Coahuila and all of Baja California, Mexico.
Natural History: This is a large keeled-scaled gray-brown lizard with a large dark gray patch on the shoulders and back. There is no other distinct pattern, but the throat has a wedge-shaped black mark. Specimens from the Baja Peninsula have conspicuous blue throat and belly tints. The desert spiny lizard is found on the lower elevations of mountains within its range and in arid arroyos where temperatures get high and there is considerable visibility. They are strong lizards capable of consuming large insects, spiders, centipedes, scorpions, and small vertebrates.
Care: House these pugnacious spiny lizards by themselves. They will thrive in almost any style of desert terrarium, including those described for collared, leopard, and horned lizards. Feed desert spiny lizards five times per week, and lightly spray the terrarium with water weekly.
Terrarium Suitability: 1

Sceloporus occidentalis Baird and Girard, 1852
Western Fence Lizard

Family: Phrynosomatidae.
Length: SVL: 3.5 in. (89 mm). TL: 4.2 in. (107 mm).
Habitat and Range: Seasonally moist forests from central Washington through most of Oregon, California, Nevada and western Utah northward into Idaho and south to northwest Baja California.
Natural History: Possibly the most commonly seen lizard in the western United States. Fence lizards are found in forest, grassland, and streamside habitats, and they are also capable of quickly burrowing into and "swimming" in loose sand. As the common name implies, these lizards are often seen on fences. Males have intense blue belly and throat patches.
Care: A trio of western fence lizards can easily be housed in a 10-gallon (38-l) terrarium. They require some shelter and sand, potting soil, or small gravel as substrate. They also need something on which to climb. Provide small crickets, mealworms, and wax worms daily. Keep the terrarium between 72° and 93° F (22° and 34° C), and humidity between 70 and 85 percent. This species does best when given full-spectrum lighting. Fence lizards may be housed with other similarly sized species.
Terrarium Suitability: 1

Sceloporus orcutti Stejneger 1893

Granite Spiny Lizard

Family: Phrynosomatidae.
Length: SVL: 4.6 in. (117 mm). TL: 10.8 in. (274 mm).
Habitat and Range: Ranges from the San Gorgonio Pass south into southern Baja California. Found on the desert slopes of mountains, among boulders and low vegetation.
Natural History: Granite spiny lizards are large, strongly keeled lizards. The body is generally brown to rusty-red, with several broad lighter cross bands. Males may have green and/or blue coloration dorsally and on the tail; there may be a purple stripe down the spine. The bellies and throats of males are largely or wholly dark blue. Females may have yellow markings on the face and neck. Both sexes have strongly banded tails. Granite spiny lizards are active and alert, rarely allowing close approach.
Care: They do well in a mixed terrarium with other lizards of similar size, but there should be only one male per terrarium. Feed them live insects with occasional fruit or flowers added to the diet. These lizards lay 6 to 15 eggs in May to July. Eggs hatch in two to three months. Additional care as for the desert spiny lizard (*S. magister*).
Terrarium Suitability: 2

Sceloporus poinsettii Baird and Girard, 1852
Crevice Spiny Lizard

Family: Phrynosomatidae.
Length: SVL: 5.25 in. (134 mm). TL: 11.3 in. (287 mm)
Habitat and Range: Central Texas and parts of southern New Mexico south into north- central Mexico. Found in arid, rocky habitats.
Natural History: This species was named for the Smithsonian scientist for whom the plant poinsettia was named. Like collared lizards, the crevice spiny lizard likes rocky hillsides and arroyos. Like the chuckwalla, crevice spiny lizards inflate the body while in the rocky cracks, making their removal very difficult for predators. This large spiny lizard is similar in appearance to the mountain spiny lizard (*S. jarrovii*), also having large keeled scales and a dark, light-edged collar. However, the crevice spiny is dusky brown and tan, the darker hue forming distinct crossbars on the back.
Care: They do well in a mixed terrarium with other lizards of similar size and need both live insects and occasional fruit or flowers added to the diet. Care as for the desert spiny lizard (*S. magister*).
Terrarium Suitability: 1

Sceloporus undulatus Daudin, 1802
Eastern Fence Lizard

Famliy: Phrynosomatidae.
Length: SVL: 3.5 in. (89 mm). TL: 7.25 in. (184 mm)
Habitat and Range: A resident of pine, deciduous, and palmetto forests from extreme southern New York into central Florida, and west to eastern Kansas, Oklahoma, and Texas. It is the lizard most likely to be encountered in the states north of Virginia.
Natural History: This widespread species is most often encountered on warm sunny days when they are seen on shrubs, fences, fallen logs, and large rocks or concrete blocks. Though they can climb well, they rarely climb trees more than a few feet (about 1 m), usually only enough to avoid a pursuer. The bark-colored back has a distinct series of smaller markings forming irregular bands. The throat and belly of males are intense blue.
Care: Eastern fence lizards are non-aggressive, and a trio can easily be housed in a 10-gallon (38-l) terrarium. They require some shelter, such as bark strips or light logs, and sand, potting soil, or small gravel as substrate. They also need something on which to climb. Provide small crickets, mealworms, wax worms, and other soft-bodied insects twice weekly. Keep the terrarium between 72° and 93° F (22° and 34° C), and humidity between 75 and 100 percent. Provide full-spectrum lighting.
Terrarium Suitability: 1

Uma inornata Cope, 1895
Coachella Fringe-Toed Lizard

Family: Phrynosomatidae.
Length: SVL: 4.7 in. (119 mm). TL: 10.3 in. (262 mm).
Habitat and Range: Sandy desert habitat of Riverside County, California.
Natural History: Coachella fringe-toed lizards are residents of sandy places surrounded by some of the most "posh" real estate in the United States. This has, unfortunately, made the lizards an endangered species through habitat loss. The third and fourth toes possess comb-like scales that aid the lizard in moving through loose sand. The eyelids are slightly enlarged and form a tight seal when closed. The ear is partially concealed by a fleshy flap, and the upper jaw extends over and anterior to the lower; both of these modifications help keep sand out of the lizard's ear and mouth. Coachella fringe-toed lizards are the only United States species that has open sandy dunes as its preferred habitat. Though active during the day, they often take cover in rodent burrows or excavate refuges in the sand. They feed on a variety of insects and small spiders, and consume small berries and bits of fruit when available.
Care: Would probably fare well in a desert vivarium with a loose sandy substrate, but the species' protected status makes keeping it inappropriate for hobbyists.
Terrarium Suitability: 5

Uma notata Baird, 1858
Colorado Desert Fringe-Toed Lizard

Family: Phrynosomatidae.
Length: SVL: 4.8 in. (122 mm). TL: 9.6 in. (245 mm).
Habitat and Range: Southeastern California from the Salton Sea east to the Colorado River, and south into extreme northeast Baja. They inhabit open areas with lose sand and sparse vegetation.
Natural History: Very similar to *Uma inornata* in appearance, behavior, and habitat. Like that species, *U. notata* possesses long comb-like scales on the third and fourth toes that aid the lizard in moving through loose sand. Males have large orange patches on the belly, with a large black bar about midbody. Fringe-toed lizards are wary and may run or dive under the sand when threatened. The modified toes allow them to run well in very lose sand, but they really do not run particularly fast when compared with species that live on firmer substrates. They can, however, run on just their hind legs. They feed on a variety of insects and small spiders, and consume small berries and bits of fruit when available.
Care: Fringe-toed lizards are rarely available in the pet trade. Keep them much like other desert lizards, but house them singly—they can be very aggressive toward each other. Provide a deep substrate of loose sand and a large terrarium. Full-spectrum lighting is necessary.
Terrarium Suitability: 3

Urosaurus ornatus (Baird and Girard, 1852)
Ornate Tree Lizard

Family: Phrynosomatidae.
Length: SVL: 2.25 in. (57 mm). TL: 5.1 in. (130 mm).
Habitat and Range: Widely distributed in dry forest habitats of Utah, western Colorado, western New Mexico, Arizona, southwestern Texas and Coahuila and Sinaloa, Mexico.
Natural History: This is a slender lizard with a pale gray ground color on which are two irregular dark stripes of black blotches. In males the belly is blue; the throat may be blue, green, or yellow. Common in areas where plants such as pines, mesquite, eucalyptus, and cactus provide habitat. They are excellent climbers, but may forage on the ground.
Care: This is a small, swift-moving insect eater that requires a tall enclosure and plenty of branches on which to explore. Males usually stake out a particular tree as a territory, so they are best housed with one male per group of two or three females. Provide considerable heat in the range of 90° to 115° F (32° to 46° C) and 10 to 14 hours of full- spectrum lighting daily. Spray branches twice weekly to provide moisture and some humidity. Feed a mixture of fruit flies, other flies, month-old crickets, and other insects four times per week. May safely be kept with ground dwellers such as horned lizards, western fence lizards, and western skinks.
Terrarium Suitability: 2

Uta stansburiana Baird and Girard, 1852
Side-Blotched Lizard

Family: Phrynosomatidae.
Length: SVL: 2.5 in. (63.5 mm). TL: 5.5 in. (140 mm).
Habitat and Range: Widely distributed in several arid habitats from desert grasslands to open pine forest to rocky canyons in central Washington south through Oregon, southwestern Idaho, Nevada, Utah, Arizona, New Mexico, western Texas, and southern California into all of Baja, Zacatecas, and Sinaloa, Mexico.
Natural History: One of the best-studied lizards because it is easy to observe in nature and to maintain in captivity. Side-blotched lizards have small keeled scales on a brown or tan body with an irregular and very variable pattern. There is a characteristic dark blue or black spot on the flank just behind the arm in both sexes.
Care: Side-blotched lizards are comfortable on flat sandy desert or in rocky canyons or among low dry shrubs, so almost any desert terrarium style will accommodate them. Provide considerable heat in the range of 90° to 115° F (32° to 46° C) and 10 to 12 hours of full-spectrum lighting daily. They are active and feed on large numbers of tiny insects—they have been seen to catch flies on the wing—so they must be fed daily. They can be safely kept with other small desert lizards. Provide a small shallow dish of water, and gently spray the terrarium weekly.
Terrarium Suitability: 1

Xantusia henshawi Stejneger, 1893
Granite Night Lizard

Family: Xantusiidae.
Length: SVL: 2.8 in. (71 mm). TL: 6.2 in. (156 mm).
Habitat and Range: This species has a very small range in south-central California and adjacent Mexico. The habitat is as delicate as the small lizard, for it dwells in the crevice of exfoliating granite; searching for these night lizards invariably results in damaged habitat.
Natural History: A flat body, large lidless eyes, and large dark spots on a pale tan body characterize this beautiful lizard. This lizard has a broad head with large head scales. It differs from other night lizards in having a flatter body and large (vs. tiny) black spots. Unlike the geckos with which it may be confused, there are no sticky toe pads in night lizards. This species produces one to four live young.
Care: Granite night lizards rarely enter captivity because their habitat—they live under flakes of rock—is very fragile. In addition, the species is protected by law. Those that do enter captivity are best housed only with other granite night lizards. They need rock flakes under which to hide, plus a variety of small insects. Gently spray the terrarium twice weekly. Heat should be provided by a heat rock and heat pad under only one end of the terrarium. These lizards are strictly nocturnal, so avoid use of heat lamps.
Terrarium Suitability: 3

Xantusia riversiana Cope, 1883
Island Night Lizard

Family: Xantusiidae.
Length: SVL: 4.2 in. (107 mm). TL: 7.6 in. (192 mm)
Habitat and Range: Restricted to the Santa Barbara, San Clemente, and San Nicolas Islands off the California coast.
Natural History: This species was long known as *Klauberina riversiana*. It is the largest of the night lizards and also the bulkiest. There is color variation among the island populations, one being striped, the other spotted. There is still fairly little known about this species. This species occupies most of the habitats, from grassland to forest, on its small island homes. Consequently, most variations of forest or grassland terrarium should suffice. The islands are subject to strong cold winds, but rocks can get very warm.
Care: Heating by heat rock and under-terrarium pads is recommended. Provide clean water in a dish. Feed daily, offering insects, small pieces of fruit, and the occasional pink mouse. This species bears live young.
Terrarium Suitability: 2

Xantusia vigilis Baird, 1858
Arizona Night Lizard

Family: Xantusiidae

Length: SVL: 2.75 in. (70 mm). TL: 5.9 in. (150 mm).

Habitat and Range: An arboreal species found under loose bark, on yucca plants, and in rocky crevices of desert areas of the northern half of Baja California into southern California and east through Nevada and into central Arizona.

Natural History: The Arizona night lizard is similar in size to the granite night lizard, but its head is more box-shaped and blunt at the tip. The dorsum is pinkish or tan with tiny black specks instead of large black spots. This is a common but very secretive lizard that rarely shows itself during the day and almost never strays more than a few inches (cm) from some type of shelter. It feeds on nocturnal insects, and females produce one to three live young.

Care: Similar to that described for the granite night lizard. Provide considerable daytime heat in the range of 90° to 115° F (32° to 46° C) and one to four hours of full-spectrum lighting daily. Lizards sometimes shelter under rocks that have some sunlight entering, presumably to absorb UV light. House only with their own species, as they are nervous lizards and easily prone to losing their tails. Captives will take tiny insects.

Terrarium Suitability: 4

Additional species that occur in the United States (many are not native). Given are the locations in the U.S. where they occur; you may find a species account for these lizards in the region section given in parentheses.

Ameiva ameiva (**Region 4: South America and the Galapagos**): Miami-Dade County, FL

Anolis cristatellus (**Region 2: Caribbean Islands**): Miami-Dade County, FL

Anolis cybotes (**Region 2: Caribbean Islands**): Miami-Dade and Broward Counties, FL

Anolis equestris (**Region 2: Caribbean Islands**): Miami-Dade and Broward Counties, FL

Anolis garmani (**Region 2: Caribbean Islands**): Miami-Dade and Lee Counties, FL

Basiliscus vittatus (**Region 3: Mexico and Central America**): Miami-Dade and Broward Counties, FL

Chamaeleo calyptratus (**Region 8: Southern Asia and the Middle East**): southwest FL

Chamaeleo jacksonii (**Region 9a: Continental Africa**): Los Angeles, San Diego, and San Luis Obispo Counties, CA and HI

Cnemidophorus lemniscatus (**Region 3: Mexico and Central America**): Miami-Dade County, FL

Cosymbotus platyurus (**Region 7: Southeast and Eastern Asia**): Pinellas County, FL

Emoia cyanura (**Region 5: New Guinea, New Zealand, and Oceania**): HI

Gambelia copei (**Region 3: Mexico and Central America**): South-central CA

Gekko gecko (**Region 7: Southeast and Eastern Asia**): Oahu Island, HI, and Miami-Dade and Broward Counties, FL

Iguana iguana (**Region 4: South America and the Galapagos**): southern FL (including Keys); Rio Grande Valley, TX; Oahu and Maui, HI

Lacerta viridis (**Region 10: Europe and Northern Asia**): Shawnee County, KS

Leiocephalus carinatus (**Region 2: Caribbean Islands**): Palm Beach and Miami-Dade Counties, FL

Podarcis sicula (**Region 10: Europe and Northern Asia**): West Hempstead, NY; Philadelphia, PA; and Topeka, KS.

Caribbean Islands

Cuban iguana
(*Cyclura nubila*)

A popular region for tourists and naturalists alike, the Caribbean islands offer some of the world's smallest lizards and some of its largest. The widely distributed disc-toed geckos are almost all tiny species under 2 inches (5 cm) in total length, while the rock iguanas typically grow up to 3 feet (90 cm) and are commonly seen on many beaches. Most conspicuous, though, are the many species of anoles that inhabit branches, shrubs, and the ground near low vegetation cover.

The reptiles of the Caribbean are largely derived from South American ancestors that either were isolated as the ocean levels rose or colonized islands via rafting and other transport methods. Caribbean lizards are active all year long, except during heavy rains, and do not all require careful searching to see. Geckos are common near outdoor lights where they hunt night insects. Anoles, curly-tails, iguanas, and skinks are common on resort grounds. Most islands have a unique assortment of species, with many restricted to just one or a few islands. The number of species on an island is related to island size, with Cuba having the greatest diversity and islands such as the Caymans having the least.

Anolis allisoni Barbour, 1928
Blue Anole

Family: Polychrotidae.
Length: SVL: 3 in. (75 mm). TL: 8.8 in. (220 mm).
Habitat and Range: A common species found in any forested or semi-forested area, including near human dwellings, in Cuba and the islets east of Honduras.
Natural History: The males of this blue to green anole are particularly distinctive, having a small crest on the nape and a dewlap that is pink to red only on the rear half. In other respects, this species resembles the green anole of the U.S. (see Region 1: North America).
Care: Another good beginner's lizard when it's available. Provide a roomy, tall terrarium—a 10-gallon [37.9-l] aquarium (larger is better) for a trio of one male and two females—with plenty of branches and live plants for climbing and perching. Gently spray plants daily, as these lizards rarely drink from a dish. Provide small crickets, mealworms, wax worms, and other soft-bodied insects on a daily basis. Keep terrarium warm, between 72° and 93° F (22° and 34° C). It is recommended that you provide full-spectrum lighting to this species and other anoles.
Terrarium Suitability: 1

Anolis conspersus Garman, 1887
Grand Cayman Anole

Family: Polychrotidae.
Length: SVL: 2.7 in. (69 mm). TL: 8 in. (203 mm).
Habitat and Range: Grand Cayman Island, in trees, bushes, and among plants near buildings.
Natural History: Grand Cayman anoles are among the most frequently studied species of lizards. While this is probably due to their wonderful coloration, their beautiful habiatat must play a large part in attracting field herpetologists! These are handsome lizards that may occur in one of three natural color morphs: green, blue, and brown. The specific coloring in a population is dependent upon the annual rainfall of the particular microhabitat, but all forms have a conspicuous "salted" pattern of small white specks. Males have a blue dewlap. Males are larger than females, eat larger insects, and tend to be higher up on trees than either females or young. They are most active at late afternoon and just before twilight. They feed on small insects and consume flowers and nectar occasionally.
Care: Care for this species is similar to that of the other Caribbean anoles, such as *Anolis allisoni*. Feed gut-loaded live insects daily. Lightly mist the terrarium each day, provide a dish of drinking water, and house no more than one male per enclosure.
Terrarium Suitability: 2

Anolis cristatellus Duméril and Bibron, 1837
Crested Anole/Puerto Rican Crested Anole

Family: Polychrotidae.
Length: SVL: 5.2 in. (131 mm). TL: 10 in. (255 mm).
Habitat and Range: Puerto Rico and Hispaniola, and introduced into Mexico and southern Florida. They prefer tree trunks in semi-arid forested habitats.
Natural History: Males of this species have a sail-like crest on the upper surface of the tail (larger in males), and often a much less-developed sail on the neck and spine. Dewlaps of males are striking, with a strawberry-green center surrounded by a very broad red border. Look for them on tree trunks, where they tend to face the ground. These are powerful anoles that feed not only on a variety of insects but also on other anoles.
Care: Care of these lizards is similar to that of other anoles, such as *Anolis allisoni*. Use a substrate of soil or other moisture-retaining medium to maintain humidity between 70 and 90 percent. Crested anoles need thick vertical climbing surfaces with plenty of leafy cover near the top. The terrarium should be at least 3 ft (0.9 m) in height and allow good air ciculation. Males should be housed alone or with groups of adult females. Feed a variety of gut-loaded insects daily.
Terrarium Suitability: 2

Anolis cybotes Cope, 1862
Large-Headed Anole

Family: Polychrotidae.
Length: SVL: 3.2 in. (77 mm). TL: 9 in. (226 mm)
Habitat and Range: Widely distributed on Hispaniola, and recently introduced into southern Florida.
Natural History: This is a primarily ground-dwelling anole, found among logs and low plants in all but arid habitats. Large-headed anoles will take lookout positions low on tree trunks, usually in a head-down posture with the head extended at right angles to the tree. Color variable, mainly some shade of gray or tan, but changes to an orange. Males may have a green dorsal patch, and both sexes may have a series of bow tie-shaped light bars on the back. In many respects similar to that for the green anole, with which it is easily confused.
Care: Make sure terrarium has some ground cover, such as leaf litter and bark strips. Spray terrarium three to four times per week, as lizards rarely drink from a dish. Provide small crickets, mealworms, wax worms, and other soft-bodied insects on a daily basis. Keep the terrarium warm, between 72° and 93° F (22° and 34° C), and humidity between 75 and 90 percent. Large-headed anoles should have daily access to full-spectrum lighting.
Terrarium Suitability: 1

Anolis equestris Mertens, 1820
Knight Anole/Cuban Anole

Family: Polychrotidae.
Length: SVL: 5.25 in. (134 mm) TL: 12 in. (305 mm).
Habitat and Range: This native of the forests of Cuba and adjacent islands has also become established in southern Florida.
Natural History: This is one of the largest anoles; it derives its specific scientific name from the (supposedly) horse-shaped head. Unlike most other anoles, this species has a distinct ridge between each eye and the snout tip. The body is generally pale green but may turn grayish brown; there is a yellowish triangular marking on each shoulder. The dewlap is present, but comparatively smaller than in other anoles. These lizards are excellent climbers, almost entirely restricted to trees and bushes.
Care: Knight anoles are extremely hardy reptiles that do well in a forest-style terrarium. Provide plenty of branches and plants. Keep the humidity above 80 percent and air temperature between 82° and 100° F (28° and 38° C). Provide full-spectrum lighting. Males can be quite aggressive towards other lizards, especially other male knight anoles, so house them singly or with one or two adult females. Feed daily, providing large insects, such as adult crickets and cockroaches, and pink mice.
Terrarium Suitability: 1

Anolis garmani Stejneger 1899
Jamaican Giant Anole

Family: Polychrotidae.
Length: SVL: 5.2 in. (131 mm). TL: 10 in. (255 mm).
Habitat and Range: Semi-arid forest habitats in Jamaica, and introduced into Bermuda, Grand Cayman, and in Florida's Lee and Miami-Dade counties.
Natural History: This beautiful green species is unusual among anoles in that there is a distinct crest of low keeled scales along the nape (these may be lacking in females); the crest becomes shorter as it runs along the spine to the tail. The tail has strong keels, and the sticky toe-pads are large. They are capable of changing color to brown, black, or marbled, and males have a large bright orange throat fan with a pale green border. They feed on a wide variety of insects and occasionally consume flowers and nectar.
Care: Terrarium animals should be fed gut-loaded live insects daily. They need terrarium temperatures of 79° to 95° F (26° to 35° C) and full-spectrum lighting. The terrarium must be tall and contain several thick vertical branches for perching and basking. The lizards prefer to have a lot of cover high up in the cage. Lightly mist the terrarium each day, provide a dish of drinking water, and house no more than one male per enclosure.
Terrarium Suitability: 2

Anolis gundlachi Peters, 1877

Sail-Finned Anole/Puerto Rican Crested Anole/Yellow-Chinned Anole

Family: Polychrotidae

Length: SVL: 2.7 in. (69 mm). TL: 6.3 in. (160 mm).

Habitat and Range: Forests and shaded areas near streams and ponds at higher elevations in Puerto Rico. They prefer thick tree trunks and broad-leafed plants.

Natural History: This unusual anole sports a sail-like fin on the upper surface of the tail (larger in males), making them resemble tiny basilisks. They are olive to brown with a variegated pattern, and males have a dark brown throat fan. The eyes are generally blue. These are powerful anoles that feed not only on a variety of insects, but also on snails, other anoles, and the small local frogs.

Care: Terrarium specimens need temperatures of 74° to 80° F (23° to 27° C) and full-spectrum lighting for about ten hours per day. The terrarium should contain 2 inches (50 mm) of slightly moist soil that will help maintain humidity between 70 and 90 percent. Live plants are recommended, and the lizards will need thick vertical climbing surfaces. The terrarium should be at least 3 ft (0.9 m) in height and have good air circulation. Males should be housed alone or with groups of adult females; they tend to attack other males and may eat juveniles.

Terrarium Suitability: 3

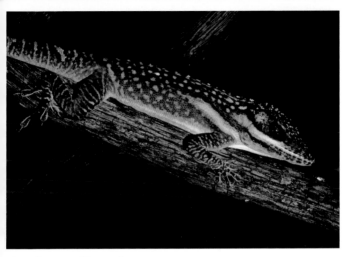

Anolis smallwoodi Schwartz, 1964
Leopard Anole

Family: Polychrotidae.
Length: SVL: 7.5 in. (190 mm). TL: 15 in. (381 mm).
Habitat and Range: Forests of extreme eastern Cuba.
Natural History and Care: This is a beautifully marked lizard, with dark brown markings on a grayish green background. The effect resembles fine stained glass work. Habits are similar in many respects to those of the knight anole, but this species also lives in drier habitats. Leopard anoles will usually be seen in trees above eye level, but also look for them on the ground. they are largely frugivorous, taking a variety of native flowers and berries in their diet, but will also eat any small prey they can overpower. Like knight anoles, these are pugnacious lizards that can give a painful bite with their strong jaws.
Care: Leopard anoles do well in a tall forest-style terrarium with plenty of branches and either live leafy plants or artificial plants. Keep the humidity above 80 percent and air temperature between 82° and 100° F (28° and 38° C). As with other anoles, provide this species with full-spectrum lighting. Males can be quite aggressive towards other lizards, especially other males, so house them singly or with one or two adult females. Feed daily, providing diced fruits, flowers, adult crickets, and pink mice. Do not house with smaller species.
Terrarium Suitability: 1

Anolis trinitatis Reinhardt and Lütkin, 1863
Trinidad Anole

Family: Polychrotidae.
Length: SVL: 2.9 in. (74 mm). TL: 7.2 in. (183 mm)
Habitat and Range: Moist, sparsely planted areas of St. Vincent Island (largely around Chateaubelair); introduced into Trinidad.
Natural History: A brilliantly colored tree lizard, with a bright green or dark blue body. The head may be yellow or have numerous red or orange spots, depending on mood and temperature. The dewlap is lemon yellow. Overall there are some 15 different color varieties of this species. They are inhabitants of the bases of trees, pillars, and fence posts and are quite active during the heat of the day.
Care: This peaceful species can be kept in a fairly small terrarium, preferably in pairs or trios (one male). Provide open basking and foraging space, along with a stout branch or tree trunk on which the lizards may climb. Keep the air temperature between 80° and 90° F (27° to 32° C) and humidity between 60 and 90 percent. Offer fruit flies and young crickets daily. Spray the terrarium heavily daily.
Terrarium Suitability: 1

Celestus stenurus (Cope, 1862)
Cope's Galliwasp

Family: Anguidae.
Length: SVL: 6.7in. (172 mm). TL: 14.3 in. (364.6 mm).
Habitat and Range: Wet forested mountain valleys of Haiti and the Dominican Republic.
Natural History: Many local people greatly fear galliwasps, believing the harmless lizards to be extremely venomous. This is a secretive, skink-like lizard that lives under leaf litter and in rotting trees, where humidity levels are high. The gray to olive body is shiny and slightly keeled, and the limbs are comparatively small. Some individuals may have thin dark stripes from the neck to mid-body or hips. When moving, the lizard appears to swim through the leaf litter. They are most active at late afternoon and twilight, when they forage for small live prey. Galliwasps feed on small arthropods, worms, millipedes, soft plants, flowers, and some fruit.
Care: They prefer lower temperatures than most lizards, with a preferred daytime range of 68° to 72° F (20° to 22° C). Daily exposure to UV light is essential to these lizards. As a substrate, use a deep layer of slightly moist soil suitable for burrowing. Females bear 1 to 6 live young, which should be fed live dusted insects and small berries and bits of fruit daily. Some galliwasps are known to live for 20 years.
Terrarium Suitability: 3

Chamaeleolis barbatus Garrido, 1982
Bearded Chameleon Anole

Family: Polychrotidae.
Length: SVL: 10 in. (254 mm). TL: 21 in. (540 mm)
Habitat and Range: Broadleaf forests along limestone hills on western Cuba.
Natural History: This large species escaped official notice until only 1982, and it remains very poorly known even today. It is similar to the Cuban chameleon anole in appearance and habits but is readily distinguished from that species by the serrated row of scales along the edge of the dewlap. The dewlap is gray, with a series of parallel white bars. Bearded chameleon anoles are known to spend considerable time in the shade; they feed on slugs and sleep on horizontal branches that are narrower than the lizard. They are generally found within 2 yards (1.8 m) of the ground. Their defense against predation is camouflage, and they blend into their environment very well.
Care: There is little available for keeping this species in captivity, but presumably care would be similar to that for the closely related Cuban chameleon anole (*C. chamaeleonides*).
Terrarium Suitability: 3

Chamaeleolis chamaeleonides Duméril and Bibron, 1837

Cuban Chameleon Anole

Family: Polychrotidae.
Length: SVL: 10 in. (254 mm). TL: 21 in. (540 mm)
Habitat and Range: Widely distributed among the moist, broadleaf forests of Cuba and its southern Isla de la Juventud.
Natural History: This is a large tree-dweller that somewhat resembles a gray knight anole. The head is similarly large, but in the chameleon anole there is a dark series of lines emanating from the eye, forming a star shape. There is also a raised vertebral crest, largest and most conspicuous on the neck. Like the Old World true chameleons, chameleon anoles are slow-moving lizards that spend almost all their time in trees. They are also capable of moving each eye independently of the other, a common feature in anoles and true chameleons.
Care: This species irequires a large well-ventilated terrarium with ambient temperatures near 86° F (30° C). Include full-spectrum lighting. Provide several upright stout branches for climbing and use as many live plants as possible. Heavily spray terrarium with water each day. Feed chameleon anoles snails, slugs, large insects, and small diced pieces of fruit three to four times per week. Do not house more than one male per terrarium.
Terrarium Suitability: 3

Chamaelinorops barbouri Schmidt, 1919
Barbour's Anole

Family: Polychrotidae.
Length: SVL: 2.2 in. (55 mm). TL: 5.4 in (137 mm)
Habitat and Range: Dwells in leaf litter of southern Hispaniola's broadleaf mountain forests, predominantly in the Dominican Republic.
Natural History: This is the most unusual of the anole-type lizards, for it is unlike all other anoles in several ways. First, Barbour's anole (named for a former herpetologist at Harvard University) does not engage in any of the display actions so typical of iguanine lizards generally. Second, it is strictly terrestrial, being most active in and under leaf litter. Third, these lizards do not run or scurry, but hop—swiftly—along the ground. Barbour's anole is poorly known and has many unusual characteristics that warrant further study.
Care: These anoles require a terrarium with a substrate of leaf litter and slightly moist soil. They rarely have access to sunlit areas, so keep the terrarium interior shaded. They feed on small insects, slugs, worms, and spiders. Preferred ambient temperature is between 70° and 81°F (21° and 27° C).
Terrarium Suitability: 2

Cyclura colliei Gray, 1845
Jamaican Iguana

Family: Iguanidae.
Length: SVL: 16 in. (406 mm). TL: 35.4 in. (900 mm).
Habitat and Range: Dry, rocky forests of extreme south-central Jamaica. Once believed extinct, but subsequently rediscovered and presently being bred by zoos.
Natural History and Care: This is perhaps the most streamlined member of the rhinoceros iguana group, and in many ways it more closely resembles the spiny-tailed iguanas (genus *Ctenosaura*) in shape. Its habitat is one of the most forbidding to humans, representing areas of razor-sharp rocky ground, sparse foliage, and intense heat in the appropriately named Hellshire Hills. Females excavate long tunnels in the soil and deposit 16 to 20 eggs that hatch about three months later. Successful hatching percentages are correlated with maternal size at laying. Only two nesting sites are known for the wild population, and plans are being drafted to try introducing the iguanas onto some small islets. The main predators are dogs, mongooses, and probably pigs.
Care: There has been considerable success in keeping and breeding this highly endangered iguana in zoos. Care is as for other *Cyclura*, although the rarity of this species prevents it from showing up in the pet trade.
Terrarium Suitability: 4

Cyclura cornuta (Bonnaterre, 1780)
Rhinoceros Iguana

Family: Iguanidae

Length: SVL: 20 in. (508 mm). TL: 43.3 in. (1,100 mm).

Habitat and Range: Hispaniola and Mona Island, in arid and hot environments.

Natural History: Rhinoceros iguanas are primarily herbivorous and are capable of feeding on even the driest of leaves and grasses in their arid habitat. They are also likely to consume carrion and small animals if the opportunity arises. These iguanas are colonial animals, and groups may number a dozen or more individuals. Males are aggressively territorial and will put on an impressive display and fight over possession of an area.

Care: All rhinoceros iguanas require large terraria, and a keeper should house no more than one adult male per enclosure. They need to be kept very warm, so provide a basking area in the range of 100° to 105° F (38° to 40° C) range. Provide 10 to 14 hours of full-spectrum lighting daily. Also, provide a large pool of water so the iguanas may completely immerse themselves. Feed them a daily assortment of fruits, vegetables, and vitamin and mineral supplements. Provide freshly killed mice or small rats from time to time.

Terrarium Suitability: 3

Cyclura cychlura (Cuvier, 1829)
Andros Island Iguana/Exuma Island Iguana

Family: Iguanidae.
Length: SVL: 21 in. (533 mm). TL: 45 in. (1,143 mm).
Habitat and Range: The Caribbean islands to the north of Cuba.
Natural History: This large gray lizard is often seen on the scenic beaches of the northern Caribbean, where colonies of several individuals may alternate sunning on the sand with shuttling to shade to cool down. Unlike other *Cyclura* species, these iguanas are not especially territorial, and fights among males are extremely rare. Adults of this species are also more likely than related species to be found climbing into the trees. Andros/Exuma Island iguanas are often seen under partial shade cover of pines. Possibly because of habitat encroachment by humans, the iguanas are found in a variety of habitats, from forests to rocky hills to beaches. Areas with sandy soils, suitable for excavating nest tunnels, seem required for egg sites. Though active on beaches, these iguanas rarely enter the water. Foods include many types of vegetation, including dry grasses, but they prefer fruits and soft green leaves.
Care: Care is as for *Cyclura cornuta*.
Terrarium Suitability: 3

Cyclura lewisi Grant, 1940
Grand Cayman Blue Iguana

Family: Iguanidae.
Length: SVL: 27 in. (686 mm). TL: 59.8 in. (1,520 mm).
Habitat and Range: Dry rocky areas and beaches of both Cuba and the Cayman Islands.
Natural History: This critically endangered lizard is called the most endangered iguana on earth by researchers. Recent surveys put wild populations at 15 to 30 individuals, though captive propagation efforts have been successful in keeping total numbers much higher. Causes of extermination include habitat destruction and predation by feral animals, notably introduced rats and cats. Unfortunately for the iguanas, their preferred habitats are also the ones favored by land developers and farmers; in Caymans researcher Fred Burton's words, these mutual interests are "making its protection socially and politically difficult." Their escape from extinction, if possible, will depend on captive breeding programs. Their diet is made up almost entirely of leaves from weeds and grasses, plus fruits that have fallen from trees.
Care: The rarity of these animals prevents them from being in the hands of private hobbyists. However, their care is similar to that of *Cyclura cornuta*.
Terrarium Suitability: 4

Cyclura nubila Gray, 1831
Caymans Islands Iguana/Cuban Iguana

Family: Iguanidae.
Length: SVL: 22 in. (559 mm). TL: 59.8. in.(1,520 mm)
Habitat and Range: The Cayman Islands and Cuba and nearby islets. Introduced to Isla Magueyes, Puerto Rico
Natural History: The Cuban and Cayman Islands populations of this species are considered distinct subspecies—*C. n. nubila* and *C. n. caymanensis* respectively—by some herpetologists. This is the largest species of *Cyclura* and among the largest land animals native to the Caribbean. They occur in a range of habitats on their home islands, including mangrove stands, wet forests, and scrub forests with rocky areas of limestone soil and sand. Males aggressively defend their territories against other males. Like other *Cyclura*, they are opportunistic feeders, taking primarily plant matter but supplementing with carrion, large insects, and small vertebrates. The Cuban subspecies is known to feed on crabs occasionally. The conservation program for this species has been fairly successful, although it is still considered endangered.
Care: See *Cyclura cornuta*.
Terrarium Suitability: 4

Gonatodes ceciliae **Donoso-Barros, 1965**
Variegated Gecko

Family: Sphaerodactylidae.
Length: SVL: 2.0 in. (51 mm). TL: 5.6 in. (143 mm).
Habitat and Range: Paria Peninsula, Venezuela, and central and north central Trinidad, in cool microhabitats of moist forests.
Natural History: Males of this handsome gecko are predominantly red, mottled with yellow and black. A distinct black-edged yellow collar encircles the neck in both sexes but is more conspicuous in males. Females are less intensely colored, being dark gray to maroon with light makings. There are four to five small spines above each eye. Variegated geckos are found on the ground, on tree stumps, and sometimes on the walls of buildings. Typical for brightly colored gecko species, variegated geckos are largely diurnal but restrict their activities to shaded places. They are sensitive to heat and will stay in areas where the maximum temperature is below 84° F (29° C). They feed on a variety of tiny insects, from ants and termites to fruit flies. Females lay a single egg per clutch but may lay every 20 to 35 days. Eggs hatch after about three months.
Care: Provide a tall tank with plenty of climbing surfaces and warm but not hot temperatures. Feed a variety of small insects—fruit flies, pinhead crickets, etc. Mist regularly.
Terrarium Suitability: 2

Iguana delicatissima Laurenti, 1768
Lesser Antilles Iguana

Familly: Iguanidae.
Length: SVL: 24 in. (610 mm). TL: 60 in. (1,522 mm).
Habitat and Range: The islands of the Lesser Antilles, southeastern Caribbean, including (north to south) Anguilla, St. Maarten, St. Barthélemey, St. Eustatius, Guadeloupe, Dominica, and Martinique.
Natural History and Care: This is another very poorly known large lizard, but it is reportedly similar in habits and ecology to the more familiar and widespread green iguana (*Iguana iguana*). Where the two species overlap in range, hybrids are common. They are known to be very adaptable to the conditions on their small islands, living in forests, cactus and rock flatlands, and dry grasslands. Iguanas are most active during the morning hours, when they search for food, but remain active until near sundown. Lesser Antilles iguanas feed on a variety of plant materials, especially prickly pear cactus (*Opuntia*). Mating occurs in spring, and eggs are laid from August through October. Females excavate long tunnels and lay up to 18 eggs that hatch in about three months. Hatchlings are arboreal, inhabiting lower branches of trees and shrubs in dense thickets.
Care: As for *Iguana iguana* (see Region 4: South America), although this species is not legally available in the pet trade.
Terrarium Suitability: 4

Leiocephalus carinatus Gray, 1827
Brown Curly-Tailed Lizard

Family: Leiocephalidae.
Length: SVL: 5 in. (130 mm). TL: 6.6 in. (169 mm).
Habitat and Range: Cuba, the Bahamas, and several Caribbean islands. It has also become an established introduction in southern Florida. It dwells in dry sandy areas where there is ample cover, including beaches—where it is common to see them—open grassy areas, and rubbish heaps.
Natural History: A common, active lizard that resembles the fence lizards of the American mainland, differing in having a low nuchal crest of triangular scales. Characteristic of the genus is the habit of holding the tail in a curl over the hips. When running, the curl is tighter and waved from side to side, possibly creating an optical illusion that confuses would-be predators.
Care: Males are aggressively territorial and should be housed one per terrarium. Curly-tailed lizards are omnivorous and can be fed flowers, fruit, seeds, insects, spiders, small prawns, and anoles. Keep temperature at 90° to 115° F (33° to 46° C) during the day, and humidity between 60 and 80 percent.
Terrarium Suitability: 2

Proctoporus shrevei **Parker, 1935**
Luminous Lizard

Family: Gymnophthalmidae.
Length: SVL: 1.65 in. (42 mm). TL: 4.1 in. (104.7 mm).
Habitat and Range: Restricted to remote mountain caves in north central Trinidad, on Mt. Aripo.
Natural History: The luminous lizard is a remarkable animal, for it has tiny silvery spots on the sides of the body that reflect light, making the lizard appear to glow. The body is brown, with large scales, and along the sides are a series of dark-rimmed "portholes." In 2002, a group of biologists finally had specimens to observe and study, and published the finding that *P. shrevei* is not capable of producing bioluminescence. Other specimens were photographed that did appear to be glowing; the question of their bioluminescence thus remains open. Luminous lizards are found in cold wet habitat and will take to the water readily.
Care: Luminous lizards should have a terrarium with several large rocks arranged to make horizontal crevices for hiding. Substrate should be a slightly moist mixture of moss and soil. Keep temperature between 69° and 73° F (20° to 23° C); at higher temperatures they become heat stressed. Keep humidity between 70 and 85 percent. Give them small gut-loaded insects daily.
Terrarium Suitability: 4

Sphaerodactylus nigropunctatus Gray, 1845
Black-Spotted Gecko

Family: Sphaerodactylidae.
Length: SVL: 1.3 in. (33 mm). TL: 2.73 in. (69.3 mm).
Habitat and Range: Very widely distributed throughout the Caribbean, including Andros Island, the Lesser Antilles, the Bahamas, Cuba, and Puerto Rico.
Natural History: A very tiny lizard that has round and sticky toe pads on the tip of each digit, and no moving eyelids. Adults are pale violet-gray with large dark spots. The unbroken tail is uniform orange or rusty brown. Juveniles are banded with cream, dark brown and chocolate brown; the pattern extends the length of the tail. Black-spotted geckos have occupied most habitats on their respective islands, from forests to beaches to hotels. They are often seen on building walls at night chasing insects drawn by lights. They are also found around the peeling bark of trees, especially palms.
Care: Black-spotted geckos do not require a large terrarium, and they can thrive in a variety of terrarium conditions. Essential for their care, though, are large quantities of very small insects—pinhead crickets and fruit flies—and shelter that will maintain humidity levels above 70 percent. Provide heat from heating tapes or a small under terrarium heat pad.
Terrarium Suitability: 3

Additional species that occur in the Caribbean but are also found elsewhere are listed below. You may find a species account for these lizards in the region section given in parentheses.

Anolis carolinensis (Region 1: North America covering the United States and Canada)
Anolis sagrei (Region 1: North America,covering the United States and Canada)
Gonatodes fuscus (Region 1: North America covering the United States and Canada)
Iguana iguana (Region 4: South America and the Galapagos)
Polychrus marmoratus (Region 4: South America and the Galapagos)

Mexico and Central America

beaded lizard (*Heloderma horridum*)

The mainland between the United States and South America is possibly the most biologically rich area on Earth. Much of the great isthmus was below sea level during prehistoric times, and as sea levels lowered, newly exposed land was colonized by species from the nearby mainlands. Mexico and Central America contain many lizard-friendly habitats, from tropical beaches to dry forests, deserts, grasslands, swamps, and rain forests, and in most places the lizards are active year-round. The largest lizards of the region are green and spiny iguanas, basilisks, and beaded lizards. Look for the smaller species on trees, in and among shrubs, in leaf litter, and on sunlit rocks.

Mexico has a combination of species whose ancestors came from both North and South America, while the more southern countries have largely South American-type faunas. There are several endemic groups in both regions, including xenosaurids. Central America contains members of all of North America's native families of lizards.

Abronia aurita (Cope, 1868)
Green Alligator Lizard/Cope's Alligator Lizard

Family: Anguidae.
Length: SVL: 5 in. (125 mm). TL: 12.5 in. (318 mm).
Habitat and Range: Montane forests of central Guatemala.
Natural History: This colorful anguid resembles the North American alligator lizards, except the body is stouter and the plate-like scales significantly larger. The body is shiny green, with darker green bands, and occasionally red spots on the head. Juveniles are light gray, with darker chevrons across the back. The head is large, broad at the rear, and distinctly triangular when viewed from above. Unlike most other members of this genus, the scales in this species are not especially rugose, except on the temples. Green alligator lizards are largely arboreal, found in shrubs and trees, where their prehensile tail helps them keep balance. All members of the genus produce live young.
Care: This beautiful lizard was very poorly known until it appeared in the animal trade in the late 1990s, and it is probably the largest lizard in the genus *Abronia*. Its diet includes insects, snails, slugs, and possibly flowers. Keep them in a humid terrarium with plenty of climbing branches.
Terrarium Suitability: 3

Abronia graminea (Cope, 1864)
Grassy Alligator Lizard/Terrestrial Alligator Lizard

Family: Anguidae.
Length: SVL: 4.1 in. (103 mm). TL: 8.6 in. (218 mm).
Habitat and Range: Occurs in the vicinity of eastern coastal Mexico, centered around Veracruz. Most *Abronia* species have very small distributions.
Natural History: Arguably the most colorful of the anguid lizards, this arboreal lizard is found in and near trees in moist and semi-arid regions but is also very likely to be seen on the ground. The grassy alligator lizard is one of the most terrestrial species of *Abronia*. The tail is strongly prehensile and is used like a fifth appendage while climbing. The large scales, emerald green coloring, and broad head distinguish this species from its relatives. It is diurnal, preferring temperatures in the 80s F (27° to 30° C), retreating to shade when it becomes too warm. Grassy alligator lizards feed on a variety of arthropods and small vertebrates and sometimes eat flowers and fruits.
Care: A rare species in captivity, these lizards can probably be kept much like *Abronia aurita*.
Terrarium Suitability: 3

Abronia mixteca **Bogert and Porter, 1967**

Mixteca Alligator Lizard

Family: Anguidae.

Length: SVL: 4.1 in. (103 mm) TL: 5.6 in. (245 mm).

Habitat and Range: Montane pine oak forests above 2000 meters in the Sierra Madre del Sur, Oaxaca, and Guerrero Mexico.

Natural History: This is a gray lizard with yellow markings on the neck and sides. Some individuals have irregular dark bars across the back. In some localities they may also sport a somewhat yellowish to orange dorsum. These lizards have a broadly triangular head and large rugose scales, making the species appear similar to the Australian shingleback skink. They prefer comparatively cool temperatures (61° to 72° F [16° to 22° C]) and a well-planted, shady habitat. They are generally slow-moving and difficult to spot. Look for them on branches in trees.

Care: Provide two to four hours of UV light at least several times per week. Mist the plant leaves and other surfaces in the morning, and keep humidity between 65 and 75 percent. Feed these lizards insects, some flowers (dandelions, daisies) and small pieces of fresh fruit. In captivity they have lived for almost five years.

Terrarium Suitability: 4

Anniella geronimensis Shaw, 1940
Baja Legless Lizard

Family: Anniellidae.
Length: SVL: 5.6 in. (142 mm). TL 11 in. (284 mm)
Habitat and Range: Loose soils, especially near and under low-growing plants, along the western half of Baja California.
Natural History: Closely related to and easily confused with the California legless lizard (see Region 1: North America), from which it differs in having a more pointed snout and a series of very thin broken black lines running down the body. Found in sand dunes and near beaches under low shrubby plants, usually within 3 in. (76 mm) of the surface. Inclined to move about on the surface in the early morning (when they may drink from dewdrops) and late afternoon.
Care: Provide loose sand, a shallow water dish, and some bark or broad live plants. Keep soil slightly moist but never damp. Prefers low temperatures, from 65° to 73° F (16° to 23° C). Feed small mealworms, young crickets, and small worms three times per week. Do not house with other species.
Terrarium Suitability: 2

Basiliscus basiliscus (Linnaeus, 1758)
Brown Basilisk

Family: Corytophanidae.
Length: SVL: 9.4 in. (240 mm). TL: 32 in. (805 mm)
Habitat and Range: Along heavily forested streams, rivers, and lakes from southwestern Nicaragua into Colombia and west-central Venezuela.
Natural History: This is a brown lizard in which males may have spectacular crests on the nape and back of similar size and shape as those of the green basilisk. Brown basilisks are largely arboreal, spending time basking and foraging in trees. When not basking to increase body temperature, they tend to avoid direct sunlight. Basilisks are active animals that require large terraria.
Care: Provide an enclosure at least four times the length of the lizard and a width twice the length of the lizard. The terrarium should also be tall with adequate climbing facilities and plenty of cover in which lizards may hide. Provide a good heat source above at least one basking site, where the temperature may reach 110° F (43.5° C). Include full-spectrum lighting. Because basilisks generally do not like direct light, be sure there is adequate filtering of the light source. Basilisks eat a variety of live foods, including insects, small rodents, and other lizards.
Terrarium Suitability: 2

Basiliscus plumifrons Cope, 1876
Green Basilisk

Family: Corytophanidae.
Length: SVL: 10 in. (254mm). TL: 35.8 in. (910 mm)
Habitat and Range: Limited to heavily forested riparian habitats in central Nicaragua, Costa Rica, and extreme northwestern Panama.
Natural History: This is the iconic species of basilisk. It is the largest species of basilisk, but it has the smallest natural range of its genus. Green basilisks show considerable sexual dimorphism, such that males have large—often double—head crests and a large vertebral crest that continues on to the tail. Females and young may have a small single head crest, but they lack the other adornments. They live in hot humid rainforests alongside streams that may be fed by water that is quite cold. The lizards spend most of their time on land or in trees, retreating to the water primarily to escape predation. They feed on smaller animals, both vertebrate and invertebrate.
Care: Green basilisks require nearly identical care as brown basilisks (*B. basiliscus*) do. Feed juveniles daily, adults three times per week. Offer live insects, slugs, earthworms, small fish (guppies or mollies), small lizards, and pink mice. It is best not to house these lizards with other species unless you have access to a very large enclosure, such as found in major zoos.
Terrarium Suitability: 3

Basiliscus vittatus Wiegmann, 1828
Striped Basilisk

Family: Corytophanidae.
Length: SVL: 5.7 in. (145 mm). TL: 23 in. (580 mm).
Habitat and Range: Coastal and southern mainland Mexico (not Baja) south to Panama and northwestern Colombia.
Natural History: This species is similar in appearance and habits to the brown basilisk, differing mainly in the shape of the male's head crest. Like other basilisks, this species has toes with enlarged wedge-shaped scales on the lower surface. The scales help distribute the lizard's weight when running, thereby making it possible for basilisks to run on the surface of ponds and streams without sinking in. When frightened, the lizards run along the surface of the water, giving them considerable distance from a would-be predator, then dive and swim away while submerged.
Care: Care is as for the brown basilisk (*B. basiliscus*). Basilisks need large terraria because they are active swimmers, climbers, and diggers. They need a large pool of water in which they can swim, and the water will need regular changing.
Terrarium Suitability: 2

Bipes biporus (Cope, 1894)
Baja Worm Lizard

Family: Bipedidae.
Length: SVL: 8 in. (210 mm).
Habitat and Range: Restricted to hard soils in southern Baja California.
Natural History: This amphisbaenian is one of only four worm lizards with limbs. A tiny pair of stubby arms lies just behind the head, each with five long clawed fingers. The head is very blunt, and the eyes are represented only by tiny dark spots. The body is covered in scales that form distinct bands that give the animal the appearance of an earthworm. Baja worm lizards burrow through soil when it has been softened by rain or erosion, living in the almost concrete-hard tunnels that result as the soils dry. They are active out of tunnels only during rainy evenings. Females lay up to four eggs in the tunnels, and these hatch after some 50 to 60 days. Hatching coincides with the rainy season when invertebrate food becomes abundant. They are rarely found above ground except during rains; they consume worms, ants, and termites.
Care: This species is rarely kept in captivity. It needs a deep soil substrate with moist bottom layers. Surface temperatures can be warm as long as the lizard can escape the heat by burrowing into cool soil.
Terrarium Suitability: 3

Coleonyx mitratus (**Peters, 1863**)
Central American Banded Gecko

Family: Eublepharidae.
Length: SVL: 3.8 in. (97 mm). TL: 8.4 in. (213 mm).
Habitat and Range: Dry habitats, from desert to scrubland, from Guatemala to Costa Rica.
Natural History: Delicate and nocturnal, these geckos belong to the family Eublepharidae, characterized by having moveable eyelids and toes without sticky pads. By day they retire under rocks, logs, and in crevices where small insects live and humidity is high. They are most active at dusk and dawn, when they move slowly in search of insect prey. When they see an insect, they can dash forward with remarkable speed. The tail, used as a fat reservoir, is thick but fragile. It will drop easily if the lizard is threatened or seized, and the gecko grows a stiff and imperfect replacement.
Care: This species can be kept as per their North American relatives (see *Coleonyx variegatus* in Region 1: North America), but also thrives in moister and less sandy terraria, too.
Terrarium Suitability: 1

Corytophanes cristatus (**Merrem, 1820**)
Large-Crested Iguana/Helmeted Iguana

Family: Corytophanidae.
Length: SVL: 4.7 in. (120 mm). TL: 15 in. (385 mm).
Habitat and Range: Forests from Veracruz, Mexico, south to northwestern Colombia.
Natural History: Large-crested iguanas are slow moving residents of moist forests, generally observed in a vertical posture on tree trunks and branches. They depend on cryptic coloration as defense and so may allow close approach before dashing away. From their perches they look for the large insects that make up their prey, at which time they quickly lunge to attack. Jonathan Campbell has noted that this species is so lethargic that liverworts and filamentous algae may grow on individuals' backs. When basking, large-crested iguanas favor indirect sunlight. The three to five eggs are laid in nests in the soil and take about five months to hatch. *Corytophanes hernandezi* (Wiegmann, 1831) is a close relative with a similar range (but not south of Panama) and habitat requirements. In coloring, though, it is different, having a brown to reddish body with a pale head crest.
Care: Terrarium heat should come from an infrared source, and provide full-spectrum lighting daily. Keep the humidity high. This species has a very poor survival rate in captivity.
Terrarium Suitability: 4

Crotaphytus dickersonae Schmidt, 1922
Mexican Collared Lizard

Family: Crotaphytidae
Length: SVL: 4.6 in. (116 mm). TL: 11 in. (279 mm).
Habitat and Range: Dry rocky areas on Isla Tiburón and coastal Sonora, Mexico.
Natural History: This large and conspicuous lizard has a very limited distribution. Very little is known about this species in the wild. Like other collared lizards, males tend to grow larger and are more colorful than females, often having blue-green bodies with bright white speckling. This is the only collared lizard with an almost turquoise coloration, making identification easy. Mexican collared lizards are aggressive and can give a painful nip if handled. They feed on insects, centipedes, and smaller lizards.
Care: Keep terrarium daytime temperatures between 85° and 110° F (29.5° and 43.5° C). Care is as for other *Crotaphytus* (see Region 1: North America).
Terrarium Suitability: 2

hatchling

adult

Ctenosaura hemilopha (Cope, 1863)
Western Black Iguana

Family: Iguanidae.
Length: SVL: 13.5 in. (343 mm). TL: 38.4 in. (975 mm).
Habitat and Range: Eastern and southern Baja California and the western coastal mainland of Mexico.
Natural History: Western black iguanas are the Mexican tourism industry's "poster reptile" on brochures and television ads. These sleek black-banded, slate gray lizards are impressive and conspicuous residents near many of the most popular resorts, and their large size and colonial habits make it very likely even casual ecotourists will spot them. Mating generally occurs in the early spring (March to April) and egg laying takes place a month or so later.
Care: Western black iguanas require very roomy enclosures, and males—which are extremely territorial—must be housed alone or only with females. Given their adult sizes, territoriality, and relative activity, these animals should be housed in terraria no less than 9.8 feet (3 meters) square, and 6.6 feet (2 meters) tall. Full-spectrum lighting is essential, and exposure to natural sunlight is recommended. Temperatures should be 95° to 120° F (35° to 49° C), but humidity is less critical and may range from 35 to 100 percent.
Terrarium Suitability: 2

Diploglossus bilobatus O'Shaughnessy, 1874
Talamancan Galliwasp

Family: Anguidae.
Length: SVL: 3.6 in. (92 mm). TL: 8 in. (203 mm).
Habitat and Range: Rainforests of Costa Rica and Panama.
Natural History: This is a handsome skink-like lizard more likely
to be heard as it scampers through leaf litter than seen. The body
is bronzy to brown, with reddish sides from midbody to tail tip.
The head and neck are yellow to light orange and have several white
markings. The awl-shaped head is used to help the galliwasp push
through debris in search of the snails, slugs, and small insects upon
which it feeds. Though diurnal, the Talamancan galliwasp is not
inclined to bask in sunlight for more than a few seconds.
Care: Very little is known about the natural history or captive care of
these secretive lizards, though they are probably egg-layers.
Terrarium Suitability: 4

Gambelia copei (**Yarrow, 1882**)
Cope's Leopard Lizard

Family: Crotaphytidae.
Length: SVL: 5 in. (127 mm). TL: 11.5 in. (292 mm).
Habitat and Range: Scrub desert flatlands of Baja, Mexico, and extreme south-central California.
Natural History: Unlike other leopard lizards, this species is a dusty gray and light tan, with many tiny white specks salted on the back and nape. Darker brown blotches form irregular tail bands. It is an aggressive hunter that feeds largely on insects, but will consume any live prey it can overcome.
Care: Like other active flatland desert species, Cope's leopard lizards need large terraria with plenty of floor space—approximately 4 feet (1.2 meters) square or more—and a few large rocks and low plants that will serve as basking and ambush sites. Provide a deep sand substrate. They should only be housed with their own species, and no more than one adult male per enclosure of the size mentioned. Offer daily feedings of insects, and supplement occasionally with pink mice, small live lizards, and washed dandelion flowers. Keep the air temperature high, from 90° to 115° F (33° to 46° C) during the day, and humidity low, between 30 and 60 percent. Give these lizards daily exposure to full-spectrum lighting.
Terrarium Suitability: 2

Heloderma horridum (Wiegmann, 1829)
Mexican Beaded Lizard
Venomous

Family: Helodermatidae.
Length: SVL: 18 in. (457 mm). TL: 40 in. (1,016 mm).
Habitat and Range: Widely distributed from central Mexico south into Guatemala. Absent from Baja California. They are most likely encountered in arid forest and desert borderland, where they are both ground foragers and active tree climbers.
Natural History: This large, stocky species has scales that resemble beadwork, each scale being a small dome. Coloration is generally black with pale to intense yellow mottling, but one subspecies from lower Mexico is entirely black. There is no light coloring on the head, and the tongue is dark purple. In Gila monsters, the other *Heloderma* species, the head is mottled and the tongue is pink. The tongue is long and forked, and these lizards frequently extrude it to taste the air.
Care: Care requirements of Mexican beaded lizards closely parallel those of the Gila monster, and in fact both species may be housed together. Beaded lizards, however, are generally less placid than captive Gila monsters, so greater care should be exercised when handling lizards or cleaning the terrarium. This species likes to soak in water, so provide a large tub of water once or twice per month.
Terrarium Suitability: 4

Laemanctus longipes Wiegmann, 1834
Cone-Headed Lizard/Casque-Headed Iguana

Family: Corytophanidae.
Length: SVL: 9 in. (230 mm). TL: 27.5 in. (700 mm).
Habitat and Range: Forested areas from northeastern Mexico south to Costa Rica.
Natural History: Cone-headed lizards are elongated and slender, with very long tails. In both sexes, there is a large rounded casque on the back of the head. The similar *L. serratus* has conical spines on the casque. These are slow-moving arboreal lizards similar in some ways to chameleons. They rarely are seen on the ground unless laying eggs (four to five per clutch). Usually found singly, they seem to be territorial. They feed on insects and other invertebrates and possibly small vertebrates.
Care: Both species of *Laemanctus* do poorly in captivity, typically being stressed and dehydrated when imported from the wild. Set them up in a tall terrarium with plenty of climbing materials, cover, and ventilation. Air temperatures should be in the 80s (27° to 31°C) and about 95°F (35°C) at the basking site. Do not let humidity drop below 75 percent. Mist the lizards frequently; consider investing in an automated misting system. Full-spectrum lighting is necessary. Feed them a variety of gut-loaded insects daily. They should probably be housed singly, and do not house males together.
Terrarium Suitability: 4

Lepidophyma flavimaculata Duméril, 1851
Yellow-Spotted Night Lizard

Family: Xantusiidae.
Length: SVL: 3.8 in. (97 mm). TL: 8.4 in. (213 mm).
Habitat and Range: From Veracruz in Mexico to south-central Panama, in areas with caves or limestone deposits, particularly in moist forests.
Natural History: The night lizards of Mexico and Central America are dark-colored and have numerous longitudinal tubercles on the body. Belly scales are rectangular, larger than dorsal scales, and arranged in rows. There are no moveable eyelids, so the eyes are always open. Night lizards, as the name suggests, are entirely nocturnal and unlikely to be observed unless one inspects the interiors of caves or rotting logs. From two to six young are produced alive in southern populations, while lizards from Mexico lay eggs.
Care: These lizards are hardy, feeding on a variety of live foods, such as wax and mealworms, crickets, and small earthworms. Although from tropical climes, they live in cool, moist microhabitats, so do not overheat them.
Terrarium Suitability: 1

Petrosaurus thalassinus (Cope, 1863)

Greater Blue Rock Lizard

Family: Phrynosomatidae.
Length: SVL: 7 in. (176 mm). TL: 17.5 in. (445 mm).
Habitat and Range: Arid rocky arroyos and valleys throughout Baja California.
Natural History: "*Petrosaurus*" literally means "rock lizard," and the name describes the habitat where this handsome turquoise species lives. Greater blue rock lizards are alert, keeping watch over their arroyos from large boulders, scampering between them at any hint of danger. These lizards are insect-eaters but will also take centipedes, spiders, and small scorpions. They are most intensely colored when warm, but in the early morning the coloration may be more gray than blue.
Care: These lizards both run and climb well, so a large terrarium is essential. Provide a sandy substrate and plenty of rocks on which they can perch and between which they may hide. Keep the terrarium warm, between 90° and 115° F (33° and 46° C), and the humidity around 70 to 80 percent. Provide full-spectrum lighting. Offer a variety of live insects daily, and supplement with small washed flowers or diced fruit weekly. Suitable terrarium mates include desert iguanas, fence lizards, chuckwallas, banded geckos, and American skinks—avoid tankmates that are small enough for the rock lizard to eat.
Terrarium Suitability: 2

Potamites apodemus (Uzzell, 1966)
Brown Water Tegu

Family: Gymnophthalmidae.
Length: SVL: 1.9 in. (47 mm). TL: 4.1 in. (103.4 mm).
Habitat and Range: Moist habitats around moss-covered logs and leaf litter from central Costa Rica to extreme northern Colombia.
Natural History: This tiny species is easily overlooked, staying near shelter. When foraging it tends to stay under the cover of logs or beneath fallen leaves. It is also capable of swimming fairly well, particularly through puddles. It feeds on small insects and may capture flies out of the air. There are several species of rough-skinned water tegus from Central America to central South America, found in moist habitats from near sea level to mountain tops.
Care: Rarely collected for captivity, but presumably they require high humidity and moderate temperatures, between 68° and 75° F (20° and 24° C), provided by indirect lighting. Offer UV for two to three hours. Offer a variety of small live insects and worms daily.
Terrarium Suitability: 4

Sauromalus hispidis Stejneger, 1891
Spiny Chuckwalla

Family: Iguanidae.
Length: SVL: 14.4 in. (367 mm). TL: 26 in. (660 mm).
Habitat and Range: Restricted to rocky habitats on the islands of Ángel de la Guarda, San Lorenzo Norte, San Lorenzo Sur, and Bahía de los Angeles in the Gulf of California.
Natural History: This is a large herbivorous lizard with pointed scales and a predominantly black unmarked body. When threatened, spiny chuckwallas will dash into a crevice and inflate the body, making extrication by a predator (or human hand) difficult. If caught in the open, they may lunge and bite an intruder. As herbivores, they have extremely strong jaws that allow the lizard to bite a variety of dry plants. They feed exclusively on vegetation, including cactuses, fruits, seeds, grasses, and flowers. In the wild, the chuckwallas are less active during the hottest part of the summer day, foraging at dusk and dawn.
Care: Like other chuckwallas, this is a heat-loving species, so keep them warm (95° to 115° F [35° to 43° C]), but provide adequate cool shelter and a dish of clean water. This species needs daily access to 10 to 14 hours of full-spectrum lighting. Feed a wide variety of vegetables, fruits, and flowers, focusing on leafy greens. Males are aggressively territorial and cannot be housed together.
Terrarium Suitability: 3

Sauromalus varius Dickerson, 1919
Island Chuckwalla

Family: Iguanidae.
Length: SVL: 14.4 in. (367 mm). TL: 26 in. (660 mm)
Habitat and Range: Isla San Esteban and Roca Lobos, Gulf of California.
Natural History: The variety of island-endemic species in the Gulf of California is remarkable and has prompted many biological studies. Not one but six island chuckwallas occur in the Gulf, but nowhere do species occur together. The island chuckwalla has smaller scales than the spiny chuckwalla and differs also in having a dark gray to brown dorsum and tail mottled with pale to dark orange. Island chuckwallas are lethargic and do not forage widely for food. Groups of several individuals may occupy a single burrow and when basking may lie on top of each other.
Care: This species requires the same care as *S. hispidis* in the previous entry.
Terrarium Suitability: 3

Sceloporus hunsakeri **Hall and Smith, 1979**
Hunsaker's Spiny Lizard

Family: Phrynosomatidae.
Length: SVL: 3.4 in. (86 mm). TL: 8 in. (203 mm).
Habitat and Range: Extreme southeastern Baja California, from La Paz to the western tip of Cabo San Lucas.
Natural History: These are handsome lizards with very spiny scales. Males are greenish or yellowish with yellowish heads, a broad purple stripe from neck to tail, and black patches on the front of the shoulders. Belly marked with dark metallic blues and greens. Females and young are greenish to brown without a purple stripe, and are unmarked on the belly. Spiny lizards are found in areas with large rocks and boulders mixed with vegetation. They spend considerable time on the rocks but also climb the plants. They are most active at late afternoon and twilight, but they have also been seen active at night. They feed on small arthropods, worms, millipedes, soft plants and flowers.
Care: They need terrarium temperatures of 79° to 95° F (26° to 35° C) and UV lighting for about half the day. The terrarium must contain at least 12 inches (305 mm) of slightly moist sandy soil suitable for burrowing. Very little is known about this species, but their care is probably not that different from other desert-dwelling *Sceloporus*.
Terrarium Suitability: 3

female

male

Sceloporus malachiticus Cope, 1864
Emerald Spiny Lizard/Emerald Swift

Family: Phrynosomatidae.

Length: SVL: 3.8 in. (96.5 mm). TL: 9.6 in. (245 mm).

Habitat and Range: Restricted to a few cloud forests in central El Salvador, Honduras, Nicaragua, Costa Rica, and Panama.

Natural History: This is a beautifully colored swift that is unusual in that it lives in moist forests rather than more open grasslands and forest edges. Males are more brightly colored than females, and they have blue ventral markings and may have a bright blue tail. Color changes from gray to black are also common, especially as a function of body temperature. Because they live at high altitudes, some populations of emerald spiny lizards endure nighttime temperatures at or below freezing. However, this lizard needs warmth, and those that live in the coolest habitats exploit morning sunlight to raise their body temperatures rapidly. Unlike most other fence lizards, emerald spiny lizards produce two to six live young instead of eggs.

Care: These swifts prefer lower temperatures than most of their relatives. Keep temperatures around 75° F (24° C) with a basking spot that reaches at least 85°F (29.5°C), and humidity at 70 to 100 percent. Provide full-spectrum lighting and a varied diet of insects, worms, and other small prey.

Terrarium Suitability: 2

Xenosaurus grandis (Gray, 1856)
Mexican Knobby Lizard

Family: Xenosauridae.
Length: SVL: 4.5 in. (115 mm). TL: 9 in. (230 mm).
Habitat and Range: Semi-arid forests from central Mexico south to Guatemala.
Natural History: Knobby lizards are members of a family entirely restricted to Mexico and Central America, though a Chinese relative has occasionally been placed in the same family. These lizards are characterized by a distinctly triangular head, body covered in linear rows of slightly enlarged scales, and a thin tail slightly shorter than the SVL. Ventral scales are arranged in longitudinal rows, and reproduction is by live birth rather than laying of eggs. One to seven large young may be produced per clutch, but females apparently give birth only in alternating years. Diet includes insects and smaller lizards. A similar species is *Xenosaurus platyceps* King and Thompson, 1968, the flat-headed knobby lizard, which is more arboreal and prefers slightly more arid microhabitats.
Care: The terrarium requires plenty of shaded hiding places, an ambient temperature of 67° to 73° F (19.5° to 23° C), and humidity at 70 to 90 percent.
Terrarium Suitability: 3

Additional species that occur in Mexico and Central America but are also found elsewhere are listed below. You may find a species account for these lizards in the region section given in parentheses.

Ameiva ameiva (Region 4: South America and the Galapagos)
Anniella pulchra (Region 1: North America, covering the United States and Canada)
Anolis carolinensis (Region 1: North America, covering the United States and Canada)
Anolis cristatellus (Region 2: Caribbean Islands)
Anolis sagrei (Region 1: North America, covering the United States and Canada)
Aspidoscelis sexlineatus (Region 1: North America, covering the United States and Canada)
Aspidoscelis tigris (Region 1: North America, covering the United States and Canada)
Callisaurus draconoides (Region 1: North America, covering the United States and Canada)
Cnemidophorus lemniscatus (Region 4: South America and the Galapagos)
Coleonyx reticulatus (Region 1: North America, covering the United States and Canada)
Coleonyx switaki (Region 1: North America, covering the United States and Canada)
Coleonyx variegatus (Region 1: North America, covering the United States and Canada)
Cophosaurus texanus (Region 1: North America, covering the United States and Canada)
Crotaphytus bicinctores (Region 1: North America, covering the United States and Canada)
Crotaphytus nebrius (Region 1: North America, covering the United States and Canada)
Crotaphytus reticulatus (Region 1: North America, covering the United States and Canada)
Dipsosaurus dorsalis (Region 1: North America, covering the United States and Canada)
Elgaria multicarinata (Region 1: North America, covering the United States and Canada)
Gambelia wislizeni (Region 1: North America, covering the United States and Canada)

Gonatodes fuscus (Region 1: North America, covering the United States and Canada)

Heloderma suspectum (Region 1: North America, covering the United States and Canada)

Iguana iguana (Region 4: South America and the Galapagos)

Leiocephalus carinatus (Region 2: Caribbean Islands)

Petrosaurus mearnsi (Region 1: North America, covering the United States and Canada)

Phrynosoma cornutum (Region 1: North America, covering the United States and Canada)

Phrynosoma coronatum (Region 1: North America, covering the United States and Canada)

Plestiodon laticeps (Region 1: North America, covering the United States and Canada)

Polychrus gutturosus (Region 4: South America and the Galapagos)

Sauromalus ater (Region 1: North America, covering the United States and Canada)

Sceloporus jarrovii (Region 1: North America, covering the United States and Canada)

Sceloporus magister (Region 1: North America, covering the United States and Canada)

Sceloporus occidentalis (Region 1: North America, covering the United States and Canada)

Sceloporus orcutti (Region 1: North America, covering the United States and Canada)

Sceloporus poinsettii (Region 1: North America, covering the United States and Canada)

Thecadactylus rapidicauda (Region 4: South America and the Galapagos)

Uma notata (Region 1: North America, covering the United States and Canada)

Urosaurus ornatus (Region 1: North America, covering the United States and Canada)

Uta stansburiana (Region 1: North America, covering the United States and Canada)

Xantusia henshawi (Region 1: North America, covering the United States and Canada)

Xantusia vigilis (Region 1: North America, covering the United States and Canada)

REGION 4
South America
and the
Galapagos

green iguana
(*Iguana iguana*)

South America—along with Australia, Africa, India, and Antarctica—was once part of a great southern supercontinent known as Gondwana. Though there are many related species in those regions, South American animals have been isolated long enough to have become very distinct from all other continental faunas. South America contains mostly tropical and subtropical regions along with some of the largest forest and river systems in the world. Even cool parts of the Andes Mountains are home to a variety of lizards, many of which bear live young. Only the southern tip of the continent lacks a lizard fauna.

The large lizards of South America are largely terrestrial (tegus) or semi-aquatic (caiman lizards), except for the arboreal green iguanas. Caiman lizards are unlikely to be encountered unless one explores well into the bush. The remaining lizards are found in virtually all remaining habitats—under boards, logs, and stones, in swamps, on trees, along beaches and rivers, under leaf litter, and in buildings. Most species are active year round but are scarce during rains. Andean lizards become dormant during the winter months.

Alopoglossus atriventris Duellman, 1973
Black-Bellied Lizard

Family: Gymnophthalmidae.
Length: SVL: 2 in. (51 mm). TL: 3.3 in. (84 mm).
Habitat and Range: Under leaf litter in forests of Colombia, Ecuador, and Peru.
Natural History: Males of this skink-like teiid have black bellies that gave it the name *atriventris* (which literally means "black belly"). Females and young have cream-colored bellies. The body is covered in keeled shiny scales. The dorsum is brown, the flanks black, and there is a longitudinal cream stripe on each side of the body. These are tiny lizards that spend most of their time under leaf litter or in rotting logs, where small insects can be found and humidity levels are high. They are found in habitats near ponds or lakes, but on the drier slopes of hills, not the wetter ground surrounding those bodies.
Care: Terrarium temperatures should be kept warm by day (85° and 109° F [29.5° and 43° C]), slightly cooler at night, and humidity should be above 75 percent. Offer 5 inches (12.7 cm) or more of slightly moist substrate and cover with leaf litter and pieces of flat bark. Black-bellied lizards are active animals, so provide a terrarium with as much floor space as possible. Keep substrate shaded, but provide UV light several times per week. Feed lizards small live worms and insects.
Terrarium Suitability: 3

Amblyrhynchus cristatus Bell, 1825
Marine Iguana

Family: Iguanidae.
Length: SVL: 23.6 in. (600 mm). TL: 59 in. (1,500 mm).
Habitat and Range: Confined to the rocky coastal areas of the Galapagos Islands.
Natural History: This is a large and distinctive iguana, possessing a round head with very rough scales, a short round body, and a long, laterally compressed tail. There is a row of low scales forming a vertebral crest. Marine iguanas are the only fully marine lizards in the world, and their entire diet consists of sea plants that grow in the cold coastal waters. Though not as plentiful as they were in the nineteenth century, they are easily approached and observed by visitors to the Galapagos. Each island's population has slightly different coloring and maximum adult size, resulting in the recognition of seven subspecies. The brightly marked coral coloring of *Amblyrhynchus cristatus venustissimus* Eibl-Eibesfeldt, 1956 from Española (Hood) Island is perhaps the most attractive and familiar.
Care: The requirements of these lizards preclude their being kept successfully in captivity.
Terrarium Suitability: 5

Ameiva ameiva (Linnaeus, 1758)
Rainbow Lizard

Family: Teiidae.
Length: SVL: 5.2 in. (132 mm). TL: 16.7 in. (424 mm).
Habitat and Range: Inhabits open grasslands, fields, and village clearings from central Panama south to central South America.
Natural History: Rainbow lizards are similar in appearance and habits to North American whiptails and racerunners. They are extremely active and forage widely during the day. Movements are jerky and rapid, and when threatened rainbow llizards can run with considerable speed, being among the fastest of lizards. Though the bright colors seem gaudy, in nature the coloration helps make the lizard difficult to see.
Care: The terrarium should be kept warm by day (85° and 109° F [29° and 43° C]), slightly cooler at night, and humidity should be above 75 percent. Provide plenty of cover such as bark or hide boxes and a thick layer of soil into which lizards may burrow. Rainbow lizards feed mainly on insects, but they also take small young birds, lizards, rodents, flowers, and fruits. Because of their activity, they require considerable floor space.
Terrarium Suitability: 3

Bachia trinasale (Cope, 1868)
(No common name)

Family: Gymnophthalmidae.
Length: SVL: 3.1 in. (80 mm). TL: 4.7 in. (120 mm).
Habitat and Range: Restricted to leaf litter in loamy or loose soils in secondary forests of Ecuador and Peru.
Natural History: *Bachia* represents a very unusual lizard unlikely to be seen except in a few museum collections. At first glance, the lizard appears to be the discarded tail of an ameiva or racerunner. Closer inspection reveals the tiny blunt head with its almost invisible eyes, and two pair of extremely reduced limbs, the posterior pair almost nonexistent. Body scales are large and rectangular, with distinct keels. The long tail is quite fragile and will likely break off if the lizard is not handled carefully. These lizards apparently spend their lives away from bright light, under leaf litter and in soft soil through which they burrow. Most likely to be encountered where bulldozers are turning up earth. They produce up to two eggs, but very little is known about the biology of these lizards. Similar species are *Bachia vermiformis* Cope, 1874 and *Bachia oxyrhina* Rodrigues, Camacho, Nunes, Recoder, Teixeira, Valdujo, Ghellere, Mott, & Nogueira, 2008.
Care: No care information is available.
Terrarium Suitability: 5

Callopistes flavipunctatus (**Duméril and Bibron, 1839**)
Monitor Tegu

Family: Teiidae.
Length: SVL: 15.8 in. (402 mm). TL: 39.6 in. (1,006 mm).
Habitat and Range: Dry habitats in Ecuador, Chile, and Peru, where rocky cover and low thorny vegetation occurs.
Natural History: A very poorly known species, and much of what we do know is based on scant field observations and specimens kept in captivity. The acute snout and streamlined body recall the Old World monitors, hence the common name. However, the monitor tegu differs in having smooth broad belly scales arranged in rows, and a shorter, broader tongue than true monitors.
Care: These are active lizards that require a spacious terrarium with considerable floor space. Though monitor tegus climb well, they rarely climb more than a few meters above the ground. They also require a large pool of water in which to swim, and this must be cleaned regularly. Keep air temperature hot (85° to 98° F [29° to 37° C]), and humidity moderate, between 55 and 75 percent. Monitor tegus feed on a variety of smaller animals, carrion, and occasionally fruit. They are very aggressive lizards that should be housed alone, and keepers should be wary of their painful bite.
Terrarium Suitability: 3

Callopistes maculatus Gravenhorst, 1838
Chilean Dwarf Tegu/Spotted Dragonet

Family: Teiidae.
Length: SVL: 6.3 in. (159 mm). TL: 20 in. (510 mm).
Habitat and Range: A resident of arid rocky and montane habitats with sandy soil and low shrubby vegetation on northern and central Chile.
Natural History: This is the smaller relative of the monitor tegu that is often seen for sale in the pet trade. It closely resembles the North American racerunners in appearance and length, but is stockier. It feeds mostly on other lizards.
Care: These are highly active lizards that require a larger terrarium than do other species of similar size. Do not house with smaller animals. They are difficult to maintain in captivity unless given a large space for foraging, deep substrate for burrowing, and objects on which to climb. Do not put two males into the same terrarium. Feed them a variety of insects, baby rodents, and small lizards daily. Interior terrarium surfaces should be dry, but the terrarium's atmosphere should be slightly humid, around 50 to 65 percent—spray lightly twice per week. Keep temperatures warm, 78° to 100° F (25° to 38° C). Full-spectrum lighting is recommended for four to eight hours per day.
Terrarium Suitability: 3

Cercosaura ocellata Wagler, 1830
(No common name)

Family: Gymnophthalmidae.
Length: SVL: 2.25 in. (57 mm). TL: 7.9 in. (200 mm).
Habitat and Range: Much of the Amazonian river basin and its tributaries in South America. Found under leaf litter, bark, and other debris on dry forest floors.
Natural History: An extremely pretty lizard that is very poorly known. The bright colors and nearly iridescent white "portholes" on the flanks—especially large in males—make them resemble some of the related *Proctoporus*. Though they live in hot regions, they generally avoid direct sunlight by staying under leaf litter while foraging. The diet includes small insects such as termites and ants. They are found in Amazonia but avoid the moist and wet areas, staying in dry habitats several meters away from water. Preferred humidity level is 90 to 100 percent. Females lay two eggs per clutch.
Care: The terrarium must be kept warm, sprayed with water twice daily, and provided with both live plants and ample leaf substrate.
Terrarium Suitability: 3

Cnemidophorus lemniscatus (Linnaeus, 1758)
Rainbow Jungle Runner

Family: Teiidae.
Length: SVL: 3.9 in. (100 mm). TL: 9.25 in. (235 mm).
Habitat and Range: Open areas, from grasslands and sandy riverbanks, in Amazonia, and sometimes near coastal beaches and around human dwellings.
Natural History: Arguably the most brilliantly colored of the racerunners, males retain blue and turquoise markings—sometimes a blue tail as well—that are brown and olive in females and young. In their native haunts, the bright colors of jungle runners are excellent camouflage, and when they run the blur of color makes then seem to disappear. Jungle runners are extremely fast, active lizards that forage widely for insects, slugs, and small vertebrate prey, and they generally feed several times each day.
Care: They prefer hot temperatures (78° to 100° F [25° to 38° C]) and humidity of 90 percent. Provide captives with terraria that have considerable floor space, at least 3 ft. by 3 ft. (0.9 X 0.9 m). Provide plenty of shade, and offer UV for at least four to six hours daily. The tail is very fragile and may come off if the lizard is seized.
Terrarium Suitability: 3

Conolophus subcristatus (**Gray, 1831**)
Galapagos Land Iguana

Family: Iguanidae.
Length: SVL: 24.75 in. (629 mm). TL: 41.3 in. (1,050mm).
Habitat and Range: Inland grassy areas on Fernandina, Isabella, Plaza, and Santa Cruz Islands. They prefer open flat areas where visibility is good.
Natural History: There are three recognized species of Galapagos land iguanas, and they are very similar in form and habits. *Conolophus pallidus* is very similar to *C. subcristatus* but occurs only on Sante Fe Island. *Conolophus marthae* Gentile & Snell, 2009, is an extremely rare pinkish species first noticed by researchers in 1986 but not described and named until 2009. It is restricted to parts of Isabella Island. *Conolophus subcristatus* is a large, primarily herbivorous lizard that feeds on *Opuntia* cactus and a variety of other local flora. On occasion individuals are opportunistic enough to consume insects, small vertebrates that stumble into an iguana's burrow, and carrion. The lizards consume small cactus spines; they scrape larger spines off food with their front legs. These lizards attain adult size in three to five years; they may live for 50 or 60 years and weigh about 30 pounds (13.6 kg).
Care: Captive animals are maintained only at the Darwin Research Station in the Galapagos Islands.
Terrarium Suitability: 5

Crocodilurus lacertinus Daudin, 1802
Crocodile-Tailed Tegu

Family: Teiidae.

Length: SVL: 8.7 in. (220 mm). TL: 26 in. (654 mm).

Habitat and Range: In and near rivers, permanent streams, and lakes of Amazonia, including Brazil, Guiana, Peru, Venezuela, and far eastern Colombia.

Natural History: A very poorly known species despite its size and heavy exploitation by the leather trade. Crocodile-tailed tegus are primarily aquatic, foraging for food in or near water. In ecology and behavior they are presumably similar to *Dracaena*. They feed primarily on frogs but presumably consume any prey items—large insects, small fish, and small mammals—that they can find and overpower. When handled, crocodile-tailed tegus emit a croaking sound. This species is almost never encountered in captivity outside of South America. The few observations and photos available have come from a handful of zoo specimens. They are largely aquatic and will actively forage for food while walking along the bottom of a pond or lake bed.

Care: Provide them with snails, slugs, large crickets, and live fish such as mollies. Keep air temperature hot (85° to 98° F [29.5° to 37° C]) and the water temperature moderate (70° to 75° F [21° to 24° C]). Full-spectrum lighting may not be necessary but is recommended.

Terrarium Suitability: 4

Dracaena guianensis Daudin, 1802
Caiman Lizard

Family: Teiidae.
Length: SVL: 13 in. (335 mm). TL: 36.9 in. (936 mm).
Habitat and Range: Rivers and large lakes along the Amazonian drainage, from Colombia east to coastal Brazil.
Natural History: Almost nothing is known about this species in the wild. It is found along riverbanks where it may lie basking on branches over the water. At the first sign of danger, the lizard drops into the water and may remain submerged for several minutes. Though noted for their ability to crush and eat snails and other mollusks, caiman lizards also feed on small animals (invertebrate and vertebrate) and eggs found while foraging in trees. The similar Paraguayan caiman lizard, *Dracaena paraguayensis* Amaral, 1950, is more slender and less vividly colored, being almost uniformly tea brown.
Care: Both species need a large terrarium because they climb and dive routinely. When not foraging on land or basking on a branch, they will be in the water, often lying submerged for several minutes. Provide an intense heat source above one basking site, and allow the daytime temperature to reach 105° to 115° F (40.5° to 46° C). Areas not under basking lamps should filter light; use plants and natural cover to provide plenty of shade. There must be a large pool in which the lizards can swim.
Terrarium Suitability: 4

Gonatodes humeralis (Guichenot, 1855)
Bridled Forest Gecko

Family: Sphaerodactylidae.

Length: SVL: 1.4 in. (37 mm). TL: 3.25 in. (82.5 mm).

Habitat and Range: Broadly distributed throughout forests of South America, from Colombia to Peru.

Natural History: This is a diurnal gecko, with round pupils and no sticky pads on the toes. Males are brightly colored, with a pale blue head marked with red bands. The body is gray to olive, with a series of black lateral spots. Females are drab, mottled dark brown on a gray background, but they too have the black lateral spots. Though conspicuous, they are very active and swift and rarely allow close approach. If seized, the gecko can slough off skin and make its escape. Bridled forest geckos are extremely sensitive to heat and will stay in areas where the maximum temperature is below 84° F (29° C). They feed on a variety of tiny insects, from ants and termites to fruit flies.

Care: Provide a tall tank with plenty of climbing surfaces and warm but not hot temperatures. These lizards feed on the tiniest of insects, such as flies (especially fruit flies), and young crickets. They will also take strained baby foods in captivity. Females lay a single egg per clutch but may lay every 20 to 35 days. Eggs hatch after about three months.

Terrarium Suitability: 3

Iguana iguana (Linnaeus, 1758)
Green Iguana

Family: Iguanidae.
Length: SVL: 24 in. (610 mm). TL: 72 in. (1,829 mm).
Habitat and Range: Broadly distributed from forested areas of Sinaloa in northern Mexico south into Uruguay and Paraguay, primarily in lowland (to 3,300 ft. [1,000 m]) forests.
Natural History: Green iguanas have a huge geographical range and occur in almost any habitats that have trees and at least some degree of water. Consequently there is considerable variation in scalation and coloration. Adults may vary from bright green with gunmetal blue crossbands, to animals that are predominantly orange with gray and tan markings. Adult iguanas are predominantly arboreal, spending time in trees where they can forage for leaves and flowers.
Care: Iguanas require very large enclosures, both because they become quite large and because they tend to be active. They require full-spectrum light as well as sufficient shaded cover. Daytime temperatures should range from 75° to 100° F (24° to 38° C). Diet should include some mixture of leafy green vegetables along with fruits and other vegetables. Iguanas should always have a large dish of clean drinking water available, and a container that is large enough to allow the lizard to immerse itself completely is advised.
Terrarium Suitability: 4

132

Liolaemus nigromaculatus (Wiegmann, 1835)
Black-Spotted Mountain Lizard

Family: Liolaemidae.
Length: SVL: 4.2 in. (105 mm). TL: 9 in. (229 mm).
Habitat and Range: Grasslands and rocky areas in the mountains of western Chile.
Natural History: An extremely variable species with twelve named subspecies, and they are all difficult to distinguish from similar related species. Black-spotted mountain lizards are subject to extremes in temperature and weather in the wild, and they have become proficient burrowers. They dig to provide shelter from wind and sun and to seek the small arthropods they feed upon. Specimens also take flowers.
Care: Daytime temperatures should be 78° to 100° F (25° to 38° C) but should drop at night to about 68° F (20° C). Provide these lizards with four to seven hours of UV light per day. These lizards are more cold-tolerant than many other lizards and are adapted to cold winters, so keepers may wish to give them a cooling period of three months. Females produce several live young, but little is known of the species' biology. Provide a shallow dish of drinking water, and house only one male per terrarium.
Terrarium Suitability: 2

Morunasaurus annularis (O'Shaugnessy, 1881)
Ringed Spiny-Tailed Lizard

Family: Hoplocercidae.
Length: SVL: 4.5 in. (115 mm). TL: 9 in. (230 mm).
Habitat and Range: Heavily forested regions of Amazonian Ecuador and Peru.
Natural History: The three species in this genus (the others are *Morunasaurus groi* Dunn, 1933, of Panama and northwestern Colombia and *Morunasaurus peruvianus* Köhler, 2003, of Peru) are very similar in appearance to the Madagascar iguanas of the genus *Oplurus*. Both genera have large heads, small round body scales, and whorls of large spines the length of the tail. The body is gray, with dark cross bands that make the lizard resemble a piece of tree bark. Ringed spiny-tailed lizards are found in moist rainforest on trees or on the ground near tree buttresses. Males are aggressively territorial; they will first display, then charge a trespasser.
Care: The terrarium should be tall, with several upright branches and plenty of shade. There should be some lateral ventilation. Keep humidity above 70 percent and provide six to ten hours of UV light. Keep temperature at 75° and 102° F (24° and 39° C). Diet includes insects, some fruits, and flowers, and lizards should be fed daily.
Terrarium Suitability: 3

Polychrus gutturosus Berthold, 1846
Large-Scaled Anole/Bush Anole/Monkey Lizard

Family: Polychrotidae.
Length: SVL: 6.5 in. (165 mm). TL: 14.3 in. (363 mm).
Habitat and Range: Dense moist rainforests of Honduras south to Ecuador.
Natural History: The five species of large-scaled anoles lack the sticky toe pads of the genus *Anolis* and have comparatively larger scales and much smaller dewlaps. Like true chameleons, large-scaled anoles are slow-moving lizards that depend on stealth and camouflage to survive. The tail is slightly prehensile; it is used as a fifth appendage and is not easily lost. Also as with chameleons and other anoles, each eye can rotate independently of the other. Males are very aggressive towards each other and must be housed in separate terraria. Large-scaled anoles feed on a variety of large invertebrates and will also take diced fruit pieces.
Care: These lizards are almost totally arboreal, so they need a tall terrarium with several lateral and vertical climbing objects. Keep the enclosure ventilated and warm: 75° to 102° F (24° to 39° C) provided by indirect lighting, and the lizards should have daily access to 10 to 14 hours of full-spectrum lighting. Mist the terrarium daily. This species is susceptible to rapid and dangerous dehydration.
Terrarium Suitability: 4

Polychrus marmoratus (Linnaeus, 1758)
Monkey Anole

Family: Polychrotidae.
Length: SVL: 6.5 in. (165 mm). TL: 13.5 in. (350 mm).
Habitat and Range: Inhabits moist forests of Brazil, Colombia, Ecuador, French Guiana, Guyana, Isla Margarita, Peru, Suriname, Tobago, Trinidad, and Venezuela.
Natural History: Look for these large green anoles on trees, where they will spend considerable time basking on narrow horizontal branches. The tail is prehensile and may be seen wrapped around a branch. Monkey anoles can vary in color from pale green with light gray-green bands to darker gray or tan. The dewlap is long and thick, making it conspicuous even when not distended. When alarmed, monkey anoles can move quite quickly and may leap from branch to branch to escape a predator. They prefer heavily shaded areas that offer dappled spaces of sunshine for basking. They feed on large insects, the occasional worm and spider, and a variety of flowers, berries, nectar, and soft leaves.
Care: Terrarium specimens do well with a varied diet of crickets, wax worms, earthworms, berries, diced fruits, and soft leafy vegetables. Keep under the same conditions as *Polychrus gutturosus* in the previous entry. All of the *Polychrus* are challenging to keep.
Terrarium Suitability: 4

Proctoporus ventrimaculatus **Boulenger, 1900**
Coral Dwarf Tegu

Family: Gymnophthalmidae.
Length: SVL: 1.7 in. (42.4 mm). TL: 5.5 in. (140 mm).
Habitat and Range: Moist, cool, mossy habitats in the Andes Mountains from southern Colombia to central Peru.
Natural History: Another small tropical American lizard about which almost nothing is known regarding its natural history. Coral dwarf tegus have come to light recently because they are being collected in Ecuador in large numbers for the live animal market. They are slender, large-scaled animals that spend their time foraging through moss, leaf litter, and the insides of fallen trees in search of insect prey. In captivity they will excavate long burrows in slightly moist soil. They are crepuscular and nocturnal and thus rarely seen in the open.
Care: Terrarium temperature should stay between 68° and 75° F (20° and 24° C), provided by indirect lighting. These are delicate lizards that should have a constant supply of fruit flies and other small prey.
Terrarium Suitability: 3

Teius teyou (Daudin, 1802)
Giant Jungle Runner

Family: Teiidae.
Length: SVL: 5.7 in. (144 mm). TL: 18.4 in. (461 mm).
Habitat and Range: Grasslands, pampas, and sparsely planted hill and mountainsides from southern Brazil west to Argentina.
Natural History: The giant jungle runner is very similar in appearance and behavior to the rainbow jungle runner, but lizards in the genus *Teius* have only four toes on each hind foot instead of five. The anterior half of the lizard is generally brown, while the rear half and tail are green. A longitudinal white or cream stripe extends down each flank from the eye to the hip. This is a highly active lizard almost never seen standing still, even when basking. It moves in short rapid bursts and may forage for food throughout the day.
Care: Captives need daily feedings of large insects such as katydids and roaches, supplemented with pieces of diced fruits. Temperatures should range from 75° to 102° F (24° to 39° C), and there should be equal areas of shaded and exposed substrate. Keep humidity between 60 and 80 percent.
Terrarium Suitability: 2

Thecadactylus rapidicauda (Houttuyn, 1782)
Turnip-Tailed Gecko

Family: Gekkonidae.
Length: SVL: 5 in. (127 mm). TL: 9 in. (230 mm).
Habitat and Range: Widely distributed in a variety of habitats from central Mexico south to central South America.
Natural History: One of South America's largest geckos, the turnip-tailed gecko is strictly nocturnal. It frequents habitats that provide ample shelter from daytime heat and light, such as inside trees, under bark, and beneath discarded wood, but it also lives near human dwellings. Best seen at night near lamps, drawn by the moths and flies coming to the light. Females lay two eggs per clutch and may do so at two- to three-month intervals year round.
Care: Turnip-tailed geckos do very well in terraria, taking a variety of live foods and jarred foods such as strained peaches and applesauce. Keep them warm at 75° to 102° F (24° to 39° C), provided by indirect lighting. The terrarium should be heavily shaded. Humidity should range from 80 to 100 percent. They have strong toe pads, so they are able to scale glass and walls as easily as bark.
Terrarium Suitability: 2

Tropidurus hispidus (Spix, 1825)
Spiny Rock Lizard

Family: Tropiduridae.

Length: SVL: 4.8 in. (122 mm). TL: 12.3 in. (312.3 mm).

Habitat and Range: South America in the northeastern Amazonian region from southern Venezuela to central Brazil, in a variety of habitats. Most likely observed in open grasslands, where it may bask on logs, fence posts, and tree trunks.

Natural History: This medium-sized lizard resembles fence lizards (genus *Sceloporus*) in appearance and habits but has much smaller scales. These are very common lizards where they occur. The gray to gray-brown basking lizards encountered by tourists are most likely this species. They are active during most of the day, though they retreat to cool shelter more frequently during the hottest hours. Spiny rock lizards are exclusively insectivorous; they can capture and consume surprisingly large insects, including roaches, katydids, locusts, and walking sticks. The similar-looking lava lizards of the Galapagos Islands were long classified as *Tropidurus*, but now have their own genus, *Microlophus*. This species is sometimes confused with *Tropidurus torquatus* (Wied, 1820).

Care: Temperatures must range between 75° and 102° F (24° and 39° C), and the lizards should have daily access to 10 to 14 hours of full-spectrum lighting.

Terrarium Suitability: 1

Tupinambis merianae (Duméril and Bibron, 1839)
Black Tegu/Black and White Tegu

Family: Teiidae.
Length: SVL: 23 in. (585 mm). TL: 51.2 in. (1,300 mm).
Habitat and Range: A resident of grasslands, particularly near permanent freshwater sources in southern Amazonian Brazil south to northern Argentina, Bolivia, Paraguay, and Uruguay.
Natural History: This is the largest of the tegus. Though similar to the Colombian tegu (*T. teguixin*), the Argentine species can be readily distinguished by its small bead-like (vs. smooth, skink-like) scales and distinct pale line from the nape to the tail on each side of the body. This species runs, digs, swims, and burrows well but is disinclined to climb. Black tegus have a considerable southern distribution and are among the most cold-tolerant of the giant lizards.
Care: This large and active species requires an enormous terrarium. Because of their digging activity, provide either enough substrate for burrow contruction or no substrate except a thin layer of paper or similar easy-to-clean material. Keep daytime temperatures at 80° to 95° F (26.5° to 36° C), and allow a nighttime drop of 10° to 15°F (6 to 8°C). Provide a varied diet of insects, small rodents, canned cat or dog food, vegetables, and fruits at least three times per week.
Terrarium Suitability: 2

Hatchling *T. merianae* have bright green heads and forequarters. These fade to the adult colors within a few months of hatching. The benefit for this juvenile coloration is unknown, but it may provide the babies with additional camouflage when they are small and vulnerable to predation. This species is captive bred for the pet trade in fairly large numbers.

Tupinambis rufescens (Günther, 1871)
Red Tegu/Golden Tegu

Family: Teiidae.
Length: SVL: 19.4 in. (492 mm). TL: 48.4 in. (1,230 mm).
Habitat and Range: Northern Argentina, Paraguay, and the southern half of Brazil.
Natural History: This is a spectacular large lizard, for it comes in two distinct color varieties. One is predominantly a golden tan marbled on a black background (sometimes called *Tupinambis duseni*), while the other replaces gold with red. Red tegus are reported to steal into chicken houses to feed on the fowl and their eggs. They are widely hunted for their meat and the skin, which makes a highly sought source of leather. Living farther south than any other *Tupinambis* has allowed red tegus to evolve to tolerate much lower temperatures than their relatives. However, when daytime temperatures dip below 70° F (21° C), the lizards may retreat to a deep burrow or cave in rocks to prepare for hibernation.
Care: Care is similar to that required by black tegus, with some modifications. Red tegus need lower humidity (35 to 65 percent), higher daytime temperatures that may reach 120°F (49° C) at the basking spot, and more air flow. Provide a diet of large insects, cooked eggs, and appropriately-sized rodents.
Terrarium Suitability: 2

Tupinambis teguixin (Linnaeus, 1758)
Colombian Tegu/Black Tegu/Gold Tegu

Family: Teiidae.
Length: SVL: 24 in. (610 mm). TL: 56 in. (1,422 mm).
Habitat and Range: A resident of grasslands, particularly near permanent freshwater sources in northern Brazil south to near Sao Paulo.
Natural History: Though similar to the Argentine tegu (*T. merianiae*), the Colombian species can be readily distinguished by its smooth, shiny, skink-like scales, dark bands from the nape to the tail, and no distinct light dorsolateral stripes. However, black tegus are tropical animals that have little tolerance for cold temperatures. Because of their considerable size, black tegus can feed upon almost any animal prey they encounter. Their success at killing and eating chicken eggs and chicks makes them *lacertae non gratis* with farmers. Younger animals will also consume flowers and berries.
Care: Keep this large and active species in a terrarium at least four times the length of the lizard and one-and-a-half times as wide. Provide enough substrate to allow burrowing. Keep daytime temperatures at 86° to 95° F (30° to 36° C), and allow a minimal nighttime drop. Give tegus full-spectrum lighting. Keep humidity between 75 and 90 percent. Provide a varied diet of insects, small rodents, canned cat food, vegetables, and fruits.
Terrarium Suitability: 2

144

Additional species that occur in South America but are also found elsewhere are listed below. You may find a species account for these lizards in the region section given in parentheses.

Basiliscus basiliscus (**Region 3:Mexico and Central America**)
Basiliscus vittatus (**Region 3: Mexico and Central America**)
Corytophanes cristatus (**Region 3: Mexico and Central America**)
Gonatodes ceciliae (**Region 2: Caribbean Islands**)
Potamites apodemus (**Region 3: Mexico and Central America**)

The Pacific includes widely distributed islands spread over an area far larger than Asia, but they equal a much smaller total land mass. Large islands, such as New Zealand and New Guinea, were once part of the supercontinent Gondwana, while most of the smaller island groups are volcanic in origin. In this region only New Guinea, the Solomons, Fiji, and Tonga are home to populations comprising a range of skinks, geckos, monitors, agamids, pygopodids, and dibamids. Only skinks and geckos are almost universally distributed among the remaining islands. The region is home to the world's largest gecko, skink, and (possibly) monitor. New Caledonia has a diverse gecko fauna, including the planet's largest species. New Zealand's geckos are intensely colored animals that bear live young. New Zealand is also the last home to the living tuatara (not actually a lizard, but it is covered here). Fiji and Tonga are home to the only iguanas between the Galapagos and Madagascar. Each of the areas in the Pacific has unusual faunal features quite distinct from each other, and no area has been particularly well studied.

crested gecko (*Rhacodactylus ciliaris*)

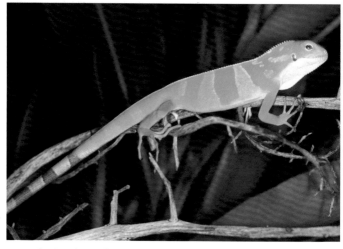

Brachylophus fasciatus (Brongniart, 1800)
Fiji Banded Iguana

Family: Iguanidae.
Length: SVL: 10.6 in. (270 mm). TL: 35.4 in. (900 mm).
Habitat and Range: Fiji.
Natural History: Banded iguanas are largely arboreal and may change color to match shadow patterns on their skin. Males are more intricately colored, with grayish blue bands on a bright green body. The nostrils and bellies of both sexes are yellow. The diet of this species is limited, consisting of bananas, hibiscus leaves and stamens, and pawpaw fruits. Note: *Brachylophus bulabula*, described in 2008, occupies a large range in Fiji and closely resembles *B. fasciatus*, so the two species may be easily confused with each other.
Care: Keep these arboreal lizards in tall enclosures with plenty of climbing branches. They require temperatures ranging from 75° to 100°F (24° to 38°C), high humidity, and full-spectrum lighting. There has been considerable success in breeding banded iguanas in captivity, at least in zoo settings. Eggs are kept in vermiculite to water in a 3:2 ratio by volume; they will incubate in five to five and a half months if kept at 75° to 80.5° F (24°to 27° C). Young are aggressive toward each other and should be separated until sexes can be determined.
Terrarium Suitability: 4

Brachylophus vitiensis Gibbons, 1980
Fiji Crested Iguana

Family: Iguanidae.
Length: SVL: 11.8 in. (300 mm). TL: 35.8 in. (910 mm).
Habitat and Range: Extremely limited to a few well-forested tiny islets of Fiji's western group: Mamanucas and Yasawas to Mali; Macuata
Natural History: Similar to the more widespread banded iguana, but with more complex and variable coloring and a pronounced set of vertebral spines. The body stripes are white and narrow on a green body that can quickly turn charcoal black when the lizard is annoyed. The belly is mottled creamy white and pale green. The nostril is yellow, and the dewlap is larger than that of the banded iguana. There is no significant sexual dimorphism in the crested iguana, but males do have larger and more pronounced femoral pores.
Care: Care similar to that for the banded iguana (*Brachylophus fasciatus*). It seems that the two species hybridize readily in captivity, and many zoo specimens look like hybrid animals.
Terrarium Suitability: 5

Carlia fusca Duméril and Bibron, 1839
Iridescent Skink

Family: Scincidae.

Length: SVL: 2.3 in. (58 mm). TL: 5 in. (128 mm).

Habitat and Range: Forests and forest edges among leaf litter and debris in southern New Guinea.

Natural History: This is a medium-sized skink, and one that is most likely to be encountered in forests. Microhabitats include areas where plant life is thriving—look for them around tree trunks and on low vines and leaves. They avoid dry places, such as isolated dry logs and woodpiles. They can climb but rarely go more than 6 feet (2 m) from the ground. The bronzy dorsum may appear blue or violet as sunlight is refracted through the scales. Iridescent skinks are active year round, but are most likely to be spotted during the weeks following rains. They feed on small insects and spiders. This species is part of a complex of several similar-looking skinks.

Care: They need plenty of cover in the form of flat bark, leaf litter, and broadleaf plants. They will drink from a dish, and they lap water drops from terrarium props. Daytime temperatures should range from 75° to 100° F (24° to 38° C). Humidity should range from 65 to 100 percent. Offer a daily feeding of small insects, finely diced fruits, or strained baby foods.

Terrarium Suitability: 4

Corucia zebrata Gray, 1855
Solomon Islands Skink/Prehensile-Tailed Skink/ Monkey-Tailed Skink

Family: Scincidae.
Length: SVL: 13.8 in. (350 mm). TL: 30.3 in. (770 mm).
Habitat and Range: Restricted to the Solomon Islands.
Natural History: This is the world's largest known skink and is a truly arboreal species, spending time only in trees except occasionally when giving birth. Though it sometimes feeds on snails, its primary diet consists of leaves, particularly of the creeper pothos (*Epipremnum aureum*). The tail is fully prehensile, used as a fifth limb, and it is both strong and very unlikely to be dropped. One or, rarely, two large live young are produced at roughly two-year intervals. Juveniles stay with the parent group for up to three years. Though they are disinclined to bite, they can do so if harassed, and the bite may require stitches.
Care: They are nocturnal, so terrarium animals should get heat from red or ceramic bulbs. They seem to prefer elevated hide boxes, such as large cork bark hollows suspended from the wall or ceiling of the terrarium. Offer fruits, leafy greens, and other vegetable matter daily. Daytime temperatures should range from 75° to 100° F (24° to 38° C). Humidity may range from 40 to 100 percent. It is critical to offer prehensile-tailed skinks a tall terrarium, with both vertical and horizontal perches.
Terrarium Suitability: 3

Diporiphora bilineata Gray, 1842
Two-Lined Dragon

Family: Agamidae.
Length: SVL: 3.9 in. (100 mm). TL: 9 in. (230 mm)
Habitat and Range: Widely distributed through both wet and dry forests of northern Australia and the southern half of New Guinea.
Natural History: Perhaps only the Australians would call so small and inconspicuous a creature a dragon. Two-lined dragons love hot weather and will be seen active during midday, when they hunt all manner of small insects, from ants to flies to wasps. These lizards are mainly terrestrial, found on open ground, at the base of grass and spinifex tufts (a coastal grass of Australia and Indonesia), and on rail fences. They rely on camouflage, so they tend to allow close approach. When they do run, however, they are swift and may climb a short distance up a tree or dive into thick brush.
Care: Because this small creature forages widely and eats so many small insects per day, it is difficult to maintain for long in the terrarium. They require a hundred or more insects the size of ants, termites, fruit flies, or pinhead crickets. They rarely drink from a dish, so spray the terrarium lightly once per week. Daytime temperatures should range from 75° to 100° F (24° to 38°C). Humidity may range from 40 to 100 percent. Provide 8 to 12 hours of UV light per day.
Terrarium Suitability: 3

Emoia cyanura (Lesson, 1830)
Blue-Tailed Skink

Family: Scincidae.
Length: SVL: 2.2 in. (56 mm). TL: 3.7 in. (95.2 mm).
Habitat and Range: In forest edges, along beaches, and near houses on the islands of Ninigo, the Admiralties, Bismarcks, Solomons, and Vanuatu, through Polynesia, the Marshalls, Wake, Midway, Hawaii, Clipperton, Kapingamarangi, Cocos, Tahiti, and Guam.
Natural History: A tiny, delicate skink that is somewhat flattened, has a triangular head, and glossy scales. The body is dark brown to black and has three cream or yellow stripes down the body, one on the vertebral line, the other two over the dorsolateral region. The tail is brilliant pale blue. Some island populations may be nearly uniformly golden or light brown, lacking stripes. These are active, nervous lizards that may bask in sunlight for short periods, then dash under leaf litter or other available cover. Though sometimes found on beaches, they stay away from the surf or rocks that are wet by waves. They feed on tiny insects.
Care: Provide cover in the form of flat bark, leaf litter, and plants. They will drink from a dish and lap water drops from terrarium props. Daytime temperatures should range from 75° to 100° F (24° to 38° C). Humidity should range from 65 to 100 percent. Offer a daily feeding of small insects, finely diced fruits, or baby foods.
Terrarium Suitability: 3

Eugongylus albofasciatus (Günther, 1872)
White-Banded Skink/Solomon Islands Ground Skink

Family: Scincidae.
Length: SVL: 6.4 in. (162 mm). TL: 15.9 in.(405 mm)
Habitat and Range: Moist forests and grasslands of extreme northern Queensland, Australia and southern New Guinea into the Solomon Islands.
Natural History: This is a medium-sized skink with very smooth glossy scales. When held in the hand, the smooth scales make it difficult to grasp the skink firmly, and it will roll until it can obtain a grip on you with its jaws. Only the nip of a large specimen can break the skin. This is a diurnal skink, heard running through leaf litter, where they search for insects, slugs, and sometimes small flowers.
Care: Terrarium animals need plenty of room for foraging. Provide indirect lighting or use a ceramic heat lamp and low-wattage or fluorescent lighting. Provide a dish of clean water; these skinks will often soak themselves. Cover should include flat bark, leaf litter, and broadleaf plants. There should be 8 to 10 in. (22 to 28 cm) of dry to very slightly moist soil in which the lizards can burrow. Daytime temperatures should range from 75° to 100° F (24° to 38° C). Humidity should range from 65 to 100 percent. Offer a daily feeding of small insects, finely diced fruits, or strained baby foods.
Terrarium Suitability: 4

Gekko vittatus Houttuyn, 1782
Striped Gecko/Skunk Gecko

Family: Gekkonidae.
Length: SVL: 4.4 in. (111 mm). TL: 7.9 in. (200 mm).
Habitat and Range: Much of the Indo-Australian archipelago, from Java and Borneo east to Papua New Guinea.
Natural History: An unmistakable large gecko with a lavender to brown body and a distinct Y-shaped white marking on the back, the "V" portion of the "Y" extending from behind each eye and meeting on the nape. This slender relative of the tokay gecko is less pugnacious and more lithe in appearance. It has also been very successful colonizing a broad range across southeastern Asia into New Guinea. Active from twilight onwards; look for them around night lamps to which insects are drawn.
Care: Terrarium animals need several individual hiding places and a variety of foods that includes crickets, roaches, young mice, and diced fruit. Keep humidity above 80 percent and spray the cage with water twice daily. A pair can live in a 10-gallon (38-l) terrarium, but a taller enclosure would be better. No lighting is necessary, but temperatures should range from 70° to 86° F (21° to 30°C).
Terrarium Suitability: 1

Hypsilurus dilophus (Duméril and Bibron, 1837)
Double-Crested Tree Dragon

Family: Agamidae.
Length: SVL: 6.5 in. (165.5 mm). TL: 22.8 in. (580 mm).
Habitat and Range: Dense forests of New Guinea and several of its nearby islands.
Natural History: A fantastic large agamid that looks like a resident of *Jurassic Park*, the double-crested tree dragon is strongly compressed and has two to five large thin spines on the back of the head. The body and tail are similarly covered with slightly shorter spines. Body scales are distinctly keeled, and there is a large dark brown to black dewlap. Lizards spend most of their time on branches, where they move slowly and live as ambush predators on any smaller animals they can overpower and eat. Because they depend on camouflage, they may allow very close approach—if you can spot a specimen at all—before moving away with surprising speed.
Care: They require very large terraria, with at least 6 feet (2m) of height for climbing. Temperatures should stay at 77° to 90° F (25° to 32° C) during the day and drop by a few degrees at night. Provide three to five hours of UV light on alternate days. Double-crested tree dragons require a large dish of water, and the terrarium should be sprayed twice daily.
Terrarium Suitability: 4

Lamprolepis smaragdina (Lesson, 1830)
Emerald Skink

Family: Scincidae.
Length: SVL: 4.3 in. (110 mm). TL: 9.9 in. (252 mm).
Habitat and Range: A dweller of tropical forests from the Indo-Australian archipelago the Solomon Islands, Santa Cruz Islands, and north to Taiwan.
Natural History: An active, sun-loving species found in a variety of habitats as long as live green plants are in the vicinity. Emerald skinks are commonly seen darting in short bursts between sunny gaps in the ground shade, and they will dive under leaf litter or climb tree trunks to avoid predators. Coloring varies from population to population, but all are a bright leek-green on the head and flanks. The back, flanks, and tail may be wholly or partly brown. Formerly placed in the genus *Dasia*.
Care: This species does well so long as there are numerous hiding places. Provide hide boxes as well as leaf litter, bark, or hollow logs. They live where humidity is generally above 75 percent, so spray terrarium lightly each day, and give the lizards a shallow water dish from which to drink. Allow temperatures to range between 78° and 88° F (25.5° and 31° C). Full-spectrum lighting should be offered three to eight hours daily. Be sure to offer a variety of live insects and occasional bits of chopped fruit daily.
Terrarium Suitability: 3

Lialis jicari **Boulenger, 1897**
New Guinea Legless Lizard

Family: Pygopodidae.
Length: SVL: 9.2 in. (234 mm). TL: 30.7 in. (780 mm).
Habitat and Range: New Guinea, in a variety of lowland habitats including swamps, grasslands, cleared fields, and near rivers.
Natural History: Virtually unknown. These lizards, relatives of the geckos, lack moveable eyelids, having instead a clear convex spectacle that the lizard often cleans with its tongue. Ear openings are present. Scales are large and stiff. About two-thirds of the length of the lizard is the fragile tail. The tongue is neither forked nor as long as that of a snake.
Care: Provide a natural substrate of potting soil and some live plants and a thick layer of dry grass. Flat pieces of bark or larger logs that will allow concealment sites are also needed. Substrate should be deep enough to allow lizards to burrow on occasion. Daytime temperatures should stay in the 86° to 98° F (30° to 36.5°C) range, and drop to 68° to 72° F (20° to 22°C) at night. They should receive two to four hours of UV several times per week. Feed and lightly spray daily, but reduce feeding to three times weekly during simulated dry periods, when spraying should be eliminated. Always provide a small shallow dish of clean drinking water. Foods should include a variety of insects, pink mice, and small live lizards.
Terrarium Suitability: 3

Naultinus elegans Gray, 1842
Sulfur Gecko/Jade Gecko/New Zealand Green Gecko

Family: Diplodactylidae.
Length: SVL: 2.6 in. (65 mm). TL: 5.7 in. (145 mm).
Habitat and Range: Dry, open forest and scrub where direct sunlight is available, in the southern half of New Zealand's North Island.
Natural History: Diurnal geckos that are typically bright lime-green with a series of dark-bordered white spots or dashed lines on the dorsum. An apparent genetic recessive allele leads to production of lemon-yellow individuals. While basking in sunlight, sulfur geckos may catch flies and other insects drawn near. During the winter months, sulfur geckos retreat to shelter and become inactive. They may, however, emerge on warm winter days. Diet may include flowers as well as small insects such as fruit flies and moths. New Zealand geckos are unusual in that they do not lay eggs, but produce one or two rather large live young in autumn.
Care: Due to export restrictions, this species is unavailable in the pet trade. Daytime temperatures should range from 76° to 88° F (24° to 31°C), and drop to 68° to 72° F (20° to 22°C) at night. They should receive two to four hours of UV light several times per week. Feed and lightly spray daily, but reduce feeding to three times weekly during simulated dry periods, when spraying should be eliminated.
Terrarium Suitability: 3

Prasinohaema flavipes (Parker, 1926)
Yellow-Footed Skink

Family: Scincidae.
Length: SVL: 3 in. (76 mm). TL: 6.2 in. (158 mm).
Habitat and Range: New Guinea, in moist forests and swamplands.
Natural History: Brown to olive above, but the bright lime-green belly scales make recognition of this lizard simple. The genus name means "green-blooded," and skinks in this genus are the only vertebrates that have green blood. The scales under the tail are broad and slightly sticky, similar in microstructure to gecko toe pads, and help the lizards climb. Yellow-footed skinks are both terrestrial and arboreal and can be found around forest clearings where high grass and low shrubs and vines are plentiful. Though active in the heat of the day, they are more likely to be in shaded areas at that time.
Care: Terrarium animals need cover and plenty of room for foraging. Because they are somewhat arboreal, they should have a tall terrarium with a variety of thin branches laid out horizontally and vertically. There should also be considerable floor space for these active animals; at least 3 ft. (0.9 m) square. Daytime temperatures should range from 75° to 100° F (24° to 38° C). Humidity should range from 65 to 100 percent. Lateral ventilation is essential, but avoid cool drafts. Offer a daily feeding of small insects and finely diced fruits.
Terrarium Suitability: 4

Prasinohaema virens (Peters, 1881)
Green-Blooded Skink

Family: Scincidae.
Length: SVL: 2 in. (51 mm). TL: 4.7 in. (120 mm).
Habitat and Range: Northeastern New Guinea and the Solomon Islands, in moist forests and swamplands.
Natural History: This is perhaps the smallest of the green-blooded skinks. It is found mainly in northeastern New Guinea, north of the Owen Stanley Range. The body is some shade of dull green, generally without markings, and the belly is bright lime. This species is considerably more arboreal than the yellow-footed skink and is likely to be found on leaves and branches of low trees and bushes. Green-blooded skinks feed on small insects and spiders. Though they can move swiftly, their first line of defense is to stay still and depend on their small size and cryptic coloration to avoid detection. During dry periods they retreat to rotting logs, inside trees, and other high-humidity shelters.
Care: Care for in the same manner as for *Prasinohaema flavipes* in the previous entry.
Terrarium Suitability: 4

Rhacodactylus auriculatus (Bavay, 1869)
Knob-Headed Giant Gecko/Gargoyle Gecko

Family: Diplodactylidae.
Length: SVL: 4.9 in. (125 mm). TL: 9.3 in. (236 mm).
Habitat and Range: Moist forest habitats in the southern third of New Caledonia.
Natural History: This is a member of a genus of large geckos endemic to New Caledonia. The knob-headed giant gecko is distinguished by its thin short tail and by enlarged bony knobs on the back of the head. Coloring is extremely variable, running through a variety of patterns made of brown, tan, black, and rusty red hues. The species ranges widely from forests to shoreline vegetation, spending most of its time a few meters from the ground. Active mainly in the early evening, these geckos may also spend some time basking in sunlight. They eat smaller lizards, insects, flowers, and fruit.
Care: Knob-headed giant geckos are frequently bred in captivity, to the extent that most available specimens have been produced in captivity. Temperatures should range from 75° to 85° F (24° to 29.5°C) with a small drop at night. Feed and lightly spray daily, but reduce feeding to three times weekly during simulated dry periods, when spraying should be eliminated.
Terrarium Suitability: 1

Rhacodactylus ciliatus Guichenot, 1866
Crested Gecko

Family: Diplodactylidae.
Length: SVL: 5.1 in.(130 mm). TL: 9.7 in. (247 mm).
Habitat and Range: Moist forests in southern New Caledonia and the Isle of Pines.
Natural History: Specimens of this bizarre gecko with a frill of head and neck spines were so rare that herpetologists had considered it to be extinct as recently as 1993. It was subsequently rediscovered and entered the animal trade, where it has been regularly bred. Females may lay seven to nine clutches of two eggs per year. Consequently, though it may occupy limited habitat in the wild, captive populations seem to be growing. The head is distinctly triangular, and the snout is comparatively longer and more acute than in other giant geckos. It feeds mainly on insects and other small arthropods but will take small pieces of fruit (including fruit baby food) as well.
Care: Care is similar to that of the gargoyle gecko (*R. auriculatus*). Daytime temperatures should range from 72° to 82° F (24° to 28°C), and drop to 68° to 72° F (20° to 22°C) at night. Feed and lightly spray daily, but reduce feeding to three times weekly during simulated dry periods, when spraying should be eliminated.
Terrarium Suitability: 1

Rhacodactylus leachianus (Cuvier, 1829)
New Caledonian Giant Gecko

Family: Diplodactylidae.
Length: SVL: 10 in. (255 mm). TL: 12.9 in. (326.4 mm).
Habitat and Range: Forests on the mainland and small islets of New Caledonia.
Natural History: This is the world's largest known living gecko. It is found in moist forests near water, from sea level to about 3600 feet (1100 m). It is almost exclusively arboreal and though primarily nocturnal is often active by day. Because these geckos spend most of their time in the canopy, an ecotourist will more likely hear their many vocalizations instead of seeing the lizards. Their large size allows them to feed on a wide variety of prey, including small birds, large insects, and probably other lizards. They also take fruit regularly, particularly figs.
Care: Though they reproduce in captivity, fecundity is low—about two clutches of two eggs each per year—and captives rarely produce females. Daytime temperatures should range from 72° to 82° F (24° to 28°C), and drop to 68° to 72° F (20° to 22°C) at night. Feed and lightly spray daily, but reduce feeding to three times weekly during simulated dry periods, when spraying should be eliminated.
Terrarium Suitability: 2

Sphenomorphus muelleri (Schlegel, 1839)
Müller's Skink

Family: Scincidae.
Length: SVL: 5.9 in. (150 mm). TL: 16.5 in. (420 mm).
Habitat and Range: Sulawesi east through New Guinea, in dry forests and grasslands.
Natural History: This is a large and magnificent lizard that is rarely encountered in the field owing to its secretive habits and strong burrowing ability. The head is cone-shaped, with a very sharp tip, and the thick tail ends in an awl-like point. The limbs are short but strong and stocky. Coloring varies greatly, the most common pattern consisting of a brown dorsum and black flanks, separated by a longitudinal thin cream stripe. A thicker cream stripe borders the lower flank from the brown belly. Both light stripes originate beneath the eye. Some populations lack one or the other of the light stripes, and the extreme form is an almost patternless dull pink. Almost nothing is known about this skink's natural history.
Care: Captives need at least 10 inches (25 cm) of thick loamy soil for burrowing. Diet includes live prey, such as earthworms, centipedes, grubs, roaches, mealworms, and baby mice. Daytime temperatures should range from 75° to 100° F (24° to 38° C). Humidity should range from 65 to 100 percent.
Terrarium Suitability: 3

Tiliqua gigas (Schneider, 1801)
New Guinea Blue-Tongued Skink

Family: Scincidae.
Length: SVL: 15.4 in. (392 mm). TL: 27.8 in. (705 mm).
Habitat and Range: Widespread in New Guinea and adjacent islands.
Natural History: This is the largest of the blue-tongued skinks and also the most carnivorous, taking little vegetable food. Blue-tongued skinks are recognizable by their stocky sausage-like bodies, relatively short tails, short limbs with tiny digits, and the cobalt to royal-blue tongue. They are bold and active lizards frequently seen near human settlements and in cultivated patches. They are strictly terrestrial and are much more prone to "borrow" a mammal's burrow than excavate one of their own. They are diurnal and active during the warmest parts of the day, when they frequent shady areas near cover.
Care: This hardy species does well in a variety of terrarium types, from simple designs with only a box and water dish, to larger and more elaborate forest terraria. New Guinea blue-tongued skinks are not likely to accept vegetable or fruit matter, but they will accept a variety of invertebrate and vertebrate prey.. These skinks can be safely housed in small groups, but *T. gigas* may suddenly turn aggressive towards other specimens after a time. Keep the temperature in the range of 75° to 98° F (24° to 37° C), and humidity above 75 percent.
Terrarium Suitability: 2

Tribolonotus gracilis De Rooij, 1909
Red-Eyed Crocodile Skink

Family: Scincidae.
Length: SVL: 3.9 in. (100 mm). TL: 7.7 in. (195 mm).
Habitat and Range: Widely distributed through the islands of northern Papua New Guinea, from the Admiralties through the Bismarck Archipelago; also on adjacent mainland. Most common in clearings and disturbed forest amid debris and in tree stumps.
Natural History: The crocodile skinks are the most divergent from the stereotype of skinks. The entire body and tail are covered with large keeled scales, some forming backward directed spines. They are the only lizards known to have a pair of large abdominal glands (function unknown) and glands on the soles of each foot. They are generally slow moving but can dash short distances when threatened. Females produce only one egg per clutch, and generally produce but one clutch per year. They prefer cool microhabitats near streams or other permanent water.
Care: The terrarium must be kept comparatively cool, at 68° to 80° F (20° to 26.5° C). They need UV light exposure several days weekly. Provide a deep, slightly moist soil substrate and plenty of cover. Humidity should range from 65 to 80 percent. Feed them a variety of slow-moving live prey, such as wax worms, bloodworms, earthworms, mealworms, slugs, and thin-shelled snails.
Terrarium Suitability: 3

Varanus beccarii (Doria, 1874)
Black Tree Monitor

Family: Varanidae.
Length: SVL: 11.2 in. (283 mm). TL: 37.2 in. (945 mm).
Habitat and Range: Dense wet forests of the Aru Islands, south of Indonesian New Guinea.
Natural History: These lizards spend virtually all of their time in the trees, where they feed upon a range of invertebrates, particularly ornithopteran insects. Look for them on tree trunks and branches well above the ground. Distinct and consistent differences serve to distinguish this species from the similar green tree monitor (*V. prasinus*) of the New Guinea mainland. Hatchlings are black, with transverse rows of light green spots that gradually fade within the first year of growth. Adults are uniformly black, though the snout tip may be yellowish to pinkish.
Care: These are notoriously active lizards, given to frequent dashes across the terrarium and often rubbing their snouts raw. They need plenty of space and a tall terrarium that allows climbing on fairly stout objects, such as natural logs. They also require a variety of hiding places. Keep the temperature in the 86° to 95° F (30° to 35° C) range, but allow it to drop to about 70° F (21° C) at night. . Humidity should be 75 to 90 percent, and mist the terrarium every other day. These hyperactive lizards need live foods daily, including roaches, crickets, small mice, and lizards.
Terrarium Suitability: 3

Varanus doreanus (Meyer, 1874)
Blue-Tailed Monitor

Family: Varanidae.
Length: SVL: 18 in. (457 mm). TL: 47.4 in. (1,204 mm).
Habitat and Range: Throughout New Guinea and adjacent islands, particularly near the western portion of the island. They inhabit forested areas near water and are rarely found on the ground.
Natural History: This species resembles the widespread mangrove monitor (*Varanus indicus*) but differs in having a pale yellow tongue, rounded snout, and blue or pale blue-gray bands around the tail. There are alternating irregular dark and light bars on the lips. Beyond that there is considerable variation in color pattern. Blue-tailed monitors are highly arboreal, rarely spending time on the ground. Where both species occur together, mangrove monitors are typically seen along riverbanks, while blue-tailed monitors will be high in the trees. Foods include tree frogs, large insects, and bird eggs.
Care: Give them a roomy and tall terrarium that allows climbing on fairly stout objects, such as natural logs. They are almost totally confined to tree tops, high branches, and the roofs of huts in the wild, so be sure they have plenty of above-ground walking space. They also require a variety of hiding places. Care is otherwise similar to that of *Varanus beccarii* in the previous entry.
Terrarium Suitability: 4

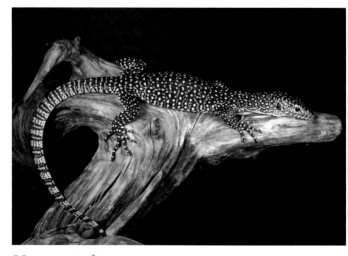

Varanus indicus (Daudin, 1802)
Mangrove Monitor

Family: Varanidae.

Length: SVL: 21 in. (533 mm). TL: 56.5 in. (1,435 mm).

Habitat and Range: This species has arguably the broadest distribution of all monitors, ranging from New Guinea and Palau south into northern coastal Australia and east through the Solomon Islands. Look for this species along waterways in mangroves.

Natural History: Mangrove monitors are typically found in groups, with lizards climbing trees and foraging on the ground near water. Though common in mangroves and quite capable of swimming in the ocean, they also occur considerable distances inland along riverbanks. Mangrove monitors are excellent climbers and swimmers. Though not as skittish as tree monitors, they are still capable of bursts of quick speed.

Care: A large terrarium is a must, preferably one with at least 9.8 x 6.5 ft (3 x 2 m) of floor space and 6.5 ft (2 m) tall or taller. The temperature in the upper areas of the cage should be in the 85° to 105° F (29.5° to 40.5° C) range, but the bottom should stay well below this range. Provide six to ten hours UV light daily. Provide a large pool of clean water in which lizards may submerge. Feed them small rodents (freshly killed), large insects (roaches, adult crickets, and locusts are good choices), and chopped boiled eggs.

Terrarium Suitability: 3

Varanus jobiensis Ahl, 1932
Peach-Throated Monitor

Famly: Varanidae.
Length: SVL: 17 in. (432 mm). TL: 48.5 in. (1,231 mm).
Habitat and Range: Broadly distributed in lowland New Guinea and nearby large islands, excepting the eastern island groups.
Natural History: This species can appear very similar to the mangrove monitor but is readily distinguished in having a dark head with no upper markings, a pink tongue, and a pronounced longitudinal stripe through the eye. The throat is orange, pale pink, or yellowish orange, without markings. Some specimens have brilliant blue markings on the tail and limbs.
Care: A large terrarium (suggested 6 ft./1.8 m square minimally, and at least 6 ft./1.8 m tall) that allows climbing on fairly stout objects, such as natural logs, is required for this largely tree-dwelling species. The temperature of the upper areas should be allowed to get in the 85° to 105° F (29.5° to 40.5° C) range, but the substrate area should stay below 85° F (29.5° C). Provide six to ten hours UV light daily. Let nighttime temperatures drop to about 80° F (21° C). Provide a large pool of clean water in which lizards may submerge. The terrarium should be well misted daily during a simulated wet season. Feed them small rodents, large insects, and smaller lizards.
Terrarium Suitability: 4

Varanus panoptes **Storr, 1980**

Argus Monitor

Family: Varanidae.
Length: SVL: 24.4 in. (620 mm). TL: 58 in. (1,448 mm).
Habitat and Range: Much of the northern half of Australia and lowland New Guinea in almost any habitat.
Natural History: Argus monitors are equally likely to be found around the noisy power generator near a station as in the remote and pristine outback. Foods include almost anything of animal origin that they can find, from carcasses of road-killed mammals to eggs to snakes. Although they are often seen patrolling along beaches on the Great Barrier Reef—Lizard Island is named for this species—Argus monitors seem loath to actually enter the water. When disturbed *V. panoptes* raises on stiffened legs and slowly and ominously hisses, occasionally lashing the tail at the intruder. However, even if grabbed these lizards are reticent to bite.
Care: This hardy species has been successfully maintained and bred by many herpetoculturists. Because these monitors are expert diggers, there should be a deep substrate of slightly moistened sand so they can excavate tunnels. Keep temperatures at the hot spot near 120° F (49° C). Provide 8 to 12 hours UV light daily. Humidity may safely range from 30 to 100 percent. If gently handled regularly, Argus monitors become docile and are good animals to use in educational shows and presentations.
Terrarium Suitability: 2

Varanus prasinus (Schlegel, 1839)
Green Tree Monitor/Emerald Monitor

Family: Varanidae.
Length: SVL: 10.3 in. (260 mm). TL: 34.4 in. (874 mm).
Habitat and Range: Lush forests of New Guinea generally, and several offshore islands.
Natural History: These are speedy, wary, active lizards that seem to be forever foraging. The diet consists mainly of large stick insects, supplemented with grasshoppers, beetles, and large moths. Green tree monitors are reportedly seasonally active, being most conspicuous just after the rains and becoming secretive during the dry season.
Care: All tree monitors are nervous, active species that respond to any disturbance by rushing around the terrarium. Green monitors need large and tall facilities. Provide solid vertical climbing materials with stout horizontal branches. Hide boxes on the "tree" will simulate natural tree hollows, a favored refuge and nest area for the lizards. Provide a diet made up of gut-loaded large insects. Captives have also eaten small banana pieces and earthworms. The temperature of the upper cage areas should be allowed to get in the 85° to 105° F (29.5° to 40.5° C) range, but the substrate area should stay below 85° F (29° C). Offer 4 to 12 hours of UV daily. Care is very similar to that of *Varanus beccarii*.
Terrarium Suitability: 3

Varanus salvadorii (Peters and Doria, 1878)
Tree Crocodile Monitor

Family: Varanidae.
Length: SVL: 31 in. (790 mm). TL: 111 in. (2,820 mm).
Habitat and Range: Throughout New Guinea, in fairly remote forest areas where disturbance by humans is minimal.
Natural History: In parts of New Guinea the local name for this species translates into "death from above," in reference to its alleged ferocity. The adults are almost entirely arboreal, found among the branches and canopies of the tallest trees in dense forest. They have also been reported from caves, and it is surmised that bats comprise a major staple in their diet. Though it is available in the pet trade, almost nothing is known of the natural history of this lizard.
Care: This species is hardy in captivity and is readily available through specialty reptile importers. However, tree crocodile monitors are enormous, extremely dangerous animals. Their teeth are like those of no other living animal, and even a small lizard is able to bite with both ferocity and the ability to be very damaging. Crocodile monitors require a very large (suggested 12 ft./3.8 m square minimally) and tall terrarium that allows climbing on stout objects, such as natural logs. Allowing for the differences in size and for the danger this species poses to keepers, the care is similar to that of *Varanus beccarii*.
Terrarium Suitability: 5

Sphenodon guentheri

Sphenodon guentheri (Buller, 1877)
Sphenodon punctatus (Gray, 1842)
Tuatara
(Not lizards)

Family: Sphenodontidae.
Length: SVL: 11.6 in. (296 mm). TL: 25.6 in. (650 mm).
Habitat and Range: Very limited in distribution to a few small islets off the northern coasts of both main islands of New Zealand; recently repatriated to parts of the coastal mainland of North Island.
Natural History: Tuatara are not lizards but are included here because they are lizard-like icons of New Zealand's fauna and likely to be encountered by ecotourists to that nation. They differ from lizards in having a lower bony skull arch, a longitudinal vs. a transverse (front to rear vs. left-to right) cloacal opening, and no male copulatory organ. Tuatara ("tuatara" is both the singular and plural) represent the last known living representatives of the Rhynchocephalia, a group of lizard-like reptiles that predate the ancestors of lizards and most dinosaurs by millions of years. Most died off around 65 million years ago, so it came as a shock to scientists when live tuatara were discovered in the nineteenth century. Like most diurnal lizards, tuatara have a pronounced

Sphenodon punctatus

parietal (third) eye on top of the head, and this organ probably helps "read" ultraviolet light exposure. Living as far south as they do, tuatara are functional at some of the lowest temperatures for reptiles, as low as 52° F (11° C).

Care: Tuatara are strictly protected endangered species that are available for keeping only by zoos approved by the government of New Zealand.

Terrarium Suitability: 5

Additional species that occur in New Guinea, New Zealand, and Oceania but are also found elsewhere are listed below. You may find a species account for these lizards in the region section given in parentheses.

Chlamydosaurus kingii (**Region 6: Australia**)
Cosymbotus platyurus (**Region 7: Southeast and Eastern Asia**)
Cryptoblepharus litoralis (**Region 6: Australia**)
Cryptoblepharus virgatus (**Region 6: Australia**)
Egernia frerei (**Region 6: Australia**)
Gehyra dubia (**Region 6: Australia**)
Gekko gecko (**Region 7: Southeast and Eastern Asia**)
Hydrosaurus amboinensis (**Region 7: Southeast and Eastern Asia**)
Hydrosaurus weberi (**Region 7: Southeast and Eastern Asia**)
Lialis burtonis (**Region 6: Australia**)
Lophognathus temporalis (**Region 6: Australia**)
Physignathus cocincinus (**Region 7: Southeast and Eastern Asia**)

REGION 6
Australia

perentie (*Varanus giganteus*)

Australia is the only nation to fully occupy a continent, and the majority of that continent is low-lying desert or near-desert terrain. Though often called "the land that time forgot," Australia contains both unique and shared species of fauna, just like other continents. However, more ancestral species have survived and evolved than in most other places. The number of lizard species in each group is considerable, and this continent is the home to the greatest number of monitor species anywhere. Portions of the far north are rainforests or dry scrub forest. The latter may become verdant and flooded during periodic rains, but they are otherwise quite dry and have sparse vegetation. The temperate southeast is home to many lizard species that tend to be inactive during the cooler months. Australia prohibits the export of its fauna, so the majority of Australian lizards are not available outside the country. However, several Australian lizards are common in the global pet trade because of the captive breeding of specimens collected before the export ban was put in place.

Amphibolurus muricatus (White, ex Shaw, 1790)
Jacky Lizard

Family: Agamidae.
Length: SVL: 4 in. (100 mm). TL: 12 in. (300 mm).
Habitat and Range: Found in shrubs and dry rocky areas throughout Victoria and in coastal New South Wales and southern Queensland, east of the Blue Mountains.
Natural History: This is a common species that is active on particularly warm days. Jacky lizards resemble thin bearded dragons but lack the extensible "beard." They can be found on the soil, where their coloring makes them difficult to spot, but are more easily observed on shrubs, low brush, and on tree stumps. Jacky lizards are active foragers that require a roomy terrarium with enough space to allow running and climbing. They can tolerate a broader temperature range than many other Australian reptiles (75° to 108° F [24° to 42° C]) as well as a range of humidity (60 to 100 percent). Water is generally taken from morning dew, so daily morning mistings are recommended. Diet includes a variety of small arthropods, including flies that they swiftly snatch as they fly by.
Terrarium Suitability: 2

Amphibolurus nobbi Witten, 1972
Nobbi Dragon

Family: Agamidae.
Length: SVL: 3in. (75 mm). TL: 10 in. (254 mm).
Habitat and Range: Dry scrub outback of eastern Queensland, much of New South Wales, northwestern Victoria, and far eastern South Australia.
Natural History: Similar to the jacky lizard, but differs in having a pair of distinct eggshell stripes that extend from over each ear to the hips. Ground color is gray, and the scales are smaller and less keeled than in the jacky lizard. Look for them basking on low branches and tree trunks, generally near the ground. When frightened, they may take cover under loose bark or fallen wood. They are insectivorous and may also take other small arthropods such as centipedes and spiders.
Care: Give these active lizards a terrarium with considerable floor space (for example, 3 ft. by 2 ft./ 0.9 m by 0.6 m), and use at least 10 in. (22 cm) of very slightly moist sand—firm enough so lizards can excavate burrows—as substrate. Keep the terrarium warm (80° to 98° F [27° to 36.5° C]) and humidity moderate (40 to 60 percent). These lizards require strong basking lights and benefit from five to ten hours of daily full-spectrum lighting.
Terrarium Suitability: 4

Carlia amax Storr, 1974
Two-Spined Rainbow Skink

Family: Scincidae.
Length: SVL: 1.4 in. (35 mm). TL: 4.2 in. (107 mm).
Habitat and Range: Among leaf litter, under fallen trees, discarded lumber, and other ground debris from northern Western Australia through the western Cape York Peninsula.
Natural History: This species has four fingers and five toes. The body is bronzy-brown with no conspicuous markings, but sunlight refracts to produce small rainbow colors on the scales. Small, active, and highly secretive, this lizard is difficult to spot unless specifically being sought. All one generally spies is a streak of greenish brown as the lizard darts from refuge to refuge. Though two-spined rainbow skinks live in dry habitats, they prefer moist microhabitats, such as in or under logs, where humidity may exceed 80 percent. These small lizards are insectivorous but probably also consume other small arthropods.
Care: Give these active lizards a spacious terrarium and use at least 10 in. (22 cm) of slightly moist sand as substrate. Keep the terrarium warm (80° to 98° F [27° to 36.5° C]) and humidity moderate (40 to 60 percent). Provide full-spectrum lighting. Captives would need daily offerings of tiny live food items such as fruit flies, month-old crickets, and small mealworms.
Terrarium Suitability: 3

182

Carlia jarnoldi Covacevich and Ingram, 1975
(No common name)

Family: Scincidae.
Length: SVL: 1.6 in. (40 mm). TL: 4.8 in. (120 mm).
Habitat and Range: Dry forests and forest edges under logs, fallen trees, leaf litter, and under bark low on trees in northeastern Queensland.
Natural History: This is an intricately marked skink. The body is brown to copper, with white spots or a series of longitudinal white stripes on the back. The flanks are black, dark brown, or (in males) greenish, with numerous white flecks. The head is solid bronze. *C. jarnoldi* has four fingers and five toes. This is a small, swift, secretive lizard best observed when basking on rocks or logs, usually very near cover. Look for it in arid rocky areas.
Care: Care is similar to that of *Carlia amax*, but the keeper must provide a layer of dried leaf litter on top of the deep substrate. Humidity under the leaf litter should approach 75 to 85 percent. Keep the terrarium warm (80° to 98° F [27° to 36.5° C]) and ambient humidity moderate (40 to 60 percent).
Terrarium Suitability: 4

Chelosania brunnea Gray, 1845
Chameleon Dragon

Family: Agamidae.
Length: SVL: 3.5 in. (90 mm). TL: 8.8 in. (225 mm).
Habitat and Range: Open savannah woodland in extreme northern Western Australia east to just over the Queensland border.
Natural History: This unusual species, the only member of its genus, was known only from a few preserved specimens until the mid 1980s. Chameleon dragons range in color from light gray to yellow, with indistinct pale brown makings on the flanks and nape. There is a distinct crest of nuchal scales. The limbs are comparatively short, the body is laterally compressed, and the lizards generally move slowly. Though largely arboreal, they do come to the ground to forage and, presumably, dig burrows in which they lay eggs. They are slow-moving and largely arboreal lizards, giving them the name "chameleon" dragon.
Care: Little is known about their natural history, and they have not been kept in captivity. They feed on insects and other arthropods, and possibly smaller lizards, flowers, and eggs. Care may be similar to that of chameleons from similar habitats, such as *Furcifer oustaleti* and *Chamaeleo calyptratus*.
Terrarium Suitability: 5

Chlamydosaurus kingii Gray, 1825
Frilled Lizard

Family: Agamidae.
Length: SVL: 14.5 in. (368 mm). TL: 35.8 in. (910 mm).
Habitat and Range: A forest dweller found in northern Australia's scrub and New Guinea's wet lowlands.
Natural History: This is possibly the world's most distinctive lizard, as it is the only species with a huge umbrella-like frill. Frilled lizards are inhabitants of scrub forest areas, where they spend most of their time on or inside trees. During the dry season, frilled lizards may retire to the insides of large hollow trees or mammal burrows in the ground, where humidity is high and the lizards can escape excessive heat. They resume activity with the coming of seasonal rains and the emergence of their prey, which includes insects, smaller lizards, fledgling birds, small snakes, and the occasional bird egg.
Care: Keep the terrarium warm (80° to 98° F [27° to 36.5° C]) and humidity moderate (70 to 80 percent). Frilled lizards enjoy strong basking lights and benefit from full-spectrum lighting. Provide deep sandy substrate for females to dig their nests. Incubate at 83° to 85° F (28°to 29° C). Young may be safely reared together as long as sufficient live foods are offered for all.
Terrarium Suitability: 2

Cryptoblepharus litoralis (**Mertens, 1958**)
Littoral Skink

Family: Scincidae.
Length: SVL: 2.2 in. (55 mm). TL: 6.3 in. (160 mm).
Habitat and Range: Coastal northeastern Australia and southeastern New Guinea.
Natural History: Littoral skinks inhabit coastal beaches and make frequent forays into tide pools and calm water in bays. Look for the small skinks on sun-exposed rocks and boulders near the ocean, where they may occur in large colonies. Sunlight reflecting from their scales gives a rainbow of colors. These skinks feed on insects, such as beach flies and bees, as well as small marine creatures, such as tiny crabs, snails, and gobies.
Care: These hyperactive lizards rarely sit in one spot for more than a few seconds, so they need a terrarium with considerable floor space (for example, 3 ft. by 2 ft./ 0.9 m by 0.6 m). Substrate may consist of clean sand, crushed coral, pebbles, or smooth rocks. Keep the terrarium warm (80° to 98° F [27° to 36.5° C]) and humidity high (80 to 100 percent). These lizards require strong basking lights and benefit from five to ten hours of daily full-spectrum lighting. They forage and feed almost constantly in nature, so offer them a daily variety of flies, fruit flies, small crickets, young roaches, mealworms, and wax worms.
Terrarium Suitability: 3

Cryptoblepharus virgatus (**Garman, 1901**)
Snake-Eyed Skink

Family: Scincidae.
Length: SVL: 1.6 in. (40 mm). TL: 4 in. (101.6 mm).
Habitat and Range: Eastern and southern coastal Australia and lowland New Guinea, in forests, rocky hillsides, and grassy clearings.
Natural History: Snake-eyed skinks get their name from the clear spectacle—instead of eyelids—that covers each eye. These are slender dark coppery skinks, and the intact tails have a zig-zag pattern of light and dark brown. They are typically seen basking on moss-covered boulders and around tree trunks, but rarely venture into leaf litter or open spaces. They are extremely wary and swift, and it is not uncommon to watch them snatch flies out of the air.
Care: Snake-eyed skinks are hyperactive lizards that need a terrarium with considerable floor space. This is a very arboreal species, so a tall terrarium with vertical branches is recommended. Substrate should consist of slightly moist soil, covered with leaf litter, twigs, and coconut husks. Keep the terrarium warm (80° to 98° F [27° to 36.5° C]) and humidity high (80 to 100 percent). Provide shade with small but strong basking area, and provide five to ten hours of daily UV lighting. They forage and feed almost constantly in nature, so offer them a daily variety of insects, snails, and other small prey.
Terrarium Suitability: 4

Ctenophorus fordi (Storr, 1965)
Mallee Dragon

Family: Agamidae.
Length: SVL: 2 in. (50 mm). TL: 6.6 in. (168 mm).
Habitat and Range: Dry outback desert and mallee (woody Australian shrub similar to American tumbleweed) scrub from south-central Western Australia east to central New South Wales.
Natural History: These small lizards are ground-dwellers best seen on sandy soils and gravel. They are generally found in close proximity to the sharp-leafed porcupine and spinifex grasses. Look for them near ant nests or foraging ant columns, as the tiny insects are their predominant prey items. They are expert burrowers that will have tunnels with several entrances that go under the prickly local plant flora. Males have black markings on the belly and throat.
Care: Their near-exclusive consumption of ants makes them unsuitable for most terrarium keepers. If you do keep them, provide at least 10 in. (22 cm) of very slightly moist sand as substrate. Keep the terrarium warm (80° to 98° F [27° to 36.5° C]) and humidity moderate (40 to 60 percent). These lizards require strong basking lights and benefit from five to ten hours of daily full-spectrum lighting. They are egg layers, with laying taking place in the spring. There is little information on captive care.
Terrarium Suitability: 4

Ctenophorus pictus (Peters, 1866)
Painted Dragon

Family: Agamidae.
Length: SVL: 2.75 in. (70 mm). TL: 6.9 in. (175 mm).
Habitat and Range: Lives in desert outback regions of inland New South Wales, South Australia, and bordering areas of Western Australia, Queensland, Victoria, and the Northern Territory.
Natural History: This is a beautifully colored lizard that is also peculiar in its wariness. One can drive a truck within meters of basking painted dragons and observe and photograph them, but it is extremely difficult to approach within 20 feet (6 m) while on foot! Males are brightly colored and vary considerably, especially in throat and ventral coloring, within a single population. The tail has several thin very pale bands. Painted dragons are found in large groups that maintain considerable intervals from each other where small insect prey is common.
Care: Care is largely the same as for the mallee dragon (*Ctenophorus fordi*). Feed the lizards a variety of small to medium-sized live insects daily.
Terrarium Suitability: 4

Ctenotus atlas Storr, 1969
(No common name)

Family: Scincidae.
Length: SVL: 2.8 in. (70 mm). TL: 8.6 in. (218 mm).
Habitat and Range: A long, narrow swath of the Australian outback, from central Western Australia east to central New South Wales.
Natural History: The genus *Ctenotus* contains over 90 species of medium-sized skinks. Look for them in mallee scrub, near sharp-leafed porcupine and spinifex grasses (*Triodia*). These robust skinks are iridescent in bright sunlight and may reflect many colors. However, their ground coloring is black with a series of cream to pale green longitudinal stripes that extend from the head to the tip of the tail. They are active, feeding on whatever small live prey they can capture. They lay eggs.
Care: Because of their wide-ranging foraging behavior, they require a terrarium with considerable floor space and several inches (about 10 cm) of slightly moist sand substrate. Humidity should be less than 50 percent. Ambient air temperature should be 80° to 98° F (27° to 36.5° C). There is little information available on captive care.
Terrarium Suitability: 4

Ctenotus robustus Storr, 1970
Robust Skink

Family: Scincidae.
Length: SVL: 4.7 in. (120 mm) TL: 16 in. (395 mm).
Habitat and Range: The crescent of northern and eastern Australia, from the Western Australia-Northern Territory border to eastern South Australia. They occupy a variety of non-forest habitats, including scrub, desert, and coastal areas.
Natural History: These pretty skinks are large enough to give a person a slightly painful nip, but when handling them there is the far greater chance that the lizard will injure itself. When seized, robust skinks squirm and twist vigorously in an effort to slip away, at which time they may lose their tails. They are most active in late afternoon into twilight. Their foods include insects, smaller lizards, and some flowers.
Care: These skinks should be housed only with their own kind in a terrarium with plentiful cover consisting of rocks, hollow logs, flat bark, and leaf litter. They require four to eight hours of UV light several times per week, and temperatures should range between 80° and 98° F (27° to 36.5° C).
Terrarium Suitability: 1

Cyrtodactylus louisiadensis (**De Vis, 1892**)
Ring-Tailed Gecko

Family: Diplodactylidae.

Length: SVL: 6.3 in. (160 mm). TL: 15.7 in. (399 mm).

Habitat and Range: Limited to the rainforests of the coast and associated mountains of far northeastern Queensland.

Natural History: This is Australia's largest gecko; it bears a superficial resemblance to American banded geckos. The tail is conspicuously and symmetrically banded. Members of this genus lack toe pads, but their long slender digits allow them to climb quite well. Ring-tailed geckos are most often encountered moving on the ground or along horizontal rock formations. This species is also commonly seen in and near caves. Ring-tailed geckos feed on any smaller animals they can capture—mainly insects but small mammals, too.

Care: The terrarium needs to offer considerable floor space, but height is not an important factor. Daytime lighting should be filtered, with UV provided for four to six hours daily. Ring-tailed geckos are prone to rapid dehydration, so the cage needs frequent mistings and hide spots that retain humidity in excess of 85 percent. Air temperature should range from 80° to 98° F (27° to 36.5° C). Food should be regularly dusted with calcium supplements; this is particularly essential for breeding females.

Terrarium Suitability: 2

Delma butleri Storr, 1987
Butler's Legless Lizard

Family: Pygopodidae.
Length: SVL: 3.5in. (90 mm). TL: 12.4 in. (315 mm).
Habitat and Range: Much of the southern half of Australia in mallee scrub near spinifex.
Natural History: These legless lizards are members of the gecko group, despite the very different appearances. Legless lizards may seek refuge in loose sand but are more inclined to seek shelter in existing burrows or among the leaves of shrubs on the ground. When threatened, this species may spring into the air until it can escape into nearby cover. The tail may be 200 percent or more of the total length and is easily dropped if the lizard is grasped.
Care: Butler's legless lizards feed on insects and small spiders and require warm temperatures from 80° to 98° F (27° to 36.5° C). Keep terrarium humidity at 55 to 70 percent, and provide plenty of low cover, such as bark or flat rocks, for this shy species. Humidity under cover should range from 60 to 85 percent. Terrria should have several inches of very slightly moist sandy substrate to accommodate the lizards' burrowing. Provide a standard heat lamp and hot spot area and five to ten hours of UV light daily. Legless lizards lay one or two hard-shelled eggs, but there is almost nothing known about their reproduction.
Terrarium Suitability: 2

Delma torquata Kluge, 1974
Legless Lizard

Family: Pygopodidae.
Length: SVL: 2.6 in. (65 mm). TL: 9 in. (229 mm).
Habitat and Range: A burrower found in a variety of habitats, from suburbs to open grassland, in southeastern Queensland.
Natural History: This small and delicate limbless lizard is one of several species that mimic the color and pattern of young eastern brown snakes (*Pseudonaja textilis*), one of Australia's most venomous animals. This coloring probably confuses predators who mistake the harmless lizard for the deadly snake and leave it alone. It is unusual for flap-footed lizards in that it is largely fossorial and makes its own tiny burrows. It feeds on arthropods and small lizards. Legless lizards lay one or two hard-shelled eggs, but there is almost nothing known about the reproduction of this species.
Care: Keep terrarium at 80° to 98° F (27° to 36.5° C), and humidity at 55 to 70 percent. Provide plenty of cover. Humidity under cover should range from 60 to 85 percent. Terraria should have several inches (about 10 cm) of very slightly moist sandy substrate to accommodate the lizard's burrowing. Provide a standard heat lamp and a small hot spot area, and five to ten hours of UV daily. Feed them calcium-dusted small insects daily.
Terrarium Suitability: 4

Diplodactylus elderi Stirling and Zietz, 1893
Jeweled Gecko

Family: Diplodactylidae.
Length: SVL: 1.8 in. (45 mm). TL: 2.75 in. (70 mm).
Habitat and Range: Found in hot, sandy, arid habitats of much of central Australia, from central coastal Western Australia east to extreme southwest Queensland, and from slightly north of Alice Springs to far southern South Australia. Habitat is limited to particular types of spinifex grasses.
Natural History: This is a small gecko that has a pattern resembling that of Australia's diamond pythons; a black or dark gray background with darker-ringed cream to yellowish spots. The neck is short and thick, as is the tail. The tail is able to squirt a defensive liquid (see *Diplodactylus spinigerus*), but lacks dorsal spiny scales. In addition, the short tail is prehensile and is used to help the lizard climb and stabilize on the thin grasses that are its habitat. This is a nocturnal lizard that feeds on a variety of small insects. Females lay up to three clutches of two eggs each year.
Care: Terrarium care is similar to that for the western spiny-tailed gecko (*D. spinigerus*).
Terrarium Suitability: 2

Diplodactylus spinigerus Gray, 1842
Western Spiny-Tailed Gecko

Family: Diplodactylidae.

Length: SVL: 2.75 in. (70 mm). TL: 4.7 in. (119 mm).

Habitat and Range: Found in heath and wooded habitats of extreme southwestern Western Australia.

Natural History: This is an elongate species with a gray or slate gray body and sometimes a dark vertebral stripe. The peculiar feature is the tail, which bears two parallel rows of sharp spines. When threatened, the gecko secretes a foul-smelling sticky fluid from glands at the bases of the spines, and this deters most would-be predators. The tail can be lost and regenerated, complete with new secretory glands. They have no adhesive toe pads, and the tiny claws can be retracted into toe sheaths. Spiny-tailed geckos are arboreal, spending their time in vegetation, where they take shelter under loose bark during the day. They feed on small invertebrates, including ants, beetles, moths, and spiders.

Care: Terrarium animals require plenty of cover in the form of live or artificial woody (strong-stemmed) plants. Provide a small bowl of drinking water at all times, and lightly mist the terrarium with water weekly. Keep the temperature between 85° and 90° F (29.5° and 32° C) and the humidity between 50 and 85 percent. Feed the geckos large gut-loaded insects daily.

Terrarium Suitability: 2

Diplodactylus steindachneri Boulenger, 1885
Box-Patterned Gecko

Family: Diplodactylidae.
Length: SVL: 2.2 in. (55 mm). TL: 3.7 in. (94 mm).
Habitat and Range: Much of Queensland and central New South Wales, Australia. They inhabit a variety of habitats but favor leaves, debris, and other cover on or near the ground.
Natural History: This is a small gecko that is brown with several large, roundish pale markings from between the eyes to the tail tip. The tail is moderately long and thin (when compared with its close relatives) and lacks any spines; it is also somewhat prehensile. This is a nocturnal lizard that feeds on a variety of small insects. They use the burrows of other animals and cracks in the ground for shelter. Females lay up to three clutches of two eggs each year. Eggs are buried in the ground and incubate for about 55 days.
Care: There should be no more than one male per terrarium, but groups that contain several females will do well. They require a deep substrate of slightly moist loamy soil or a sand and soil mixture. A layer of leaf litter and broad flat bits of bark will provide cover. The terrarium should be warm 73° to 86° F (23° to 30° C) by day and several degrees cooler at night. Provide daily feedings of gut-loaded live insects and lightly mist the terrarium weekly.
Terrarium Suitability: 3

Diporiphora australis (Steindachner, 1867)
Tommy Round-Head

Family: Agamidae.
Length: SVL: 3.7 in. (95 mm). TL: 11 in. (285 mm).
Habitat and Range: Found in most habitats of coastal and northern Queensland.
Natural History: These small agamid lizards are true heat lovers, most likely seen at midday when temperatures may reach 100° F (38° C). Look for them near or on the ground, on fallen logs, boards, tree stumps, and boulders. Though they generally allow close approach, they will dash away swiftly once an observer gets too close. While active, they spend considerable time chasing tiny insect prey. The body is gray-brown with a pair of thin light stripes, between which are rectangular brown markings. Females lay up to eight eggs in a deep burrow, and these hatch 75 to 90 days later.
Care: Keep terrarium at 80° to 90° F (27° to 32° C), with a hot spot that allows substrate to become 120° F (49° C). Humidity should range from 50 to 70 percent. Provide access UV light daily. Provide plenty of cover, such as bark or large stones. Terrria should have 12 inches (30 cm) of slightly moist sandy substrate for burrowing. Feed these lizards a variety of calcium-dusted small insects daily. Supplement with flowers and finely diced bits of fruit.
Terrarium Suitability: 3

Egernia cunninghami (Gray, 1845)
Cunningham's Skink

Family: Scincidae.
Length: SVL: 10in. (255 mm). TL: 19 in. (483 mm).
Habitat and Range: Lives in arid rocky habitats in New South Wales and Victoria; southeastern Queensland; and isolated populations in Queensland's Carnarvon Range and coastal South Australia.
Natural History: This large, prickly skink is easily recognized by its pattern of gray and brown mottling and a keeled tail that tapers. It spends much of its time hidden in rocky crevices that provide shelter and also attract insects, small lizards, and small marsupials, which the lizards consume. Much of the diet is made up of flowers and seeds, and captives will take lettuce, fruits, and diced vegetables. These lizards are hardy and long-lived: Swan mentions a captive male that was about 30 years old. Four to six young are produced live.
Care: The preferred temperature range is 80° to 98° F (27° to 36.5° C) with a hot spot that reaches 120° F (49° C). Humidity should seasonally range from 50 to 80 percent. Provide 6 to 12 hours of UV on alternate days. Provide plenty of cover and a very slightly moist sandy substrate. Feed skinks a variety calcium-dusted small insects daily. Supplement with pink mice, flowers, and very finely diced bits of fruit weekly. Allow juveniles to remain with mother for first few months.
Terrarium Suitability: 1

Egernia depressa (Günther, 1875)
Pygmy Spiny-Tailed Skink

Family: Scincidae
Length: SVL: 4in. (100 mm). TL: 5.3 in. (133 mm).
Habitat and Range: Arid rocky terrain in most of Western Australia and the borders with South Australia and the Northern Territory.
Natural History: Unlike most skinks, which tend to have smooth or only slightly keeled scales, this peculiar skink has large keels over the entire body. It also has a short, thick, and very spiny tail. Coming from some of the hottest and driest areas on Earth, pygmy spiny-tailed skinks are tolerant of extremely high temperatures but will stay in cool shaded rocky recesses when they get overheated. Up to six live young are produced per litter.
Care: In the terrarium they require high temperatures (90° to 110° F [32° to 43° C]) but also several refuges where they can escape to a lower temperature. Provide humidity that varies seasonally between 25 and 50 percent, plenty of shelter, and a varied diet of insects, young rodents, green vegetables, and fruits. There should be a water dish that is large enough to allow lizards to soak. Provide UV light for four to eight hours daily. House only with their own species.
Terrarium Suitability: 1

Egernia frerei Günther, 1897

Major Skink/Mount Bartle Frere skink

Family: Scincidae.
Length: SVL: 7in. (180 mm). TL: 12.6 in. (320 mm).
Habitat and Range: The narrow strip of coastal Queensland north through the Torres Straits islands and southern New Guinea. Look for them in leaf litter and along rocks and logs in forest edges.
Natural History: Major skinks are large, wary lizards that tend to be heard rushing away through dry leaves before being spotted. Though active year round, they are most likely to be seen on hot summer and spring days. When basking, they tend to stay partially concealed. Color varies considerably among shades of brown, tan, and copper. They feed on whatever they can overpower, along with flowers, fruits, and soft grass. This is the only *Egernia* that ranges outside Australia.
Care: Care is similar to that of *Egernia cunninghami*. Humidity should range from 65 to 85 percent. Terrria should have 12 inches (30 cm) or more slightly moist sandy or loamy substrate that can allow burrowing. Feed major skinks a variety of calcium-dusted small insects daily. Supplement with pink mice, small lizards, chopped boiled eggs, flowers, and very finely diced bits of fruit weekly. This is a fairly aggressive species that rarely tolerates the presence of other skinks.
Terrarium Suitability: 1

Egernia major (Gray, 1845)
Land Mullet

Family: Scincidae.
Length: SVL: 11.9 in. (300 mm). TL: 14 in. (360 mm).
Habitat and Range: Restricted to a small area of the extreme northeast of New South Wales and far southeastern Queensland north to about Brisbane. Found in moist forests and along dry forest edges and clearings.
Natural History: The land mullet is *Egernia major* and the major skink is *E. frerei*, which can be confusing. The land mullet, however, ranges just south of the major skink, with a tiny area of overlap in Queensland. Land mullets are among the largest Australian skinks, and their black bodies and shiny scales give them their common name. Like other large skinks, land mullets have long lives that may exceed 15 years.
Care: The care for the land mullet is basically the same as that of the *Egernia cunninghami*. Up to ten large young are produced live, and care for the young is the same as for adults. Allow juveniles to remain with the mother for the first three months, then separate them. This is a fairly aggressive species that rarely tolerates the presence of other skinks.
Terrarium Suitability: 1

Gehyra dubia (Macleay, 1877)
Northern Dtella

Family: Gekkonidae.

Length: SVL: 2.8 in. (70 mm). TL: 5.7 in. (145 mm).

Habitat and Range: Found in a variety of habitats throughout the northeastern quarter of Australia. They have been introduced into New Zealand.

Natural History: Like many other small geckos, northern dtellas are common amid human habitations, capitalizing on electric lighting to draw prey near them. They are frequently first noticed because of their high-pitched vocalizations. The ground color varies from ghostly gray to a pinkish tan, and the skin is somewhat translucent. Unlike similar species, the tail has no spiny scales. They tolerate a wide range of temperature and humidity, a feature that has allowed them to successfully occupy habitats from dry outback to cool and windy reef islets. Wild specimens feed on small arthropods, flowers, nectar, and tree sap.

Care: The preferred temperature range is 80° to 95° F (27° to 35° C) during the day but should be 76° to 81° F (24° to 27° C) in the evening. Humidity should range from 65 to 85 percent. Provide plenty of cover. Feed dtellas a variety of calcium-dusted small insects daily with supplemental fruit and flowers. Males are territorial and should not be housed together.

Terrarium Suitability: 2

Gnypetoscincus queenslandiae (**De Vis**, 1890)
Rainforest Skink/Prickly Skink

Family: Scincidae.
Length: SVL: 3.2 in. (80 mm). TL: 5.7 in. (144 mm).
Habitat and Range: Restricted to wet forest areas of central Queensland, from Cooktown to Cardwell and west to the Atherton Tablelands.
Natural History: Very little is known about this species, but it is not unlikely that they will be observed in one of the national parks. They are largely nocturnal but begin activity in the early evening, when they emerge from beneath moss-covered logs and rocks. The triangular head, short keeled scales, and lack of iridescence make them easy to identify. Live young are produced. They feed on small arthropods.
Care: The preferred temperature range is 79° to 85° F (26° to 29.5° C) with a slight drop at night. A hot spot is not required. Humidity should range from 65 to 85 percent. Provide two to five hours of UV on alternate days. Provide plenty of cover, such as hollow logs, leaf litter, rocks, and live broad-leaf plants. Feed these skinks a variety of calcium-dusted small insects daily. Supplement with flowers and very finely diced bits of fruit weekly. Mating takes place in the spring, and females produce one to five live young about four months later. Males are territorial and should not be housed together.
Terrarium Suitability: 3

Hemisphaeriodon gerrardi (Gray, 1845)
Pink-Tongued Skink

Family: Scincidae.
Length: SVL: 8.3 in. (212 mm). TL: 17.7 in. (450 mm).
Habitat and Range: Found in forest or grassy habitat from central New South Wales north to the Cairns area, along the eastern coast.
Natural History: Pink-tongued skinks are elongated cylindrical lizards with rather short legs and digits and a tail longer than the snout-vent length. The tail is somewhat prehensile and helps steady the lizard when it is climbing. Unlike the related blue-tongued skinks, this species has a pink tongue. The body color is pale gray to light coral, and typically has darker bands across the back and tail. Females give birth to as many as 67 (generally 25 to 30) live young after three to four months gestation time. This is an extraordinary number of live young for a lizard species.
Care: Terrarium animals require a deep and slightly moist substrate for burrowing along with plant cover and climbing branches. Lightly spray the terrarium to maintain 65 to 80 percent humidity. Keep the terrarium warm, between 85° and 90° F (29° and 34° C) at the hot end. Provide UV lighting daily. Feed them large gut-loaded insects daily, and supplement with diced fruits and small berries weekly. Offer small mice weekly or biweekly and give snails and slugs when possible. They are very hardy lizards that live for more than 12 years.
Terrarium Suitability: 2

Heteronotia binoei (Gray, 1845)
Bynoe's Gecko

Family: Diplodactylidae.
Length: SVL: 2 in. (50 mm). TL: 4.9 in. (125 mm).
Habitat and Range: Found in areas where there is ample ground cover that includes rocks, logs, bark sheets, woodpiles, or iron sheeting, through much of Australia excluding the far southeast and extreme southwest.
Natural History: This small delicate ground dweller has a pattern consisting of irregular brown mottling on a lighter brown background. Scales are rough and there are no sticky toe pads. Many populations are parthenogenetic, meaning that they are entirely female. Bynoe's geckos occur in a variety of habitats, from moist forest and grasslands to coastal grasslands and offshore islands. In the northern half of the range they may be active year round, even on cool (68° F [20° C]) nights. They feed on insects, small spiders, and slugs. They are most likely to be observed during the day by looking under boards and logs; at night they are secretive and generally stay under grass and shrub cover.
Care: Care information is not available. Presumably these lizards have the same needs as leopard geckos and similar species: warm temperatures, plenty of hiding places, humid microhabitats, and abundant small prey.
Terrarium Suitability: 2

Hypsilurus spinipes (Duméril and Duméril, 1851)
Forest Angle-Headed Dragon

Family: Agamidae.
Length: SVL: 4.3 in. (110 mm). TL 13 in. (330 mm).
Habitat and Range: Restricted to a small area of the extreme northeast of New South Wales and far southeastern Queensland north to about Brisbane. Found in moist forests and along dry forest edges and clearings.
Natural History: Forest angle-headed dragons are peculiar creatures. Their coloration resembles tree bark, and they move uncharacteristically slowly for tree agamids. When sleeping, they may dangle in ways that resemble contorted yoga positions, adding to the illusion of being a twig or cluster of dried leaves. They are rarely seen on the ground. They are most likely to be observed during and shortly after rains in dense forests. They feed on a variety of insects, slugs, geckos, and fruits.
Care: The males of this species are very territorial, so they should be housed alone or with females. They need a stout vertical climbing object and horizontal branches, but you should also employ thick vines. Keep the terrarium at 80° to 90° F (27° to 32° C) and 65 to 90 percent humidity. Feed them large insects, including giant roaches, large crickets, butterflies, and locusts daily, and supplement with pink mice (monthly) and diced fruits (weekly).
Terrarium Suitability: 3

Lialis burtonis Gray, 1835
Burton's Flap-Footed Lizard

Family: Pygopodidae.
Length: SVL: 12 in. (300 mm). TL: 41 in. (1,050 mm).
Habitat and Range: Found throughout New Guinea and most of Australia, excepting Tasmania, Victoria, and the far southwest. Found in a variety of habitats, from forests and swamps to grasslands.
Natural History: Burton's flap-footed lizard is the largest species of the family Pygopodidae. The extemely long tail may be dropped if seized. There is a small flap—rudimentary hind limbs—on each side of the vent, and these are larger in males than females. Like snakes, these lizards lack a moveable eyelid, having instead a clear round spectacle. Unlike snakes, they possess ear openings and have a short blunt tongue. They lay hard-shelled eggs. Burton's flap-footed lizards feed on insects, centipedes, young mammals, lizards, and small snakes.
Care: A terrarium for a pair of lizards should have about 4 ft. (123 cm) square of floor space and a height of 24 in. (61 cm) or more. Provide deep sand, loamy soil, or slightly moist potting soil, and plenty of hiding places. Give the terrarium a small hotspot and direct lighting, and provide four to eight hours of UV on alternate days. Lightly spray the terrarium with water three times per week, and provide a small dish of clean water.
Terrarium Suitability: 3

Lophognathus temporalis (**Günther, 1867**)
Striped Tree Dragon

Family: Agamidae.
Length: SVL: 4 in. (100 mm). TL: 16 in. (400 mm).
Habitat and Range: Found in areas where there are trees and at least seasonal moisture in southern New Guinea and Australia's Northern Territory, northeastern Western Australia, and coastal northwestern Queensland.
Natural History: These large and conspicuous lizards are often observed basking and foraging along streets, in yards, and around car parks, but they also live in dry forests. They spend roughly equal amounts of time on the ground as in trees and shrubs and will be active at higher temperatures (95° to 115° F [35° to 46° F]) than many other local species. They swim well, run fast—sometimes on the rear legs only—and will climb to the tops of tall trees. They take all manner of live prey, from insects to young mammals.
Care: These are very active lizards and require a terrarium with considerable floor space and height. Males are aggressively territorial and should be housed singly or only with females. They need a stout vertical and horizontal branches. Keep terrarium at 80° to 90° F (27° to 32° C), with 50 to 90 percent humidity. Feed them large insects daily and supplement with pink mice (once or twice monthly).
Terrarium Suitability: 4

Moloch horridus (Gray, 1841)
Moloch/Thorny Devil

Family: Agamidae.
Length: SVL: 4 in. (42 mm). TL: 6.5 in. (165 mm).
Habitat and Range: Molochs live in Australia's most hot and sandy deserts, in places where relatively few other creatures coexist.
Natural History/Care: Molochs bear a superficial resemblance to America's horned lizards. They differ from horned lizards in having near-spherical bodies, two horned humps on the neck, and two greatly elongated horns at the front of the skull. Like horned lizards, molochs feed almost exclusively on ants, are small, and are preyed upon by many larger animals. These small lizards prefer hot temperatures, ranging from 96° to 125° F (35.5° to 51.5° C), and cloudless days. They may see liquid water only a few times in their lives, but any tiny water droplets that attach to their skin are transported by fine capillary action to the lizard's mouth. Most water comes from their food. When walking, molochs have a jerky gait that vaguely resembles a bit of mallee (local bushy plants) blowing in a gentle wind, almost certainly part of their camouflage.
Care: Because of their extremely specific diet and habitat needs, molochs are rarely kept successfully in captivity. To keep them, you must have access to large numbers of ants at all times.
Terrarium Suitability: 5

Nactus cheverti (Boulenger, 1885)
Keeled Ground Gecko

Family: Diplodactylidae.
Length: SVL: 3.2 in. (82 mm). TL: 6.5 in. (165 mm).
Habitat and Range: Lives in leaf litter and under logs, discarded plywood, and other ground cover in a variety of open habitats, from grasslands to forest edges and clearings. Distributed across the upper half of Australia's far northeastern Queensland, from Princess Charlotte Bay to Cairns and the rise of the tablelands.
Natural History: Little is known about this species, which was long considered to be part of the widely distributed *Nactus pelagicus*. Like other padless geckos, this species is primarily terrestrial, though it will climb low shrubs. Specimens exposed during daylight hours will have a dark brown body with darker mottling and a yellowish head, but at night the color is a uniform dull gray. Young are very dark brown with tiny yellowish speckling. Some populations may be parthenogenetic. Keeled ground geckos feed on small arthropods and are active year round.
Care: Care information for this species is not available but should be similar to that for tropical geckos such as *Ptychozoon* and *Gekko ulikovskii* (see Region 7: Southeast and Eastern Asia for those species)—except that *Nactus* is terrestrial.
Terrarium Suitability: 2

Nephrurus amyae Couper, 1994
Spiny Knob-Tailed Gecko

Family: Diplodactylidae.
Length: SVL: 5.3 in. (135 mm). TL: 5.7 in. (145 mm).
Habitat and Range: Found in hot, sandy, arid habitats of the inland Northern Territory, Australia.
Natural History: The spiny knob-tailed gecko is very similar in appearance to the rough knob-tailed gecko, which is why it wasn't formally recognized as a separate species until 1994. It differs from its relative in having much larger and spinier body scales, a larger adult size, and a tendency to have rusty red ground coloring. They also possess heads that appear disproportionately large, and very large eyes. Spiny knob-tails also prefer more open and sandier habitats, living not only amid rocks, but among spinifex and other protective shrubs. All members of the genus *Nephrurus* (which translates into "kidney-tail") are strictly nocturnal. This is the largest of the knob-tailed geckos. There is also very little else known about this species in the wild.
Care: Care is the same as for the rough knob-tailed gecko (*Nephrurus asper*).
Terrarium Suitability: 2

Nephrurus asper Günther, 1876
Rough Knob-Tailed Gecko

Family: Diplodactylidae.
Length: SVL: 4.5 in. (114 mm). TL: 5 in. (127 mm).
Habitat and Range: Found in hot, rocky, arid habitats of the northern third of Australia.
Natural History: This is a very distinctive lizard, in that it has a comically small tail that that ends in a small globe. The head and eyes are quite large. The body is covered in conspicuous cone-shaped scales, and there are no adhesive pads on the toes. There is very little known about this species in the wild.
Care: Terrarium animals require plenty of cover. Use rocks, bricks, and similar large objects. Provide a small bowl of drinking water at all times. Keep the temperature between 85° and 90° F (29.5° and 32° C) at the hot side of the cage, and keep humidity between 30 and 55 percent. Feed the geckos gut-loaded insects daily. Knob-tailed geckos have a life span of seven to nine years in captivity.
Terrarium Suitability: 2

Nephrurus levis De Vis, 1886
Smooth Knob-Tailed Gecko

Family: Diplodactylidae.
Length: SVL: 3.5 in. (90 mm). TL: 4.25 in. (108 mm).
Habitat and Range: Much of central Australia, from coastal Western Australia to central inland Queensland and New South Wales. Inhabits a variety of open arid areas.
Natural History: The genus *Nephrurus* consists of geckos with a short carrot-shaped tail that ends in a distinct small globe. The eyes are comparatively quite large for the blunt, rounded head. A distinct set of rear-facing chevrons adorns the neck. These lizards are strictly nocturnal and forage widely for small live prey. By day they shelter in small burrows that they excavate or appropriate from other burrowing creatures. They live in regions where daytime temperatures may exceed 110° F (43° C).
Care: Provide a terrarium of 24-in. by 18-in. (61 by 46 cm) for up to three specimens. Do not house more than one male per terrarium. Substrate should be 2 to 6-in. (5 to 15 cm) of sand, and there must be a variety of shelters on the surface. During the day temperature should be near 78° F (25.5° C). Females may lay two eggs every 15 to 20 days and may have several clutches per year. Place eggs in an incubator and keep at 82.5 ° F (28° C.); they hatch after 60 days or longer.
Terrarium Suitability: 2

Nephrurus wheeleri Loveridge, 1932
Western Knob-Tailed Gecko

Family: Diplodactylidae.
Length: SVL: 3.5 in. (90 mm). TL: 4.25 in. (108 mm).
Habitat and Range: Arid outback near rocks and spinifex grass in Western Australia.
Natural History: The tubercles on this species are the largest in the genus, giving western knob-tailed geckos a distinctly spiny appearance. They stay under cover beneath rocks or in burrows during the heat of day, emerging after dusk to hunt small arthropods. Look for them after dark, when they will be foraging on the ground. Though they live in regions where daytime temperatures may exceed 110° F (43° C), these geckos stay deep under cover at such times and are unable to survive when exposed to such heat for more than a few minutes.
Care: Terrarium specimens should be given a deep layer of slightly moist sandy soil so they may excavate burrows. Provide a terrarium of 24-in by 18-in (61 by 46 cm) for up to three specimens. Do not house more than one male per terrarium. Provide a variety of shelters. During the day, temperature should be near 80° F (27° C). Keep humidity below 65 percent. Feed a variety of live insects daily and dust with calcium powder three to four times weekly. Provide live foods daily.
Terrarium Suitability: 2

Oedura marmorata Gray, 1842
Marble Gecko/Marbled Velvet Gecko

Family: Diplodactylidae.
Length: SVL: 4.5 in. (114 mm) TL: 7.3 in. (185 mm)
Habitat and Range: Widely distributed in the northern two-thirds of Australia, absent in southern regions where winters can be cold. They prefer semi-arid terrain with rocks and low vegetation.
Natural History: Thickset geckos with a dark background with tiny white specks. Young marble geckos resemble American banded geckos, having a pale eggshell body with dark brown bands and head. Tails of adults may be thin or greatly swollen. The skin feels like velvet to the touch. These stout geckos are deceptively quick when fleeing from danger or pursuing prey. They actively forage on the ground and in low shrubs, on fences, and around debris such as fallen logs, and are most likely encountered at and for a while after twilight. Preferred foods are small arthropods, but they also consume some flowers and nectar. They are active following hot sunny days. They remain under cover during heavy rains and avoid walking through mud. Look for them near places that offer quick cover.
Care: In the terrarium, give them a variety of places to hide, including rocky crevices and large bits of bark, and plenty of places to climb. Feed them a variety of insects, including crickets, moths, and wax worms.
Terrarium Suitability: 2

216

Physignatus lesueurii **(Gray, 1831)**
Australian Water Dragon

Family: Agamidae.
Length: SVL: 11 in. (280 mm). TL: 35.4 in. (900 mm).
Habitat and Range: Found around permanent water, such as lakes, rivers, and seacoast, along most of the Australian east coast.
Natural History: A large and handsome lizard that resembles a gray iguana. A black mask extends from the eye to the throat. Males have orange ventral coloring that becomes more intense during the mating season. Water dragons are semi-aquatic, spending basking time on rocks or branches over water. They swim well and may remain submerged for several minutes. In some areas the lizards show little fear of humans and permit observers to get within about 6 feet (2 m) before moving away. These large lizards feed on a variety of foods, including smaller animals, flowers, and fruits.
Care: Males are aggressively territorial and should be housed singly or with females. They require a large, tall terrarium with stout vertical climbing branches. Keep terrarium at 70° to 90° F (21° to 32° C), with a hotspot near 97° F (36.5° C), and humidity at 65 to 90 percent. They should have at least ten hours of UV light daily. Feed them large insects daily, and supplement with pink or hopper-sized mice and diced fruits.
Terrarium Suitability: 1

Pogona barbata (Cuvier, 1829)
Bearded Dragon

Family: Agamidae.
Length: SVL: 9.8 in. (250 mm). TL: 27 in. (675 mm).
Habitat and Range: Open woodlands, dry sclerophyll, and outback habitats in most of eastern Australia, from near Cairns south to the Sydney area, then west to central Victoria; also found in southern South Australia.
Natural History: One of Australia's iconic lizards, the bearded dragon gets its name from the short prickly neck scales, which appear like a beard when the throat is inflated. Combined with wide open jaws and hissing, the display is generally a bluff to frighten predators. Color varies largely with temperature, ranging from sandy brown in cool specimens to black in warm ones. Additionally, as the lizard's body temperature passes a certain threshold, the entire belly turns black. Bearded dragons excavate or appropriate burrows between clusters of spinifex and porcupine grasses. By day, they climb low perches—boulders, tree stumps, and fence posts—to bask and spy prey. The diet includes smaller reptiles and mammals, insects, fruits, and soft green vegetation.
Care: Care is as for the more commonly available *Pogona vitticeps*.
Terrarium Suitability: 1

Pogona henrylawsoni Wells and Wellington, 1985
Outback Bearded Dragon/Lawson's Dragon

Family: Agamidae.
Length: SVL: 5.9 in. (150 mm). TL: 8.9 in. (225 mm).
Habitat and Range: Rocky arid outcrops of central Queensland.
Natural History: Very similar to *P. barbata*, but it has a less spiny "beard" and is generally lighter in coloring. Outback bearded dragons reside in the black soil plains of Queensland's outback, which is also the habitat for Spencer's monitors and black-headed pythons, both of which prey on the outback bearded dragon. These lizards like heat and are active during the day but frequently retreat to shade to avoid overheating. The diet is broad, including centipedes, spiders, insects, small eggs, other lizards, and flowers.
Care: Care is as for *Pogona vitticeps*, although this species can be housed in slightly smaller terraria. Outback bearded dragons are less prone to climbing and eat less vegetation than inland bearded dragons.
Terrarium Suitability: 2

Pogona minima (**Loveridge, 1933**)

Western Bearded Dragon

Family: Agamidae.
Length: SVL: 6.8 in. (172.7 mm). TL: 14.8 in. (376 mm).
Habitat and Range: The western quarter of Western Australia except the extreme southwest. They are found in various habitats and are often seen perching on fence posts, shrubs, and boulders.
Natural History: Western bearded dragons are significantly smaller than their more familiar eastern relatives. The enlarged scales that form the distensible "beard" are not nearly as long as those of the eastern species. They are able to tolerate temperatures that most other animals would avoid; it is not uncommon to see western bearded dragons basking on blacktop during the day.
Care: Terrarium animals require a deep sandy substrate and plenty of cover. They also need props for climbing, including wrist-thick branches or large rocks. Provide a flat shallow bowl of drinking water at all times, and lightly spray the terrarium with water weekly. Keep the terrarium warm, and provide a basking site that reaches up to 100° F (38° C). Provide about 12 hours of UV lighting daily, and keep humidity between 35 and 60 percent. Feed them large gut-loaded insects daily, and supplement with diced fruits, small berries, and leafy greens weekly. Offer small mice weekly or biweekly.
Terrarium Suitability: 2

Pogona vitticeps (Ahl, 1926)
Inland Bearded Dragon

Family: Agamidae.
Length: SVL: 9 in. (230 mm). TL: 19 in. (485 mm).
Habitat and Range: Arid areas in all eastern Australian states except for Tasmania.
Natural History: Smaller and generally lighter in color than the bearded dragon, inland bearded dragons are similar in behavior, diet, and activity patterns. They are also among the most popular lizards kept in the herpetoculture hobby, for they are hardy, feed on a variety of foods, and allow handling without becoming too stressed to feed. Bearded dragons also have strong tails that do not naturally break off, so they can be picked up by the tail (not recommended). Though they open the mouth and put on a show of defense, they are extremely unlikely to bite.
Care: All bearded dragons need warm daytime temperatures of 80° to 110° F (26.5° to 43° C). Give them plenty of shaded cover or a thick substrate of slightly moist sand for burrowing. Full-spectrum lighting is necessary. Feed a variety of foods, including a range of insects, small rodents, leafy greens, and other produce. This is probably the most appropriate species of lizard for new herpetoculturists to keep, and they are rather easy to breed. Males are very territorial and cannot be housed with other males; they are occasionally aggressive to females as well.
Terrarium Suitability: 1

Pygopus nigriceps Fischer, 1882
Hooded Flap-Footed Lizard

Family: Pygopodidae.
Length: SVL: 8.8 in. (225 mm). TL: 28.3 in. (720 mm).
Habitat and Range: Across most of continental Australia from near Brisbane to Perth but not on the coasts They are found in most habitats provided there is loose soil and at least sparse plant cover.
Natural History: This is another lizard that mimics the highly venomous brown snake (*Pseudonaja textilis*) in color and pattern. If threatened, it is capable of raising the head and neck, flattening the neck into a narrow hood, and emitting squeaking sounds. Most of the range of this lizard includes hot to very hot regions, for which reason they are most active at twilight and evening. They feed almost exclusively on insects.
Care: Captives need places for hiding and burrowing. Most water comes from their food, but a weekly light misting is suggested. They prefer temperatures of 85° to 90° F (29.5° to 32° C), and humidity at 65 to 90 percent.
Terrarium Suitability: 3

tail detail

Strophurus ciliaris (Boulenger, 1885)
Spiny-Tailed Gecko

Family: Diplodactylidae.

Length: SVL: 3.5in. (90 mm). TL: 5.75 in. (129 mm).

Habitat and Range: Most likely to be encountered in the tropical forests of the northwestern third of Australia, but also found in spinifex and scrub outback.

Natural History: Color in this species is highly variable, ranging from dull gray or brown to dark brown with orange or yellowish spots. The tail is shorter than the SVL and has a distinct set of dorsal spines. When threatened, spiny-tailed geckos can secrete a foul-tasting fluid from glands at the base of these spines, which may aid in deterring predators from attacking. Typically terrestrial, but may climb when trees or shrubs are present.

Care: Keep terrarium at 80° to 90° F (27° to 32° C) and humidity at 55 to 70 percent. These geckos should have a small hot spot area in the terrarium that reaches a substrate temperature of 98° F (36.5° C) and two to six hours of UV light on alternate days. Provide plenty of cover. Terraria should have 2 to 3 inches (5 to 8 cm) of very slightly moist sandy substrate to accommodate egg laying. Feed the geckos a variety of calcium-dusted small insects daily. Females lay one or two hard-shelled eggs that hatch after 60 to 70 days when incubated at 84.5° F (29° C).

Terrarium Suitability: 2

Strophurus intermedius (Ogilby, 1892)
Eastern Spiny-Tailed Gecko

Family: Diplodactylidae.
Length: SVL: 2.6in. (65 mm). TL: 4 in. (102 mm).
Habitat and Range: Southeastern Australia and west along the extreme southern coast to central Western Australia, where they occur in a variety of planted habitats, including sclerophyll forest, mallee and spinifex, and seasonally moist grassland.
Natural History: Though these lizards climb well, they are most likely to be encountered while foraging on the ground in the evening. The marbled slate-gray body is excellent camouflage when the lizards are on rocks or tree bark. The eye resembles an intricate cat's-eye stone, being orange with a scalloped pupil. Though small, it will aggressively threaten a human intruder, gaping and squeaking until danger passes. Voracious insect eaters that consume moths, beetles, crickets, and large ants.
Care: Identical to that of *Strophurus ciliaris* in the previous entry.
Terrarium Suitability: 2

Tiliqua adelaidensis (Peters, 1863)
Adelaide Blue-Tongued Skink

Family: Scincidae.
Length: SVL: 3.5 in. (90 mm). TL: 6.2 in. (157.5 mm).
Habitat and Range: Known only from open grassland areas in Burra and near Adelaide, South Australia.
Natural History: Here is another Australian animal about which very little is known. It was described in 1863, and very few specimens have come to light since then, leading herpetologists to think it might be extinct. Then a single specimen was discovered in 1992, and subsequent searches have led to colonies of this species, the smallest of the blue-tongued skinks. They are quite different in appearance from other blue-tongued skinks; the body is usually unicolor gray-brown to yellowish brown, though some individuals may have indistinct dark crossbands. Though they inhabit a very small range, they are apparently more common than once feared. By day they take refuge in spider holes or under debris such as plywood boards. Consumes plants, insects, snails, and possibly spiders.
Care: This species has not been kept in captivity and is quite rare. Husbandry should be the same as for other *Tiliqua*.
Terrarium Suitability: 4

Tiliqua nigrolutea Quoy and Gaimard, 1824
Blotched Blue-Tongued Skink

Family: Scincidae.
Length: 7.8 in. (200 mm). TL: 11.8 in. (300 mm).
Habitat and Range: A resident of temperate regions of southeastern Australia, including Tasmania, from sea level into the mountains. In Tasmania, this is the largest species of native lizard.
Natural History: This stocky, short-limbed lizard is conspicuous with its dark brown and yellowish mottling that helps it blend into the leaf litter. Unlike most other skinks, blotched blue-tongues can change their dorsal coloring depending on temperature. Like other blue-tongues, they are diurnal foragers that consume slugs, snails, large insects, small eggs, other lizards, and some vegetable matter, including berries, flowers and leaves. They can tolerate much lower temperatures than most reptiles, but they will seek cover and become dormant when temperature falls below 65° F (18° C). These lizards are most likely to be seen in the spring and early summer, when temperatures range from 68° to 88° F (20° to 31° C) and males are actively seeking mates. One to three large live young are produced.
Care: *T. nigrolutea* can be kept much like *T. scincoides*. These lizards are excellent burrowers that should be given terrria with a foot (30.5 cm) or more of substrate.
Terrarium Suitability: 2

Tiliqua occipitalis (**Peters, 1863**)
Western Blue-Tongued Skink

Family: Scincidae.
Length: SVL: 11.8 in. (300 mm). TL: 17.7 in. (450 mm).
Habitat and Range: Arid sandy regions from coastal Western Australia east to central New South Wales.
Natural History: This is a boldly marked skink, having a yellow to light gray ground color with four broad chocolate-brown dorsal bands and three to four solid caudal bands. Some populations also have thin dark bands between the large dorsal series. Western blue-tongued skinks are found in areas with loose soil and low vegetation that includes some combination of spinifex, porcupine grass, and shrubs. Most active in late afternoon through dusk, they may also be active during midday.
Care: Captives need high ambient temperatures (90° to 110° F [32° to 43° C]) and plenty of cooler hiding places. They do best in low humidity, about 55 to 65 percent. They feed on plants, fruits, other lizards, eggs, insects, snails, and carrion.
Terrarium Suitability: 1

Tiliqua rugosa (Gray, 1825)
Shingle-Backed Skink/Sleepy Lizard

Family: Scincidae.
Length: SVL: 11.8 in. (300 mm). TL: 14.4 in. (365.6 mm).
Habitat and Range: Found in most habitats of southern Australia west of the Great Dividing Range. Absent from Tasmania.
Natural History: Coloration in this species varies tremendously across Australia. Some lizards may be uniformly black or brown, while others are predominantly eggshell, with brown mottling or bands. They have the distinct cobalt-blue tongue of other *Tiliqua*, but they differ in having a very short tail that resembles a second head and in having keeled scales. These anatomical differences lead many herpetologists to place the shingle-back in a genus of its own, *Trachydosaurus*. The life history of this species is particularly interesting. A pair typically mates for life, sharing burrows or other refuges. The one to (rarely) three large young are born alive and may stay with the parents for a year or more. Life span may exceed 30 years.
Care: Shingle-backs eat a variety of plant and animal matter and are extremely hardy terrarium animals. Care is as for *Tiliqua scincoides*.
Terrarium Suitability: 1

Tiliqua scincoides (**Shaw, 1790**)
Eastern Blue-Tongued Skink

Family: Scincidae.
Length: SVL: 15.7 in. (400 mm). TL: 25 in. (640 mm).
Habitat and Range: Most of coastal northern and eastern Australia, with a small isolated population in northeastern South Australia. Occurs in a variety of habitats, from arid spinifex desert to moist coastal forests and backyards.
Natural History: The eastern blue-tongued skink is a generalist, being at home in almost any habitat with its large range. Despite the comically tiny limbs, the skinks can move quite rapidly. It is almost wholly terrestrial but will climb occasionally. Active during the day and feeding on a variety of foods, especially snails, slugs, flowers, and small eggs. Eastern blue-tongued skinks may live for 20 years in captivity.
Care: Provide this species with a water dish, as it is more likely to drink regularly than some of its relatives. Possibly ties with inland bearded dragons as the ideal lizard for novice keepers. Keep temperature between 75° and 100° F (24° and 38° C), and provide UV lighting on alternate days. Tolerates 65 to 90 percent humidity. Feed them some combination of large insects, small rodents, prawns, snails, and diced fruits, mixed and leafy green vegetables daily. All *Tiliqua* are live-bearing lizards; the eastern blue-tongue may produce up to 25 large young per litter.
Terrarium Suitability: 1

Underwoodisaurus milii (Bory de Saint-Vincent, 1825)
Thick-Tailed Gecko

Family: Diplodactylidae.
Length: SVL: 3.2 in. (80 mm). TL: 5.7 in. (144 mm).
Habitat and Range: Found in most habitats across southern Australia, and centrally as far north as Alice Springs, Northern Territory.
Natural History: Thick-tailed geckos closely resemble *Nephrurus* but have a longer tail and lack the terminal globe structure. These are generalist ground geckos, living in moist forests and dry sclerophyll outback. Thick-tailed geckos feed on all manner of small live prey, and take the occasional flower as well. When threatened, they rise on stretched limbs, slowly wave the tail, and may emit a long gravelly squeak, then lunge at the intruder. They live in regions where daytime temperatures may exceed 110° F (43° C).
Care: Provide a terrarium of 24 in by 18 in (61 by 46 cm) for up to three specimens. Do not house more than one male per terrarium. Substrate should be 2 to 6 in. (5 to 15 cm) of sand, and there must be a variety of shelters on the surface. During the day temperature should be near 78° F (25.5° C). Females lay two eggs that should be incubated at 82° to 86° F (28° to 30° C).
Terrarium Suitability: 2

Varanus acanthurus Boulenger, 1885

Spiny-Tailed Monitor

Family: Varanidae.

Length: SVL: 13.8 in. (350 mm). TL: 31.2 in. (805 mm).

Habitat and Range: Among rocks and hillsides of northern Australia, from western Western Australia to the Atherton Tablelands of Queensland.

Natural History: A very variable lizard, but all specimens possess a spiny tail that is about 1.2 to 1.66 times the snout-vent length. Spiny-tailed monitors frequent habitats with considerable rocky cover, from dry watercourses to roadside rock heaps. They feed primarily on other lizards and large arthropods, such as locusts and centipedes, but will also consume eggs of lizards or small birds. It is not unusual to see them active when it is 104° F (40° C). Spiny-tailed monitors are wary and extremely quick to bolt into cover.

Care: Terrarium animals should have as much floor space as one can provide and 12 to 24 in. (31 to 61 cm) of very slightly damp sandy substrate in which to burrow. Keep the terrarium very warm by day (90° to 104° F [32° to 40° C]) with a hotspot that may reach 130° F (54.5° C). There must be plenty of cover and areas that are much cooler than the hotspot. Always provide a dish of clean drinking water. Feed these lizards dusted crickets, roaches, and other insects daily and offer small mice weekly.

Terrarium Suitability: 2

Varanus baritji **King and Horner, 1987**
White's Spiny-Tailed Monitor

Family: Varanidae.
Length: SVL: 13.9 in. (353 mm). TL: 23.6 in. (600 mm).
Habitat and Range: Rocky habitats across the top third of the Northern Territory.
Natural History: Little is known about this monitor, discovered and named about 20 years ago. What is known is that its habitat, diet, appearance, and behavior are very similar to those of the spiny-tailed monitor. In coloration, though, it differs markedly, having a gray dorsum and flanks with a faint series of dark gray bands on the flanks and tiny, irregularly spaced light markings on the back. The throat is bright yellow. Very similar to *Varanus acanthurus* in coloring, but has no dark stripes on the neck. More shy than the spiny-tailed monitor. It will also be found in rocky areas, but also in places with trees.
Care: Care information seems to be the same as for the spiny-tailed monitor (*Varanus acanthurus*) although *V. baritji* is not known to be in the pet trade
Terrarium Suitability: 3

Varanus brevicauda Boulenger, 1898
Short-Tailed Monitor

Family: Varanidae.

Length: SVL: 5.2 in. (131 mm). TL: 9.8 in. (250 mm).

Habitat and Range: Sandy, arid desert regions of northern Australia from far western Western Australia east through the Northern Territory and far western Queensland.

Natural History: *Varanus brevicauda* has long held the record as the smallest monitor. It is also the only dwarf monitor in which the tail is shorter than the snout-vent length, a feature approached only by some of the largest monitors (i.e., Komodo dragons and savannah monitors). Many people include the short-tailed monitor among the spiny-tailed assemblage, but in fact *V. brevicauda* has keeled, not spiny, caudal scales. They are known to be residents of extremely harsh deserts, where they seek refuge in tunnels dug under the protective spines of spinifex clumps. They spend much of the day seeking prey, tending to keep under the shaded cover of desert plants. They feed primarily on insects and centipedes but will also consume smaller lizards they encounter. They are often active at 104° F (40° C) or more.

Care: Care is similar to that for *Varanus acanthurus*. Always provide a dish of clean water large enough for these lizards to soak themselves. Feed them dusted crickets, small roaches, or other small insects daily.

Terrarium Suitability: 3

Varanus giganteus (Gray, 1845)
Perentie

Family: Varanidae.

Length: SVL: 34 in. (861 mm). TL: 78 in. (1,982 mm).

Habitat and Range: Sandy, arid desert regions of northern Australia from far western Western Australia east through the Northern Territory and central Queensland.

Natural History: The fact that this is Australia's largest lizard is reflected in its scientific name, *Varanus giganteus*. Adults have been recorded at about 8 feet (2.5 m), though most are somewhat shorter. This is a handsome and unmistakable species, the neck and throat brightly marked in a lace-like pattern of cream rings on a dark brown background. This elongate, elegant lizard is a resident of open and spinifex deserts; it digs deep burrows or secretes itself into rocky crevices to escape the hottest sun. Perenties are active and formidable predators, and adults have few natural enemies.

Care: Perenties require very hot and roomy enclosures and are not suited to keeping by the majority of private herpetoculturists. Municipal and private zoos (such as Australia Zoo, Beerwah) have the facilities to keep these lizards in excellent health, but such facilities are large and costly.

Terrarium Suitability: 4

Varanus gouldii (Gray, 1838)
Gould's Monitor/Sand Goanna

Family: Varanidae.
Length: SVL: 25 in. (640 mm). TL: 63 in. (1,600 mm).
Habitat and Range: Most of Australia excepting Tasmania. Gould's monitors prefer arid and semi-arid habitats.
Natural History: This is probably Australia's most wide-ranging monitor. It is similar to the Argus monitor, but has a more slender build, irregular light-colored rosette markings on the back, and the last 1/4 to 1/3 of the tail is cream or some shade of yellow, without markings. A putative central Australian subspecies, *V. g. flavirufus*, is intensely marked with golden-yellow and orange flecks, the dorsal rosettes often fusing into bands across the back. They are among Australia's top predators, capable of feeding on other lizards, snakes, birds, mammals, large arthropods, eggs of lizards or small birds, and carrion.
Care: Terrarium animals should have as much floor space as one can provide and 36 in. (92 cm) of sandy substrate. Keep the terrarium (90° to 104° F [32° to 40° C]) by day with a hotspot that may reach 130° F (54.5° C). There must be several places for the lizards to hide and to escape the heat of the hotspot. Always provide a dish of clean drinking water. Provide variety in foods: dusted large crickets and roaches, mice, small rats, and fresh eggs. Feed three times per week.
Terrarium Suitability: 3

Varanus mertensi Glauert, 1951
Mertens's Monitor

Family: Varanidae.
Length: SVL: 26.7 in. (680 mm). TL: 70 in. (1,700 mm).
Habitat and Range: Found in fresh-water ponds, lakes, and billabongs of tropical northern Queensland, Western Australia, and the Northern Territory.
Natural History: Mertens's monitors are olive lizards flecked with pale spots only one to two scales large, giving the lizard an appearance of being gold-dusted. The tail is compressed, and slightly higher, than in similar monitors, and is used as a sculling organ when in the water. The nostrils also have an unusual valve in the form of a loose flap of tissue that extends along the floor on the inner nostril. When the lizard submerges, air pressure forms a bubble under this tissue, pushing it into and slightly through the nostril, making a passive flotation valve. When submerged, Mertens's monitors may actively and effectively forage for fishes, crawfish, and frogs.
Care: Their large size and high dependence upon water make these unlikely lizards for most private herpetoculturists to properly house.
Terrarium Suitability: 4

Varanus semiremex **Peters, 1869**

Rusty Monitor

Family: Varanidae.
Length: SVL: 9 in. (230 mm). TL: 23.6 in. (600 mm).
Habitat and Range: Most of east coastal Queensland, from Frasier Island to the Cape York Peninsula, near brackish water and estuaries.
Natural History: Development of much of the rusty monitor's picturesque habitat has greatly reduced its numbers, and it is considered endangered. Rusty monitors are highly aquatic, foraging for prey below the water as much as on land. They have a strongly compressed tail and valves that seal the nostril when the monitor is submerged. This species is restricted to areas of brackish water. Food includes insects, crabs, snails, small mammals, and other lizards. Rusty monitors spend much of the day basking on sturdy branches that overhang water. When frightened, they leap off the branch and dive into the water below, staying submerged for several minutes. As a consequence of living in salty water, the salt glands of rusty monitors produce considerable amounts of pale white exudate that looks like waxy tear stains.
Care: Similar to that of other semi-aquatic monitors, such as *V. indicus* and *V. salvator* (see Region 7: Southeast and Eastern Asia) but this species is much smaller than those two.
Terrarium Suitability: 3

Varanus varius (Shaw, in White, 1790)
Lace Monitor

Family: Varanidae.
Length: SVL: 33 in. (840 mm). TL: 55.5 in. (1,410 mm).
Habitat and Range: Frequents a variety of habitats as long as trees are present, from arid scrub to coastal rainforest in most of eastern continental Australia.
Natural History: The lace monitor (*Varanus varius*) may represent two or more species. This is Australia's second largest lizard and one of the few monitors in the world with a yellow tongue. Lace monitors, locally called "lacies," are generalists, equally adept at swimming, running, digging, and climbing. They spend considerable time in trees but are also likely to be observed foraging or basking next to a stream. They feed upon a variety of other animals, including insects, snakes, birds, eggs, mammals and carrion. Females lay eggs in termite nests (as do several other large species of monitors) and have been observed to return to dig the young out of the nest some nine months later.
Care: These are large and active monitors that are suited for captivity only by facilities that can provide extremely large enclosures. Because they regularly use a variety of habitats and range widely from north to south in Australia, their environmental needs probably vary based on the location from which any individual was collected.
Terrarium Suitability: 4

V. varius occurs in two distinct patterns. Pictured here is the banded form that was once considered a separate species and subspecies (*Varanus belli* or *V. varius belli*). This pattern is sometimes called the "belli phase" in reference to the defunct scientific name. Banded and spotted individuals can occur in the same clutch, and the hatchlings of both phases are banded when they first hatch.

239

Australia is home to more monitor species than any other continent. Here are six more you might see there.

Varanus glauerti Mertens, 1957

Kimberly Rock Monitor
SVL: 11.8 in. (300 mm).

Varanus pilbarensis Storr, 198

Pilbara Rock Monitor
SVL: 6.8 in. (172 mm).

Varanus rosenbergi Mertens, 1957

Heath Monitor
SVL: 20 in. (508 mm).

Varanus scalaris Mertens, 194

Banded Tree Monitor
SVL: 12.3 in. (313 mm).

Varanus spenceri
Lucas and Frost, 1903

Spencer's Monitor
SVL: 22 in. (558 mm).

Varanus storri Mertens, 1966

Storr's Monitor
SVL: 5.5 in. (139 mm)

Additional species that occur in Australia but are also found elsewhere are listed below. You may find a species account for these lizards in the region section given in parentheses.

Carlia fusca (Region 5: New Guinea, New Zealand, and Oceania)
Diporiphora bilineata (Region 5: New Guinea, New Zealand, and Oceania)
Eugongylus albofasciatus (Region 5: New Guinea, New Zealand, and Oceania)
Varanus indicus (Region 5: New Guinea, New Zealand, and Oceania)
Varanus panoptes (Region 5: New Guinea, New Zealand, and Oceania)
Varanus prasinus (Region 5: New Guinea, New Zealand, and Oceania)

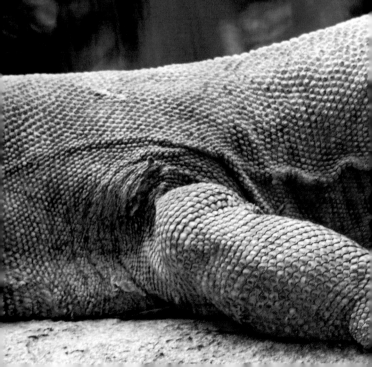
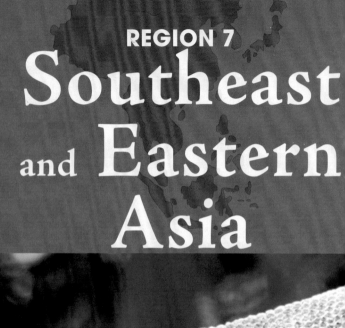

Included here are the Indonesian islands, Singapore Malaysia, Thailand, Burma (Myanmar), Laos, Cambodia, Vietnam, southern China, Japan, and the Philippines. There are several biodiversity hotspots here, home to not only a great many species but also many found only in very small areas. Families represented include amphisbaenids, agamids, geckonids, eublepharids, scincids, lacertids, anguids, dibamids, and varanids. Two additional families, Lanthanotidae and Shinisauridae, are endemics restricted to small areas of Borneo and China, respectively. The numerous mountains offer a greatly increased land area in seasonal forests and rainforests, tropical montane, and riverine habitats. The two most massive lizards, Komodo dragons and water monitors, live here; water monitors range across the entire region west of New Guinea. Sumatra and the mainland are home to the remarkable flying dragons, plus the largest variety of agamas with unusual crests, frills, and tails. There are also numerous small limbless or nearly limbless burrowers that may be found in rotting logs and loose soils or under leaf litter and mulch.

Komodo dragon
(*Varanus komodoensis*)

Acanthosaura armata (Hardwicke and Gray, 1827)
Mountain Horned Lizard

Family: Agamidae.
Length: SVL: 5.5 in. (140 mm). TL: 12 in.(305 mm).
Habitat and Range: Forests of southern Thailand to the southern tip of the Malayan Peninsula.
Natural History: These generally stationary tree dwellers rely on camouflage rather than speed for protection. Like squirrels, they will carefully move around a tree trunk to keep it between an observer and themselves. Males are territorial and will threaten and attack rivals in their area. The similar *Acanthosaura crucigera* Boulenger, 1885 generally has a pronounced triangular black neck collar and is more widely distributed across southern Burma east to Vietnam and south into Singapore. Eight to 15 eggs are laid in holes excavated in the soil by females; the eggs take 190 or more days to hatch.
Care: The terrarium must have considerable height for climbing and plenty of perches. Keep temperatures moderate, in the range of 75° to 82° F (24° to 28° C). Use lighting, but provide plenty of shade. Full-spectrum lighting is recommended. Humidity should stay above 70 percent, and the terrarium should be sprayed lightly at least once per day. Feed a variety of earthworms, crickets, and other insects.
Terrarium Suitability: 3

Acanthosaura crucigera is similar to *A. armata*, but *A. crucigera* has dark markings around the neck. This species ranges from Burma (Myanmar) to Singapore.

245

Aeluroscalabotes felinus (Günther, 1864)
Cat Gecko

Family: Eublepharidae.
Length: SVL: 3.3 in. (84 mm). TL: 6.3 in. (160 mm).
Habitat and Range: Wide-ranging in the forests of the southern Malay Peninsula and northern Sumatra to coastal Borneo, excepting the northernmost quarter of the island.
Natural History: The two species of *Aeluroscalabotes*, along with fat-tailed, leopard, and banded geckos are members of the family Eublepharidae. As such, they have moveable eyelids, long thin legs, and clawed digits without toe pads. This is a delicate- looking gecko, somewhat resembling a North American anole, with a long slender body and elongated snout. The dorsal color varies from mustard-yellow to olive to brown, with or without light flecks. The belly and lower jaw are consistently bright yellow. The tail can be tightly coiled. Cat geckos are primarily crepuscular and tend to stay on or near the ground. Diet includes a variety of tiny arthropods.
Care: Give these shy lizards a terrarium with soil substrate and a layer of moss or leaf litter on top. Also provide a variety of hiding places; live plants are a good terrarium addition. Keep temperature from 75° to 82°F (24° to 28°C) and humidity over 80 percent. Feed these lizards calcium-dusted insects daily.
Terrarium Suitability: 3

Bronchocela cristatella (Kuhl, 1820)
Green Garden Lizard

Family: Agamidae.
Length: SVL: 6.3 in. (160 mm). TL: 18.9 in. (485 mm).
Habitat and Range: Central Myanmar (Burma) east to Vietnam and south throughout the Malay Archipelago, and east to the Philippine and Nicobar islands and western New Guinea, in dense moist forests.
Natural History: These gorgeous lizards, long assigned to the genus *Calotes*, slightly resemble Cuban knight anoles. The head is elongated and tapered, with a distinct canthal ridge from the nostrils to the rear of the eye. The body changes hue throughout the range of greens, often taking on a spectacular emerald color when *B. cristatella* is basking or displaying to potential mates. Green garden lizards are easily seen while foraging for food on vines and bushes near buildings. With the aid of the extremely long tail, they can move swiftly and acrobatically through the branches. They require humidity above 75 percent and therefore tend to be scarce during the dry season. They are entirely insectivorous.
Care: Provide a tall terrarium with plenty of climbing objects and shade. Keep temperatures near 85°F (29.5° C) and humidity over 80 percent; daily access to UV light is necessary. Feed these lizards calcium-dusted insects daily.
Terrarium Suitability: 3

Calotes emma Gray, 1845
Mottled Garden Lizard

Family: Agamidae.
Length: SVL: 4.5 in. (115 mm). TL: 11.4 in. (290 mm).
Habitat and Range: Populations from eastern India and Bangladesh
east to Cambodia and Vietnam live in moist rainforests, while
populations from northern Thailand and southern China frequent
seasonally wet dry forests.
Natural History: Northern populations inhabit deciduous forest
that experience an intense rainy season followed by several dry
months, when the lizards are less active. Those from the south live in a
more stable rainforest. Both groups feed on insects. This is one of the
rare agamids that can vocalize. Breeding males have bright red areas
on the forebody, head, and the lateral stripes, while the front limbs
and anterior flanks can be jet black.
Care: Terrarium animals need both plenty of floor space and a tall cage
with climbing branches. Keep the terrarium warm by day (90° to 104°
F [32° to 40° C]). The lizards should have access to UV light daily.
Always provide a dish of clean drinking water and spray the terrarium
with water on alternate days. Do not house two males in the same
terrarium. Feed lizards dusted crickets, roaches, and other insects daily.
Terrarium Suitability: 2

Calotes versicolor (Daudin, 1802)
Bloodsucker/Indian Garden Lizard

Family: Agamidae.
Length: SVL: 5.5 in. (140 mm). TL: 19.3 in. (490 mm).
Habitat and Range: This is the most wide-ranging member of the genus, found in both seasonally moist and dry forests from southern India east to Singapore and north into southern China.
Natural History: This is a generally brown or dusky lizard with small spots or a pair of pale yellowish lateral stripes. Garden lizards are totally harmless to humans, though in some regions they are greatly feared. They are almost totally arboreal, coming to earth rarely, mainly in pursuit of prey or to lay eggs.
Care: Almost any manner of desert terrarium with numerous live or artificial branched plants will suffice. Alternatively, they may be kept as described for mottled garden lizards. Keep temperatures around 90° F (32° C). Humidity may range from 65 to 100 percent. Feed them live small insects daily. Bloodsuckers may be safely housed with other similar-sized species, especially ground dwellers such as butterfly lizards, but do not house two males together.
Terrarium Suitability: 2

Cosymbotus platyurus (Schneider, 1792)
Pacific Flat-Tailed Gecko/Flat-Tailed House Gecko

Family: Gekkonidae.
Length: SVL: 2.4 in. (60 mm). TL: 5.5 in. (140 mm).
Habitat and Range: Widely distributed throughout the southwest Pacific, southeastern Asia, and as an immigrant in parts of southern Europe and southern Florida.
Natural History: A tiny lizard that has been very successful in colonizing a large portion of the planet. They are small, inconspicuous lizards that are active from twilight until early morning, and most commonly seen around lights that attract flying insects. Where they occur, they tend to be extremely common. The intact tail is deeply flattened and bears a thin scalloped edging of loose skin. Placed in the genus *Hemidactylus* by some authors.
Care: House geckos are common in the pet trade where they are so inexpensive that they are often sold as food for other lizards or snakes. Two pair can safely be housed in a 10-gallon (38-l) terrarium. They need large quantities of small insects—young crickets and fruit flies— and shelter that will maintain humidity levels above 70 percent. Spray the terrarium with water daily. Provide heat from heating tapes or a small under terrarium heat pad. Temperatures should range from 75° to 85°F (24° to 29.5°C)
Terrarium Suitability: 1

Dendragama boulengeri Doria, 1888
Sumatran Tree Lizard

Family: Agamidae.

Length: SVL: 2.8 in. (72 mm). TL: 6.3 in. (160 mm).

Habitat and Range: Dense wet forests on mountains above 3937 feet (1200 m) of northern and western Sumatra.

Natural History: These distinctive tree lizards resemble bloodsuckers but differ in having only four or five enlarged neck spines, each distinctly separated from the others, and in having a more compressed body and larger dorsal and lateral scales. Both sexes are bright green, but males can change color to brown or black as well.

Care: As mountain dwellers, they prefer cooler temperatures than other tropical forest lizards. Keep the terrarium temperature between 68° and 75° F (20° and 24° C), and humidity at 65 to 80 percent. They like basking sites in direct sunlight but require plenty of shaded cover. Provide full-spectrum lighting, but make sure the lizards can get out of it when they wish. They are largely insectivorous but may take flowers and diced fruits.

Terrarium Suitability: 3

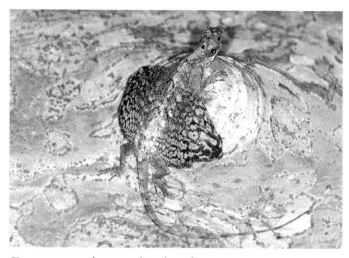

Draco maculatus whiteheadi **Musters, 1983**
Spotted Flying Dragon

Family: Agamidae.
Length: SVL: 3.3 in. (84 mm). TL: 7.5 in. (190.5 mm).
Habitat and Range: Found in moist forests and along forest edges from southern China through Tibet, the northern half of India, Myanmar (Burma), Laos, Vietnam, Thailand, and western Malaysia.
Natural History: This cryptic species matches the tree bark. The "wings" (technically patagia) are dark and have black spots. The throat fans of both sexes are very long. Wings may be displayed if dragons are courting or threatening rival males. Look for them in moist forests on trees with considerable shade-forming foliage. Though primarily insect-eaters, flying dragons have also been observed taking nectar and small berries on occasion.
Care: Like other flying dragons, they make very difficult terrarium subjects. Successful keepers report that flying dragons do well when given very tall terraria with considerable shade and a network of branches in the upper third of the enclosure, and a few inches (10 cm or so) of peat, moss, or potting soil on the ground. Cages should have lateral ventilation, but no strong breezes. Mist frequently and keep humidity above 75 percent. Keep temperature fairly stable around 78° to 88° F (25.5° to 31° C). Provide full-spectrum light.
Terrarium Suitability: 5

Draco maximus Boulenger, 1893
Giant Flying Dragon

Family: Agamidae.
Length: SVL: 3.9 in. (98 mm). TL: 12 in. (305 mm).
Habitat and Range: Dense moist forests of Malaysia south to Sumatra, Borneo, and Sunda Islands.
Natural History: Though most books that discuss flying dragons mention only one species, *Draco volans* (which translates to "flying dragon"), there are more than 20 species in this large genus of southeast Asian tree dwellers. The "wings" are made of lateral skin and extremely long ribs; as the lizard expands the ribs, the skin is pulled out and taut, forming a wing. The lizards use the wings as paragliders; when they leap off a tree, the wings open and allow the lizard a slow and controlled descent to another perch or the ground. The giant flying dragon is one of the largest species, and it is characterized by a lichen-green to olive body, five broad black bands from the nape to hips, and no spines over each eye. The throat is black. The wings and dewlap are used by males in displays to threaten other males or to attract females. Diet is restricted to small insects, especially tree ants and moths.
Care: Captives fare poorly. See *Draco maculatus* for details. All *Draco* need large quantities of small insect prey on a daily basis.
Terrarium Suitability: 5

Draco volans Linnaeus, 1758
Flying Dragon

Family: Agamidae.
Length: SVL: 4 in. (103 mm). TL: 13 in. (327 mm).
Habitat and Range: Myanmar and Southern Thailand east to Vietnam, south to the eastern Lesser Sunda Islands of Indonesia, and north into the Philippines. Restricted to forest habitats.
Natural History: To most people interested in herpetology, *Draco volans* is the flying dragon. The *Draco volans* group—there are a number of subspecies and closely related species—contains small-bodied lizards with a dusky gray dorsum dusted with extremely fine black speckling. The upper wing membrane is gray, with large black and yellowish spots. A single larger black spot is found on the nape. During breeding season, males' heads turn green. When threatened, these lizards are most likely to dash around a tree trunk, keeping the tree between themselves and the observer. "Flight" is actually a controlled glide; it may cover more than 150 feet (46 m). They are most likely to take wing when confronted by a nearby predator (such as a tree snake), or when in pursuit of insect prey on another branch or tree. Diet consists almost entirely of ants, termites, and aphids, which they consume in large quantities each day.
Care: Difficult to keep, but care is like that for *Draco maculatus*.
Terrarium Suitability: 5

Gekko gecko Linnaeus, 1758
Tokay Gecko

Family: Gekkonidae.
Length: SVL: 7.6 in. (194 mm). TL: 13.8 in. (350 mm).
Habitat and Range: Most of southeastern Asia in a variety of habitats from west coastal India to Vietnam and the Philippines, and south through Indo-Australia to far western New Guinea. Introduced in Florida, Hawaii, Belize, and other places.
Natural History: The tokay is one of the largest living geckos and also one of the most familiar. Its presence in many Asian homes is considered a sign of good fortune, and it is certainly useful in controlling insect numbers. Tokays were also imported to the U.S. in the 1980s as part of a fad to control roach numbers (successfully) in apartments in New York and Chicago. They are aggressive and voracious, taking insects, spiders, baby rats, subadult mice, small eggs, and young birds in the diet.
Care: Extremely hardy in captivity. Tokays may draw some blood when they bite the hand that feeds them, and they tend to hold on like bulldogs. The name "tokay" refers to the sound of their loud vocalizations and has nothing to do with the grape of the same name. These hardy lizards can handle a temperature range of 70° to 100° F (21° to 38° C), and humidity from 50 to 100 percent. Provide a tall terrarium with hiding areas. Mist several times weekly.
Terrarium Suitability: 1

Gekko ulikovskii **Darevsky and Orlow, 1994**
Golden Gecko

Family: Gekkonidae.
Length: SVL: 4.4 in. (112 mm). TL: 9.4 in. (238 mm).
Habitat and Range: A variety of habitats in southern Vietnam and adjacent Cambodia.
Natural History: The golden gecko was one of many subsequent zoological surprises to emerge from Vietnam recently, once scientists began to inventory that country's fauna. Gold geckos are much more docile lizards than tokays and quickly may allow handling without biting. They are nocturnal and pale gray-yellow by day but become yellowish green to light yellow when awake and active.
Care: They do best in warm terraria with moderate humidity (70 to 85 percent) and a daily light spray of clean water. The terrarium should be moderately tall (at least 2 ft/61 cm) and provided with a variety of climbing perches and hiding spots. They should have a temperature between 70° to 100° F (21° to 38° C) and perhaps two to four hours of UV weekly. They take a variety of live insects, diced fruit, and strained fruit baby foods. Live foods especially should be dusted with calcium powder daily, and vitamin powder weekly. Females will lay two hard-shelled eggs that should be removed and incubated at about 82° F (28° C). Young hatch after 90 days.
Terrarium Suitability: 1

Goniurosaurus araneus Grismer, Viets & Boyle, 1999
Vietnamese Leopard Gecko/Brown Goni

Family: Eublepharidae.

Length: SVL: 3.4 in. (86 mm). TL: 7.5 in. (190 mm).

Habitat and Range: Rocky valleys, hillsides, caves, and grassy forest edges in Vietnam and Cambodia.

Natural History: Very little is known about this species in the wild. The body of adults is yellow to yellowish-tan and has four wide chocolate-brown bands across the back and one on the neck that are divided by light yellow bands. Original tails are banded dark brown and white, and are about as long as the body. Functional eyelids are present, and the eyes may be brown, maroon, or dark orange. They spend considerable time on rocks but also dig well and construct long burrows. They are most active at twilight and early evening. They feed on small arthropods, worms, millipedes, smaller lizards, and sometimes soft plants and flowers.

Care: They need terrarium temperatures of 74° to 80° F (23° to 26.5° C). Do not let temperature exceed 83° F (28°C); they may tolerate nighttime lows near 60° F (15.5° C) for brief periods. The terrarium should contain a deep substrate of some humidity-retaining substrate, such as a mix of sand and sphagnum moss. Humidity should not drop below 70 percent. Offer live gut-loaded insects daily.

Terrarium Suitability: 3

Gonocephalus chameleontinus (**Laurenti, 1768**)
Chameleon Tree Dragon

Family: Agamidae.
Length: SVL: 6.9 in. (175 mm). TL: 18.3 in. (465 mm).
Habitat and Range: Moist, dense, hot lowland rainforest near permanent water sources from the Malay Peninsula and Sumatra east through Java.
Natural History: A spectacular arboreal agamid with bright colors and a docile disposition, the chameleon tree dragon will allow close approach but is still remarkably difficult to spot in the wild. Coloring is variable—almost always containing different shades of green—but males are not always distinguishable from females. Once they find a preferred perch on a branch or narrow tree trunk, chameleon tree dragons may stay in place for several days.
Care: Because of their low activity, these lizards do not require as much food as more active species of similar size. Diet includes insects, young rodents, and occasional flowers and fruits. They like warm temperatures (78° to 88° F [25.5° to 31° C]) but indirect lighting. They must have a large pool of clean water in the terrarium. Provide four to ten hours of UV light daily.
Terrarium Suitability: 3

Harpesaurus becarrii Doria, 1888
Sumatran Nose-Horned Lizard

Family: Agamidae.
Length: SVL: 3.3 in. (83 mm). TL: 9.8 in. (248 mm).
Habitat and Range: Known only from a few mountain rainforest localities at 4921 feet (1500 m) in western Sumatra.
Natural History: The first specimen of this bizarre creature was described in 1888, and very few have been collected since then. All that is known about its natural history comes from observations made on a single captive male collected in 1988 or 1989. This is a difficult animal to misidentify: there is one large, stout, curved horn at the tip of the snout followed by a thinner straight horn directly posterior. These lizards are extremely lethargic, spending most of the time on a thin branch where they can keep alert for food or danger.
Care: The only captive Sumatran horn-nosed lizard was kept at "room temperature" and fed on earthworms and small insects.
Terrarium Suitability: 5

Hydrosaurus amboinensis (Schlosser, 1788)
Sail-Finned Lizard/Soa-Soa

Family: Agamidae.
Length: SVL: 13.9 in. (352 mm). TL: 43.3 in. (1,100 mm)
Habitat and Range: In forests near rivers and streams from Java east to western New Guinea.
Natural History: This is the largest living agamid lizard and is that family's counterpart to the Central American basilisks. The back sports a row of low pointed scales, and the tail of adults has a large dorsal fin supported by elongations from the caudal vertebrae. Unlike as in basilisks, the toes of sail-finned lizards are broadly lobed, providing the lizard with a way to swim with great efficiency. Also unlike the New World basilisks, sail-finned lizards cannot run across the surface of the water. These diurnal lizards are best observed while they bask on branches overhanging water. When they feel threatened, they leap into the water and may swim away submerged.
Care: Primarily herbivorous, feeding on a variety of fruits, flowers, and soft leafy greens. Captives will also take large insects and small rodents, but the diet should still be predominantly of plant matter. A large enough pool to allow swimming is essential. Keep the temperature between 85° and 100° F (29.5° to 38° C), and provide 4 to 10 hours of UV light daily.
Terrarium Suitability: 4

Hydrosaurus weberi Barbour, 1911
Moluccan Sail-finned Lizard

Family: Agamidae.
Length: SVL: 13.9 in. (352 mm). TL: 43.3 in. (1,100 mm).
Habitat and Range: Habitats near fresh or brackish water in north-central Indonesia.
Natural History: This species is very similar to the sail-finned dragon and a third putative species from the Philippines. Herpetologists are still uncertain whether *Hydrosaurus* should be classified as three species or one. Moluccan sail-finned lizards tend to be darker than sail-finned lizards, lacking green coloring except as juveniles. The head is generally completely black. Because of their large size, an observer might at first mistake basking sail-finned lizards for water monitors. The monitors, however, are more likely to make a dash for the nearest tree unless they are very near the water already. Sail-finned lizards can swim very well and can stay submerged for at least five minutes, very probably more. The toes of these lizards are peculiar in being broad, depressed, and bearing lateral flaps of skin. They serve as paddles, giving the lizard extra strength when swimming in river currents. Eggs are laid year round, with clutches numbering up to 12.
Care: Habits and care the same as for the related *Hydrosaurus amboinensis*.
Terrarium Suitability: 4

Japalura splendida Barbour and Dunn, 1919
Lime Japalure/Dragon Agama

Family: Agamidae.
Length: SVL: 3.7 in. (95 mm). TL: 8.5 in. (217 mm).
Habitat and Range: Hills and mountains from 328 to 9842 feet (100 to 3000 m) in western southern China.
Natural History: A handsome lizard that has become common in the animal trade since 1990 despite being delicate in captivity. It dwells in seasonally dry deciduous and coniferous forests where rain may be scarce but humidity tends to be high. These lizards are largely arboreal and prefer to perch on thin branches, but they will forage for food and water on the ground. Both sexes are similar in color and pattern.
Care: Daytime temperature should hover near 80° F (27° C) and drop at night to about 68° F (20° C). Provide full-spectrum lighting. They eat small insects and small pieces of diced fruit. A large enough dish of water for them to be completely immersed is needed.
Terrarium Suitability: 3

Lanthanotus borneensis Steindachner, 1878
Earless Monitor

Family: Lanthanotidae
Length: SVL: 8.75 in. (222.25 mm). TL: 18 in. (457.2 mm).
Habitat and Range: Wet forest near streams and ponds in western Borneo, from Sarawak to central Kalimantan.
Natural History: An exceptional lizard, though whether so few have been collected because they are rare or because incorrect collecting methods have been employed is unknown. Earless monitors are found in moist lowland areas near streams, rivers, and rice paddies, where they burrow into soft soil. The tail is prehensile, and a specimen was once observed climbing a low shrub, but they tend to be largely fossorial and semi-aquatic. When submerged they can seal off the nostrils and use the prehensile tail to help fight currents. They are known to feed on earthworms and slugs, while captives have taken strips of raw fish. Mating has been observed while lizards were in the water. Two, possibly more, large eggs are laid. Young are steel blue-gray but turn brown as they mature.
Care: Not known to be in the pet trade, and their care is unknown.
Terrarium Suitability: 5

Leiolepis belliana (Gray, 1827)
Butterfly Agama

Family: Agamidae.

Length: SVL: 6.4 in. (162 mm). TL: 18 in. (462 mm).

Habitat and Range: Southern Vietnam and southeastern Thailand south to Singapore, plus Bangka and Sumatra and nearby small islets. They inhabit particularly warm open areas, from grasslands to beaches.

Natural History: Butterfly agamas have flanks that can be extended and flattened to a considerable degree when they are basking in the sun, and the flanks are brightly marked with red or orange and dark gray to black bands. Males may have bluish markings on the legs and groin. Butterfly agamas are, like their close relatives the mastigures (genus *Uromastyx*) among the most heat-loving of reptiles. They excavate or appropriate long burrows in loose sand to avoid excessive heat and for nighttime retreat. Butterfly agamas are herbivores, feeding on leaves, seeds, and fruits.

Care: The terrarium should offer lizards considerable floor space and a deep sandy substrate. Cluster hiding places at opposite ends of the terrarium, leaving open, flat space for running. Keep daytime air temperature between 88° and 112° F (30° to 44.5° C) with a hotspot of up to 140° F (60° C). Humidity should stay below 65 percent. Provide full-spectrum lighting daily. Feed a mixture of chopped vegetables, small birdseed, and occasionally small insects daily.

Terrarium Suitability: 3

Physignathus cocincinus Cuvier, 1829
Green Water Dragon/Chinese Water Dragon/ Asian Water Dragon

Family: Agamidae.
Length: SVL: 16.3 in. (413.5 mm). TL: 40.7 in. (1,035 mm).
Habitat and Range: Lowland moist forests throughout southeast Asia, from Burma (Myanmar) and extreme southern China east through Vietnam, Malaysia, Indonesia, and far western New Guinea.
Natural History: Water dragons are sexually dimorphic, with males having a short series of pronounced femoral pores, massive jowls, and pinkish lips and cheeks during the mating season. They are generally found on logs or branches near still or slow-moving fresh water and will dive into the water and stay submerged at any sign of a threat. They feed mainly upon other animals—fish, frogs, snails, insects, and smaller lizards—but they also eat flowers and soft green leaves.
Care: The terrarium should be large and include high climbing space and a large pool of clean water. Do not house small animals with adults and keep no more than one adult male per enclosure. Provide them with some combination of chopped vegetables, fresh fruits, fresh fish and prawns, gut-loaded large insects, and freshly thawed or live small rodents. Preferred temperature range is 78° to 90° F (25.5° to 32° C). Provide full-spectrum lighting daily. Keep the humidity above 80 percent.
Terrarium Suitability: 2

Pseudocalotes khaonanensis Chan-ard, Cota, Makchai and Laoteow, 2008

Khao Mountain Lizard

Family: Agamidae.

Length: SVL: 4.1 in. (104.5 mm). TL: 8.85 in. (225 mm).

Habitat and Range: Cloud forests of the Khao Mountain region of Thailand, at elevations above 3608.9 ft (1100 m); possibly more widely distributed.

Natural History: This is the largest species of the genus *Pseudocalotes* and was named only as recently as 2008. The head is acute, forming a sharp-tipped cone. The ear is tiny and exposed, and the body is covered in comparatively large and keeled scales. A white stripe extends along the upper lips. The dorsum is brown with triangular light brown bands on the flanks. The tail is prehensile and used like a fifth limb to hold onto twigs. Khao Mountain lizards are slow moving and easily overlooked on branches where they blend in well. Look for them on thin branches hiding among the leaves and vines. The few known specimens were collected on tree trunks no higher than 15.7 ft. (4 m) off the ground. They feed on small soft-bodied insects.

Care: Care is unknown at the present time. Try keeping like *Chamaeleo jacksoni* or *C. quadricornis* (see Region 9a: Continental Africa).

Terrarium Suitability: 4

Ptychozoon kuhlii Stejneger, 1907
Kuhl's Flying Gecko

Ptychozoon lionotum (Annandale, 1905)
Parachute Gecko

Family: Gekkonidae.
Length: SVL: 5.2 in. (133 mm). TL: 7.4 in. (190 mm).
Habitat and Range: Forests of southern Burma (Myanmar), Thailand, and Vietnam south to Singapore and offshore islands.
Natural History: These two lizards are so similar in size, color, distribution, and habits that they sometimes confuse the experts. They can best be told apart if they have complete original (not regrown) tails: *Ptychozoon lionotum* has scalloped folds along the entire length of the tail, while *P. kuhlii* has scalloped edges on the first three-quarters of the tail, but the tip is a single spatula-like flap. Neither species flies, nor do they glide as do the *Draco* lizards. Rather, they may leap from heights and the loose skin folds serve as a parachute, greatly reducing speed of fall, an interesting habit not likely to be seen in a terrarium.
Care: These are hardy, active, nocturnal geckos that will eat all manner of small live arthropods and take water both as drops on leaves and from a dish. They need warmth, with temperatures around 85° F (29.5° C) and humidity over 70 percent.
Terrarium Suitability: 1

male

female

Salea horsfieldi Gray, 1853
Green Mountain Lizard

Family: Agamidae.
Length: SVL: 3.7 in. (95 mm). TL: 13.6 in. (345 mm).
Habitat and Range: Forest and grasslands in mountainous regions above 5,900 ft. (1800 m) of India, Myanmar, and extreme southern China. They dwell in trees and shrubs.
Natural History: Though apparently fairly common, green mountain lizards are poorly known, probably because they live in remote areas. There is a crest of large pointed scales on the neck; in males, it is interrupted at the shoulders, then continues out to the tail. They spend considerable time on horizontal branches to bask in sunlight. They will sometimes be found in shallow water and are active at temperatures that most other reptiles would find too cold. The diet, as far as known, consists of insects, flowers, and soft grasses.
Care: Provide the lizards with deep moist soil and add leaf litter to the floor. Use of large, hardy live plants is recommended. Climbing branches are necessary. Terrarium animals probably need comparatively low temperatures of 64° to 75° F (18° to 24° C), and humidity around 70 percent. Provide UV light daily. Males are quite territorial, so should be housed alone or with females. Feed them gut-loaded insects daily, and supplement with diced fruits weekly.
Terrarium Suitability: 3

Shinisaurus crocodilurus Ahl, 1930
Chinese Crocodile Lizard

Family: Shinisauridae.

Length: SVL: 8.6 in. (218.4 mm). TL: 19.6 in. (500 mm).

Habitat and Range: Known from Kwangsi Province in southeastern China, and in parts of northern Vietnam. Found near ponds and slow-moving streams in forested areas.

Natural History: Barely a dozen specimens of this large semi-aquatic lizard had been collected from 1930 until about 1988. Then, in 1988, these lizards became available from the Chinese market, and herpetoculturists and zoos have been breeding them ever since. They resemble box-headed miniature crocodiles, having a brown body with longitudinal rows of enlarged dorsal scales and triangular plates down each side of the tail. The jaws are immensely powerful and can easily crush snail, freshwater clam, and crawfish shells.

Care: They must have a large pool in which they can swim, mate, and forage. Captives prefer earthworms, mealworms, wax worms, and roaches; they have difficulty capturing swift insects such as crickets. Two to 12 young are born alive per clutch, and there is a degree of parental care given to the young. Keep the terrarium temperature between 68° and 75° F (20° and 24° C) and humidity at 65 to 80 percent. Provide UV lighting.

Terrarium Suitability: 3

Takydromus sexlineatus Daudin, 1802
Long-Tailed Grass Lizard

Family: Lacertidae.
Length: SVL: 2.4 in. (60 mm). TL: 14.8 in. (375 mm).
Habitat and Range: Widely distributed in a variety of grasslands and forest clearings from southern China and far northeastern Burma (Myanmar) south and east through Malaysia, Java, and Borneo.
Natural History: Despite a maximum adult size of over 14 inches (356 mm), long-tailed lizards are actually small animals, with tiny pointed heads. The incredibly long tail may be lost to predators but is a valuable counterbalance for these lizards as they run through tall grasses. The back and upper flanks may be brown, dark tan, or olive, with up to six cream or yellow stripes that extend from the eyes to some distance beyond the hips. The belly ranges from pale yellow to light green. A beautiful green species, *Takydromus smaragdinus* Boulenger, 1887 is found in the Ryukyu Archipelago of southern Japan. Its care and natural history are similar to those specified for the long-tailed lizard.
Care: Captives are remarkably hardy if provided with tiny insect foods such as fruit flies and young crickets. Give them a spacious terrarium with planted or dry grasses, and keep humidity above 70 percent. A low water dish and a few branches are also required.
Terrarium Suitability: 2

Tropidophorus grayi Günther, 1861
Spiny Water Skink

Family: Scincidae.
Length: SVL: 3.9 in. (100 mm). TL: 8.3 in. (210 mm).
Habitat and Range: Restricted to moist areas along small rivers, streams, lagoons, and lakes of the Philippine islands of Cebu, Leyte, Luzon, Masbate, and Negros.
Natural History: This is a commonly seen waterside lizard that may be observed basking on branches or rocks, foraging along the water's edge, or swimming to evade predators. Unlike most skinks, spiny water skinks have large keeled scales on the body; many head and body scales have a glossy sheen. Though they may bask in bright sunlight for short periods, they prefer shaded microhabitats and reach peak activity late in the day. They feed on all manner of small invertebrates, including insects, crawfish, small prawns, worms, and spiders.
Care: The terrarium should be planted with soft, moist mosses and bark for shelter. Temperatures should range between 68° and 75° F (20° and 24° C), with humidity from 65 to 80 percent. Feed a variety of small insects and other invertebrates daily.
Terrarium Suitability: 2

Varanus auffenbergi Sprackland, 1999
Peacock Monitor

Family: Varanidae.
Length: SVL: 8.4 in. (212 mm). TL: 28 in. (700 mm).
Habitat and Range: Forests and planted areas among trees and tall grasses around villages on Rotti Island, near Timor, Indonesia.
Natural History: These lizards differ from the brown Timor monitor in being slate gray or black with turquoise rosette markings on the back and bright yellow and orange spots on the limbs. Females build small mound nests of soil and leaf litter, in which eggs may be communally laid.
Care: Peacock monitors are rarely tame monitors suitable for demonstrations; they require housing that offers both plenty of hiding places and limited exposure to the eyes of curious humans. These lizards require daily feedings of crickets, king mealworms, locusts, pink mice, beef strips, and scrambled eggs. They are active and ravenous feeders when healthy. Though they like heat above 90° F (32.5° C), and humidity over 85 percent, they also must have considerable shade and canopy cover to shield them from too much direct lighting. These lizards rarely swim but will soak in a water dish. They also burrow well.
Terrarium Suitability: 3

Varanus dumerilii (Schlegel, 1839)
Duméril's Monitor

Family: Varanidae.
Length: SVL: 16.5 in. (420 mm). TL: 51.2 in. (1,300 mm).
Habitat and Range: Moist forested regions, especially near streams, of the Malay Peninsula, Sumatra, Borneo, and neighboring islands.
Natural History: Juveniles are breathtaking: the straw-colored body has solid, broad black bands, and the head is neon orange. These dramatic colors (which may serve as a mimic to the colors of the deadly red-headed krait) fade rapidly as the young lizard grows into a tan and brown-banded adult. Duméril's monitors are largely aquatic, inhabiting fresh-water streams and salty mangroves. They have a flap inside each nostril that closes when the lizard is submerged, and monitors may walk along underwater in search of prey. Among their favorite foods are crabs and snails, which they crush readily in their strong jaws.
Care: Duméril's monitors are among the most mellow of monitors in captivity. Give them a large terrarium with a pool in which they can swim. Duméril's monitors need a deep soil substrate. Keep air temperature between 85° and 100° F (29.5° to 38° C) and provide a lit hotspot kept around 135° F (57° C). Feed lizards freshly killed rodents, roaches, and locusts twice weekly; given them fresh thawed prawns, small crabs, and fresh fish on alternate days.
Terrarium Suitability: 2

Hatchling *V. dumerilii* are much more brightly colored than the adults (see photo on previous page). The bright colors may provide the vulnerable hatchlings with protection from predation. The colorful pattern closely mimics that of the deadly red-headed krait (*Bungarus flaviceps*), which shares much of its range with the monitor.

Varanus komodoensis Ouwens, 1912
Komodo Dragon/Ora

Family: Varanidae.
Length: SVL: 61.3 in. (1,555 mm). TL: 122.5 in. (3,112 mm).
Habitat and Range: Indonesia's Lesser Sunda Islands of Komodo, Rinca, Gili Dasami, Gili Motang, and western coastal Flores.
Natural History: Komodo dragons may eventually yield their title as the world's longest lizards to a New Guinea species, but they have no competition as the world's heaviest and bulkiest living lizard. A large adult may weigh 165 lbs (75 kg). The Komodo dragon's habitat includes dry deciduous forest and savannahs. Their bites may lead to severe infections. Researchers demonstrated in 2002 that these lizards possess a virulent bacterial "cocktail" in the saliva, a result of the carrion they eat. They can be seen in the wild only at Komodo National Park and in western Flores, the former only in the company of park rangers. Though attacks are rare, Komodo dragons have injured and killed humans.
Care: The species is now often bred in zoos but has not yet entered the commercial animal trade. The care of these large and dangerous reptiles is beyond the scope of private hobbyists.
Terrarium Suitability: 5

Varanus olivaceus Hallowell, 1856

Gray's Monitor

Family: Varanidae.

Length: SVL: 23.6 in. (600 mm). TL: 64 in. (1,626 mm).

Habitat and Range: Dense monsoon forests of northern parts of the Philippines, notably on Luzon Island.

Natural History: This lizard became famous when it was learned that its diet was made up largely of fruits—at the time, it was the only known fruit-eating monitor However, the majority of its diet consists of large tree snails. Like many other large monitors, this species undergoes ontogenetic tooth change, meaning the curved, sharp teeth of young lizards convert to broad, molar-like teeth in adults. The species is predominantly arboreal. Eggs are often laid in excavated burrows near the bases of trees.

Care: Gray's monitor is a fairly docile species. The terrarium should be large and very tall. Provide a large pool in which they can immerse themselves completely. They are expert diggers and need a deep soil substrate. Keep air temperature between 85° and 100° F (29.5° to 38° C), provide full-spectrum light daily, and include a lit hotspot reaching 135° F (57° C). The primary foods for adult lizards are fruits and large snails; supplement as necessary with freshly killed rodents, large roaches, and locusts twice weekly.

Terrarium Suitability: 4

Varanus rudicollis (Gray, 1845)
Rough-Necked Monitor

Family: Varanidae.
Length: SVL: 19 in. (484 mm). TL: 63 in. (1,600 mm).
Habitat and Range: Dense rainforests of Southeast Asia, including Burma (Myanmar), Thailand, Malaysia, Borneo, and the extreme southern Philippines.
Natural History: Hobbyists and professionals alike often confuse this species with Duméril's monitor, though they are quite different in appearance. Roughnecks are black and have white markings (often only on the posterior of the body); they have greatly elongated snouts and huge, slit-like nostrils. The neck is covered with large pyramid-like scales (vs. round and only slightly keeled scales in *V. dumerilii*), and the tail is exceptionally long and thin. These are almost exclusively arboreal monitors found in rainforests, swamps, and mangrove stands. Although they are large lizards, they seem to feed mostly on insects—including ants and termites—and frogs and their eggs.
Care: In contrast to Duméril's monitor, roughneck monitors are more fragile in captivity, especially as young individuals. They arrive from overseas severely dehydrated and carrying enormous parasite loads. Care is nearly identical to that for *Varanus dumerilii*, except that *V. rudicollis* is much more shy and nervous.
Terrarium Suitability: 4

Varanus salvator (**Laurenti, 1768**)
Water Monitor

Family: Varanidae.

Length: Water monitors show considerable range in adult size, from 3.5 to 4 feet (1,067 to 1,219 mm) in some small island populations to nearly 9.5 feet (2,896 mm) in peninsular Malaya and parts of Borneo.

Habitat and Range: Water monitors form a complex of "subspecies" that range from Sulawesi in central Indonesia, north to the Philippines, and west into Burma and southern China, with remote populations in eastern coastal India and the island of Sri Lanka.

Natural History: Taxonomists have only recently begun studying the variation and relationships of these lizards, so for now the subspecies designations remain as convenient labels for regional populations. Some of these populations are quite distinctive, such as the intensely patterned kabaragoya (*V. s. salvator*) of Sri Lanka.

Care: Juveniles are notoriously difficult to maintain because they are field-collected in huge numbers and housed by the hundreds in communal pens with no food or water and little hygiene. It is best to hold out for subadult lizards at least 20 to 24 inches (559 to 610 mm) long. Care for as the Duméril's monitors, but use a much larger terrarium—12 ft. by 15 ft. (366 cm by 457 cm) of floor space—for the adults.

Terrarium Suitability: 4

Varanus timorensis (Gray, 1831)
Timor Monitor

Family: Varanidae.
Length: SVL: 10.2 in. (258.6 mm). TL: 28 in. (700 mm).
Habitat and Range: Restricted to both wet and dry forested areas and sometimes grassy areas on Timor Island.
Natural History: The small Timor monitor becomes active after rains, perching on tree stumps and fence posts. It feeds on a host of smaller animals, particularly insects and smaller lizards. Unlike most other forest monitors, Timor monitors have tails that are round in cross-section, lacking a double keel along the upper ridge. They burrow well, and females are known to build small mound nests of soil and leaf litter, in which eggs may be communally laid.
Care: Captives are rarely docile, and they require housing with hiding places and limited exposure to the eyes of curious humans. Once acclimated to captivity, these lizards require daily or alternate daily feedings of crickets, king mealworms, locusts, pink or fuzzy mice, beef strips, and scrambled eggs. They are active and ravenous feeders when healthy. Though they like heat above 90° F (32° C), and humidity over 85 percent, they also must have considerable shade and canopy cover to shield them from too much direct lighting. These lizards rarely swim but will soak in a water dish.
Terrarium Suitability: 3

Varanus yuwonoi **Harvey and Barker, 1998**

Tri-Colored Monitor

Family: Varanidae.
Length: SVL: 32 in. (813 mm). TL: 72 in. (1900 mm).
Habitat and Range: Forests of Halmahera, central Indonesia.
Natural History: *Varanus yuwonoi* looks like a piece of art. The head is dark green to black, with cream sutures between the scales, while the neck is dark green with large darker green spots. The forebody is dark green to black and lacks a distinct pattern, while the rear half sports light cream to yellow spots that form distinct crossbands. The tail is black, with gray to pale turquoise bands. Though not nearly as aggressive as *V. salvadorii* (which they somewhat resemble), they are still not known to be particularly good animals for handling and remain skittish for a considerable time.
Care: The terrarium should be large and tall, with a pool in which these monitors can immerse themselves completely. Care is very similar to that specified for *Varanus dumerilii*. Do not house with other species, and only house similar-sized tri-colored monitors in a single enclosure. Tri-colored monitors are quick to bite and do so repeatedly. The primary foods for adult lizards are freshly killed rodents, roaches, and locusts given daily. Feed young specimens smaller versions of the same food.
Terrarium Suitability: 4

Additional species that occur in southeast and eastern Asia but are also found elsewhere are listed below. You may find a species account for these lizards in the region section given in parentheses.

Gekko vittatus (Region 5: New Guinea, New Zealand, and Oceania)
Lamprolepis smaragdina (Region 5: New Guinea, New Zealand, and Oceania)
Teratoscincus scincus (Region 8: Southern Asia and the Middle East)
Varanus bengalensis (Region 8: Southern Asia and the Middle East)
Varanus nebulosus (Region 8: Southern Asia and the Middle East)
Zootoca vivipara (Region 10: Europe and Northern Asia)

Southern
Asia and the
Middle East

Low humidity, high temperatures, and vast open spaces characterize much of this region. Most areas at lower altitudes are warm enough that lizards will be active year-round, but in higher elevations the temperatures can become quite cold and lizards become dormant. India, with its varied terrain that runs from deserts to high-elevation mountains, has an incredible diversity of lizards, and no doubt many species still await discovery. Most of this region was part of the vast prehistoric supercontinent Laurasia, but India represents a fragment of Gondwana that drifted northward until it crashed into Laurasia; the results of that collision are seen as the Himalayan Mountain chain. Lizards from this region thrive at some of the highest temperatures anywhere, particularly in the Arabian Peninsula. More cold-tolerant species are found in the mountains, including the lower elevations of the Himalayas. Chameleons are found in the extreme eastern and western parts of this region but are absent in between. Agamids and geckos are particularly abundant and diverse in the region. The largest lizards are the local monitors and mastigures.

young leopard gecko
(*Eublepharis macularius*)

Ailuronyx seychellensis (Duméril and Bibron, 1836)
Seychelles Gecko

Family: Gekkonidae.
Length: SVL: 5.4 (138 mm). TL: 9.8 in. (250 mm).
Habitat and Range: In coconut palm trees and in buildings throughout the Seychelles.
Natural History: This stocky gecko has a very unusual defense mechanism. If seized, it can slough off large sections of skin to effect an escape. A similar attribute is seen in the day gecko group (genus *Phelsuma*) as well. Color is variable and may change depending on mood, light, and temperature. The basic color is bronze to pale olive green, with black mottling and sometimes very tiny white specks on the flanks. Seychelles geckos are active and aggressive geckos that may be heard making squeaks and barks as they chase each other or intimidate intruders. They are nocturnal insect eaters.
Care: They need a tall terrarium with several stout branches on which to climb. Only one pair should be kept per terrarium, and even so the geckos will tend to fight, though they do very little damage to each other. Provide heat via indirect lighting, with temperatures between 72° and 86° F (22° and 30° C). Keep humidity over 70 percent. Food for adults and young should be dusted with calcium and vitamin supplements at least thrice weekly.
Terrarium Suitability: 2

Calotes calotes (**Linnaeus, 1758**)
Green Garden Lizard/Green Bloodsucker

Family: Agamidae.
Length: SVL: 5.1 in. (130 mm). TL: 24.8 in. (630 mm).
Habitat and Range: A nearly totally arboreal resident of forests and gardens in southern India and Sri Lanka.
Natural History: This distinctive species has a single large row of spine-like scales running along the center of the back, the highest on the nape. The body is bright green, with four or five very thin white bands. During the breeding season, males take on a rich red head, forebody, throat and cheek coloring, hence the name "bloodsucker." The scales are large and keeled. The extremely long, thin tail is used to help this lizard in its acrobatic foraging in trees and along thin branches. It is an active diurnal predator, taking insects along with some flowers. Most likely observed during the morning, when basking in the sun but before foraging begins.
Care: They need a large terrarium that also provides height for climbing. Males are quite aggressive towards others in the garden lizard group. Feed them daily, offering large insects and the occasional small piece of fruit. Provide plenty of natural or artificial foliage and keep temperatures around 90° F (32° C) at the hottest spot of the terrarium. Humidity may range from 65 to 100 percent. Water should be provided by misting the terrarium.
Terrarium Suitability: 2

Ceratophora stoddarti Gray, 1834
Cone-Nosed Lizard

Family: Agamidae.
Length: SVL: 3.7 in. (94 mm). TL: 6.7 in. (170 mm).
Habitat and Range: Among leaf litter in mossy mountain rainforest habitats of the Sabaragamuva and Hiniduma regions of Sri Lanka.
Natural History: The three species of *Ceratophora* are entirely endemic to Sri Lanka and are threatened or endangered because of widespread modification of habitat. Cone-nosed lizards have a tapered horn on the tip of the snout. The two other species are *Ceratophora aspera* Günther, 1864 and *Ceratophora tennentii* Günther, 1861. *C. aspera* has a short, can-shaped horn on the snout, while *C. tennentii* has a laterally compressed leaf-shaped nose appendage. All are slow-moving, found on the ground or low on trees, and feed on soft-bodied insects and small beetles. The peculiar snout appendage serves as a sexual identifier—it is well-developed in males, small or absent in females and young—but has no other known function. Cone-nosed lizards prefer undisturbed forest habitat.
Care: There is virtually no information on care of these lizards in captivity; presumably they should do well if cared for in a manner similar to that described for flying dragons (*Draco*) (see Region 7: Southeast and Eastern Asia).
Terrarium Suitability: 4

Chamaeleo calyptratus Duméril and Bibron, 1851
Veiled Chameleon/Yemeni Chameleon

Family: Chamaeleonidae.
Length: SVL: 11.8 in. (300 mm). TL: 24.4 in. (620 mm)
Habitat and Range: Native to Yemen, Aden, and southwestern Saudi Arabia; the species was introduced in parts of southwestern Florida.
Natural History: This large chameleon lives in harsh environments that include sandy desert, shaded valleys, and dry grasslands. It can climb well but is usually encountered within 10 feet (2 m) of the ground. Veiled chameleons are slow-moving, strictly diurnal, and quite aggressive; males are especially aggressive towards other males of the species. Males are easily recognized by their very high head casques, tarsal spurs on the ankle regions, and pronounced hemipenial bulges at the base of the tail. Their ability to change colors is pronounced and is dependent upon temperature, mood, and activity of the lizards. They feed on smaller creatures they can snare with their long tongues.
Care: Captive lizards require a large terrarium with some lateral airflow and high humidity. Preferred temperatures range from 73° to 97° F (23° to 36° C), and full-spectrum lighting is required. They only drink from dripping water, so mist several times a day. Feed them a wide variety of insects. This chameleon will also eat some fruit and leafy greens. House chameleons one per cage.
Terrarium Suitability: 3

Eublepharis macularius (Blyth, 1854)
Leopard Gecko

Family: Eublepharidae.
Length: SVL: 5.7 in. (146 mm). TL: 9.8 in. (250 mm).
Habitat and Range: Broadly distributed across steppes and grasslands with loose sandy soils from eastern Iran to northwestern and western coastal India.
Natural History: Another of the geckos with moveable eyelids, thick tails, and no sticky toe pads, the leopard gecko resembles a large version of the American banded geckos (genus *Coleonyx*), except that in the former the body is covered by distinct tiny tubercles. Through much of their range local people, who believe them to be highly venomous, fear leopard geckos. Actually, these are docile and harmless lizards. A thick tail, constricted at the base, is a sign of fat reserves stored for lean times.
Care: Though nocturnal, they will become active for daytime food offerings of insects and usually adjust to gentle handling quite quickly. Breeders have produced a bewildering assortment of color morphs. Give leopard geckos a sandy substrate, preferably deep enough so they may dig, and a few shelters such as pieces of curved bark. A water dish is suggested, along with light misting during shed cycles. The temperature at the hottest spot in the cage should reach about 85°F (29.5°C).
Terrarium Suitability: 1

Laudakia stellio Linnaeus, 1758

Hardun/Pyramid Agama/Clown Agama

Family: Agamidae.
Length: SVL: 5.8 in. (147 mm). TL: 13.4 in. (340.4 mm).
Habitat and Range: Wide-ranging in the Middle East and far eastern Europe: Cyprus, Egypt, Greece, Iraq, Israel, Jordan, Lebanon, Saudi Arabia, Syria, and Turkey.
Natural History: Though often associated with deserts, harduns are mostly seen near boulders, in rocky areas, and along stone walls and houses. They dwell in crevices, and leave to forage or find mates. The head is large and nearly round, and the grayish body is covered in distinctly keeled scales. Capable of marked color change, from yellow to dark brown.
Care: Terrarium animals require plenty of cover. Use rocks, bricks, and similar large objects. Keep the terrarium warm, between 85° and 90° F (29.5° and 32° C). Harduns should also have a hot basking site of 105° F (40.5 ° C). Provide about 12 hours of UV lighting daily, and keep humidity between 30 and 60 percent. Feed them large gut-loaded insects daily, and supplement with diced fruits, small berries, leafy greens, and other vegetables on alternate days. Offer small mice weekly or biweekly. With gentle handling, these lizards become quite tame, almost as calm as bearded dragons.
Terrarium Suitability: 2

Phrynocephalus mystaceus (Pallas, 1776)
Toad-Headed Agama

Family: Agamidae.
Length: SVL: 4.9 in. (125 mm). TL: 9.8 in. (250 mm).
Habitat and Range: Sandy and desert regions of western Asia, from the Caspian Sea east to Afghanistan.
Natural History: Toad-headed agamas are a diurnal species with intermittent activity periods during the day. They excavate temporary burrows to escape heat and spend the night, but they also dive or wriggle under the sand to avoid excessive heat or elude predators. A large flap of skin lies along the rear of the mouth and expands into a wide "beard" when the lizard gapes to threaten predators. They live in areas where daytime temperatures may exceed 120° F (49° C), and humidity is lower than 30 percent. They feed on a variety of arthropods such as spiders, centipedes, scorpions, and insects.
Care: The terrarium should be at least 3 ft. by 4 ft. (90 cm by 122 cm) for up to three adult lizards, with a deep sandy substrate. The lizards tend to prefer making their own burrows for retreat. Keep air temperature between 82° and 112° F (28° to 44.5° C) with a hotspot near 140° F (60° C) during summer; allow temperatures to drop to 46° to 52° F (8° to 11° C) during winter. Humidity should stay below 60 percent. Provide daily UV light. Feed gut-loaded insects daily.
Terrarium Suitability: 3

Scincus scincus (Linnaeus, 1758)
Sandfish

Family: Scincidae.
Length: SVL: 4.3 in. (110 mm). TL: 7.9 in. (200 mm).
Habitat and Range: Deserts of Northeastern Africa east to Iran, and south through the Arabian Peninsula to Yemen.
Natural History: Sandfish is a particularly apt name for this lizard. It has glossy scales and spends most of its life swimming through the sands of relatively inhospitable deserts. It is one of the few vertebrates to be encountered in the dunes of the Sahara. The head is flattened and acutely pointed, and the lower jaw is countersunk into the upper jaw, preventing sand from getting into the mouth. There are no external ear openings, the eyes are small, and the short stout limbs end in fringed digits.
Care: Sandfish are not the best of terrarium animals, because they will spend most of the time buried under the sand, require high air temperatures (86° to 112° F [30° to 44.5° C]), and often refuse food. They eat a variety of arthropods, including insects, spiders, and scorpions, and derive all of their water from their prey.
Terrarium Suitability: 2

Sitana ponticeriana Cuvier, 1829
Four-Toed Lizard

Family: Agamidae.
Length: SVL: 3.1 in. (80 mm). TL: 9.4 in. (240 mm).
Habitat and Range: Deserts, rocky hillsides, and dry grasslands of eastern India and Sri Lanka.
Natural History: Four-toed lizards are unique as the only agamid lizards with fewer than five digits on the feet. They are small animals with very long thin tails and are mostly terrestrial. They can often be seen basking on desert sand when the temperature is 120° F (48° C), or foraging for the ants that make up the vast bulk of their diet. Males have a large dewlap, generally white or dull gray, with a bright blue anterior. Four-toed lizards closely resemble another lizard from Sri Lanka, *Otocryptis weigmanni* Wagler, 1830, but the latter has five toes and an orange and red dewlap. Both species are nervous and extremely wary and can run swiftly on the back legs.
Care: Care for this lizard is virtually unknown. Like most other ant-eating desert lizards, four-toed lizards are probably difficult to keep.
Terrarium Suitability: 4

Teratoscincus scincus (Schlegel, 1858)
Frog-Eyed Gecko

Family: Gekkonidae.
Length: SVL: 3.7 in. (94 mm). TL: 6.7 in. (170 mm).
Habitat and Range: Lives in dry sandy deserts around the sparse vegetation, and sometimes into the dunes, of northern Iran and southern Russia east to northern Pakistan and far western China.
Natural History: Frog-eyed geckos are found in some of the most arid and inhospitable environments, where daytime temperatures may reach or exceed 120° F (49° C). They survive this heat by living in deep burrows where sand is slightly moist and emerging only after dark to hunt nocturnal arthropods. The deserts where they live become quite cold during the winter months, during which time the geckos will hibernate. Unlike the majority of geckos, frog-eyed geckos and their kin have very large plate-like scales on the body, but these scales feel velvety to the touch.
Care: Frog-eyed geckos are somewhat delicate in captivity, but they are captive bred in fairly good numbers. Provide a desert terrarium with a deep sand substrate. The lower layers of the sand should be moist and cool, while the surface is dry and warm—about 90 to 95F (32° to 35°C). Room temperatures are fine at night. Feed gut-loaded insects dailiy. Never house males with other males.
Terrarium Suitability: 2

Teratoscincus scincus has three recognized subspecies. *T. scincus keyslingeri* (pictured here)—usually called the giant frog-eyed gecko—is the most commonly kept and bred in captivity. It reaches an adult size of about 8 inches (203 mm) total length. This subspecies ranges from the Arabian Peninsula to Afghanistan and Pakistan; generally it occurs south of the range of *T. scincus scincus* (shown on previous page). The third subspecies, *T. s. rustamowi,* is poorly known in nature and in captivity.

Uromastyx hardwickii Gray, 1827
Indian Spiny-Tailed Lizard/Indian Mastigure

Family: Agamidae.
Length: SVL: 12 in. (305 mm). TL: 19.25 in. (489 mm).
Habitat and Range: Deserts of northern India, Pakistan, and Bangladesh.
Natural History: As is the case for most other spiny-tailed lizards, this species tends to live in isolated colonies across its range. Groups of these lizards reside in sandy regions where they can dig deep burrows to escape the hottest sun, and they feed on whatever foods are available. The diet includes all manner of plants, including stems, flowers, and seeds, plus insects. They retreat to their burrows and hibernate for the winter.
Care: Spiny-tailed lizards can be very hardy in captivity provided several conditions are met. They must have a hot terrarium, at least in an area under a heat lamp. The temperature must reach 110° to 135° F (43.5° to 57° C) at the hotspot. There must be a deep substrate of sand or soil. Keep air humidity below 50 percent, but keep the burrow moist (stick a funnel in the soil and pour in some water to keep the lower levels moist). Allow the lizards daily access to full-spectrum lighting. Do not house two males in the same enclosure. Feed the lizards a daily variety of mixed green leafy vegetables plus corn kernels, small birdseed, washed dandelions, and fruit.
Terrarium Suitability: 2

Varanus bengalensis (Daudin, 1802)
Bengal Monitor

Family: Varanidae.
Length: SVL: 37 in. (940 mm). TL: 80.5 in. (2,045 mm).
Habitat and Range: Widespread from Pakistan and India, south to Sri Lanka and east to Singapore and Java.
Natural History: Juveniles are largely arboreal but will come to the ground to hunt. Subadults and adults are predominantly terrestrial and may excavate deep burrows to use as daytime retreats and in search of prey. Tooth shape and prey taken changes radically as the lizards grow. Juveniles have long, sharp teeth and consume insects, while adults have flat molar-like teeth and can crush snails, clams, and large animals.
Care: Terrarium setups can be kept simple with a wooden, glass, or laminated floor and a box large enough for the lizard to take refuge in. Daytime temperatures should be in the 85° to 95° F (29.5° to 35° C) range, with seasonal increases to 103.5° to 113° F (40° to 45° C), but it may be lowered considerably at night. Humidity should be low—30 to 50 percent—and a large dish of clean water always available. Natural diet includes almost any manner of animal food—including venomous snakes, the bites of which have no apparent effect—from eggs to carrion. They will hiss and lash the tail, putting on an excellent façade of aggression, but rarely bite even if seized.
Terrarium Suitability: 2

Varanus nebulosus (Gray, 1831)
Cloudy Monitor/Indian Monitor

Family: Varanidae.
Length: SVL: 25.7 in. (653 mm). TL: 63 in. (1,600 mm).
Habitat and Range: Semi-arid grasslands and open forest areas from Pakistan south through India to Sri Lanka and east to Java and western Borneo.
Natural History: Clouded monitors differ from the similar Bengal monitor in the following features: the snout is more elongate, the supraocular (above the eye) scales are larger than the surrounding scales, the head has a distinct yellow coloring (at least in young animals), and the body has distinct, often tricolor bands (that tend to fade with age). In contrast, Bengal monitors have a truncated snout, lack distinctly enlarged supraoculars, and have simple bands only in the young. Bengal monitors also tend to grow larger than clouded monitors.
Care: Care as for the Bengal monitor. This, too, is both a very hardy terrarium animal and a species that allows handling. Be sure to provide a variety of foods, spanning insects, boiled eggs, turkey sausages, snails, and freshly killed rodents.
Terrarium Suitability: 2

Varanus yemenensis Böhme, Joger, and Schätti, 1989
Yemeni Monitor

Family: Varanidae.
Length: SVL: 23.2 in. (59 cm). TL: 45.3 in. (1150 mm)
Habitat and Range: Dry deserts and rocky canyons in Yemen in the southwestern corner of the Arabian Peninsula, at elevations above 984 ft (300 m).
Natural History: Poorly studied, but known to frequent valleys and regions where sparse vegetation is prevalent, providing places for perching and attracting the large insects and snails that make up the bulk of its prey. Yemeni monitors are similar in appearance to the African savannah and white-throated monitors, and they represent the easternmost range for that African monitor group. They are stocky, blunt-headed, and relatively short-tailed predators and scavengers. Yemeni monitors can climb and burrow well and typically excavate extensive burrows in the desert sand. They actively forage for food among logs and rocks, and near standing water. Activity occurs in the morning and late afternoon to early evening.
Care: Few specimens have been kept in captivity, but their care is similar to that of Bengal and cloudy monitors.
Terrarium Suitability: 3

Additional species that occur in southern Asia and the Middle East but are also found elsewhere are listed below. You may find a species account for these lizards in the region section given in parentheses.

Calotes emma (Region 7: Southeast and Eastern Asia)
Calotes versicolor (Region 7: Southeast and Eastern Asia)
Chamaeleo chameleon (Region 10: Europe and Northern Asia)
Draco maculatus (Region 7: Southeast and Eastern Asia)
Eumeces schneiderii (Region 9a: Continental Africa)
Gekko gecko (Region 7: Southeast and Eastern Asia)
Tarentola mauritanica (Region 9a: Continental Africa)
Uromastyx aegyptia (Region 9a: Continental Africa)
Varanus griseus (Region 9a: Continental Africa)
Varanus salvator (Region 7: Southeast and Eastern Asia)

Africa is the largest landmass given its own section in this book and is home to some comparatively large and conspicuous agamas, chameleons, plated lizards, and monitors. There are also small colorful geckos, larger desert-dwelling geckos, sand-swimming skinks, legless plated lizards, armadillo lizards, and many others. African lizards belong to families including amphisbaenids, agamids, chameleons, geckonids, eublepharids, scincids, and lacertids; armadillo lizards (Cordylidae) are endemic to mainland Africa, while the plated lizards (Gerrhosauridae) are found only in both Africa and Madagascar. On a continent where there remain so many deadly insect-borne illnesses, lizards are probably important disease vector controls.

The geology of Africa has had a profound effect on its fauna, especially among the smaller animals. Lizards on different mountaintops, though not very far apart, may represent distinct species. Africa's lizards have not been nearly as well studied as its large mammal fauna, and undoubtedly have many fascinating behaviors yet to be described.

rainbow lizard
(*Agama agama*)

Acontias gracilicauda Essex, 1925
Thin-Tailed Legless Skink

Family: Scincidae.
Length: SVL: 9.5 in. (242 mm). TL: 12.2 in. (310 mm).
Habitat and Range: Restricted to areas with compacted soil in South Africa.
Natural History: This thin limbless lizard is unlikely to be encountered unless one is specifically looking for it or comes across one in freshly turned earth. Thin-tailed legless skinks spend most of the time underground, often in burrows they excavate with the firm and pointed head. Color ranges from yellow to olive to brown, without a distinct pattern, but always with dark-edged dorsal and lateral scales. They feed on small insects and worms and produce up to 12 live young. The related striped legless skink, *Acontias lineatus* Peters, 1879, is found in the western and northwestern Cape area, is smaller (to 7 inches [180 mm]), and generally has a series of very thin dark stripes along the length of the body.
Care: Rarely kept in captivity, and little information is available.
Terrarium Suitability: 4

Acontias plumbeus Bianconi, 1849
Giant Legless Skink

Family: Scincidae.
Length: SVL: 17.5 in. (445 mm). TL: 21.7 in. (550 mm).
Habitat and Range: Restricted to open forest areas with loose soils of eastern and extreme southeastern South Africa.
Natural History: According to South African herpetologist Bill Branch, this is the world's largest limbless skink. Unlike most of their relatives, adult giant legless skinks have thick bodies and solid patternless dark coloring, and they can consume a wider variety of prey that includes large insects, centipedes, and small vertebrates. They spend most of their lives underground, where temperatures are cooler than at the surface and humidity levels higher. Females may produce 14 live young per season.
Care: These animals and their relatives are rarely kept in captivity, in part because all a keeper would see is a terrarium with a thick layer of soil; the lizards very rarely come above ground. Keep one with a deep soil substrate. Surface temperatures should be warm, but the lower layers of the substrate must remain cool.
Terrarium Suitability: 2

Adolfus jacksoni (**Boulenger, 1899**)
Jackson's Forest Lizard

Family: Lacertidae.
Length: SVL: 3.3 in. (85 mm). TL: 10.2 in. (260 mm).
Habitat and Range: Lives in a variety of humid forest habitats up to an altitude of 9842 feet (3000 m) in eastern Africa from Kenya to Tanzania and west to the Democratic Republic of the Congo.
Natural History: One of the most common lizards where it occurs, Jackson's forest lizard will be found on trees, fences, rock piles, roadsides, and other places where it may bask in direct sunlight. They can be seen foraging for small arthropods at temperatures up to 98° F (37° C). These relatively large lacertids only lay up to five eggs per clutch, but often do so in communal nests that may contain dozens of eggs.
Care: The terrarium should be tall enough to allow several vertical climbing branches as well as considerable floor space. They prefer direct light and should have UV light exposure for 4 to 10 hours daily. These very active lizards spend much of their time foraging for small live insect food, so they should be fed once or twice daily. Spray terrarium lightly to keep the humidity moderate to high.
Terrarium Suitability: 3

Agama agama (Linnaeus, 1758)
Rainbow Lizard

Family: Agamidae.
Length: SVL: 7.9 in. (200 mm). TL: 16.3 in. (415 mm).
Habitat and Range: Lives in fairly open, generally dry areas throughout much of Africa excepting the Sahara, south central, and southwestern regions.
Natural History: These lizards vary tremendously in color depending on sex, season, age, and activity. Females and young are often mottled brown, cinnamon, and ashy gray. Males tend to have a black, gray, or bluish body and tail, and the head may become bright yellow, orange or coral. These lizards are omnivorous, feeding on arthropods, small mammals, spiders, other lizards, flowers, and fruits. In areas with plenty of cover, near rocks or trees, a single adult male may live in a colony with many females and young. Adult males are fiercely territorial and will chase other males and unwanted females.
Care: The terrarium should be at least 3 ft. by 4 ft. (90 cm by 122 cm) for up to three adult lizards, with a sandy or soil substrate of at least 6 in. (15 cm.) Keep air temperature between 80° and 112° F (27° to 45° C) and a hotspot up to 140°F (60°C) during summer, allow it to drop to 50° F (10° C) for three to four months of winter. Humidity should stay below 60 percent. Provide UV light daily. Feed insects daily.
Terrarium Suitability: 2

Chamaeleo dilepis Leach, 1819
Flap-Necked Chameleon

Family: Chamaeleonidae.

Length: SVL: 5.9 in. (150 mm). TL: 15 in. (381 mm).

Range and Habitat: Found over most of southern and central Africa, from Nigeria east to Somalia and south to northern South Africa. Most common in dry forests, but this species may be found in most habitats within its range.

Natural History: *Chamaeleo dilepis* takes its common name from the two-lobed casque on its head, which is larger in males. The lobes of the casque are somewhat mobile, and the chameleon flares them outward when threatened or defending its territory. *C. dilepis* is one of the most abundant chameleons in Africa and is the species most likely to be seen by tourists. Like other chameleons, they dwell in trees and shrubs, but they will cross the ground to get from tree to tree. In the southernmost parts of their range, flap-necked chameleons reportedly hibernate during the coolest months. At least eight subspecies have been described; in all likelihood this is a complex of several species.

Care: Wild-caught flap-necks usually are dehydrated and parasite ridden, making them challenging to keep. Captive-bred ones are hardy for a chameleon. Keeping in conditions suitable for *Furcifer pardalis* (see Region 9b: Madagascar and Indian Ocean Islands) is suggested.

Terrarium Suitability: 3

Chamaeleo (Trioceros) jacksonii Boulenger, 1896
Jackson's Chameleon

Family: Chamaeleonidae.
Length: SVL: 5 in. (127 mm). TL: 13.5 in. (343 mm).
Habitat and Range: Distributed in humid forested regions of East Africa, from Kenya to Tanzania; introduced and thriving in Hawaii, parts of southern Florida, and possibly other locations.
Natural History: Male Jackson's chameleons possess three large facial horns, one above each eye and one on the snout tip. Females either lack the horns or have only very tiny versions. Jackson's chameleons are typically green but range from bright pale green to dark Kelly green. When ill or distressed they may become dark gray or black. This species likes relatively cool and humid climates. Females give birth to up to 35 tiny live young about five months after mating. Neonates feed on very tiny insects, such as fruit flies, young crickets, ants, and termites.
Care: Their captive needs are very specific. Use a tall screen cage with climbing materials and cover. Temperatures in the 70s (21° to 26°C) with a basking spot of 90°F (32°C) and humidity above 70 percent are needed. This species drinks from dripping water; investing in an automatic mister or humidifier on a timer is a good idea. Chameleons need a more varied diet than most other types of lizards; offer a wide range of small live arthropods.
Terrarium Suitability: 3

Chamaeleo (Triceros) quadricornis Tornier, 1899

Four-Horned Chameleon/Cameroon Bearded Chameleon

Family: Chamaeleonidae.

Length: SVL: 7.3 in. (185.4 mm). TL: 15 in. (381 mm).

Range and Habitat: Montane cloud forests of Cameroon; may also range into Nigeria.

Natural History: *Chamaeleo quadricornis* are spectacular lizards. They sport a sail-like crest running from the base of the neck down to the first fifth of the tail. This sail is more prominent in males. The number of horns varies from two to six, normally arranged in pairs between the tip of the snout and the eyes. Typically only males have the horns, but some females have them. This species lives in high-altitude rainforests with an annual rainfall of at least 100 inches (254 cm).

Care: Care is much like that for the related *Chamaeleo jacksonii*, but four-horned chameleons are more delicate and sensitive to high temperatures and dehydration. Keep the terrarium temperature between 72° and 76° F (22° and 24.5° C). The basking site should not be hotter than 80°F (26.5°C). This species does not bask frequently and tends to stay hidden in plant cover. Captive breeding of this species occurs somewhat regularly; unlike *C. jacksonii*, *C. quadricornis* lays up to eight eggs per clutch, and these hatch in five to six months. Life span is up to five years.

Terrarium Suitability: 4

Chondrodactylus angulifer Peters, 1870
Namibian Sand Gecko

Family: Gekkondiae.
Length: SVL: 3.3 in. (85 mm). TL: 6.7 in. (172 mm).
Habitat and Range: Botswana, Namibia, and South Africa, in the open deserts.
Natural History: This is a large-headed gecko with a stout body, noticeable tubercules, and brownish coloration that resembles the more northern genus *Tarentola*. It differs in having much shorter toes that lack adhesive pads; instead, the undersides of the toes are lined with comb-like structures that facilitate walking across fine sand. Males have white spots surrounded by dark brown or black rings; females lack light markings.
Care: The terrarium must offer considerable floor space and a layer of sand at least 8 in. (20 cm) deep. These lizards are expert burrowers that will make their own refuges. Provide direct light and four to ten hours of UV daily. Keep air temperature between 75° and 90° F (24° and 32° C). Feed them gut-loaded insects once or twice daily. Spray terrarium lightly with water once weekly. Females may lay clutches of two eggs every 10 to 14 days. Young hatch after about 60 to 90 days.
Terrarium Suitability: 3

defensive posture

Cordylus cataphractus Boie, 1828
Armadillo Lizard

Family: Cordylidae.

Length: SVL: 3.9 in. (100 mm). TL: 8.5 in. (216 mm).

Habitat and Range: Occurs in flat sandy, open areas with sparse vegetation in western South Africa.

Natural History: Armadillo lizards are smaller, less spiny relatives of the South Africa sungazer. They are found in loose soils that allow them to dig burrows. The scales at the rear of the sides of the head are large and spiny; those on top of the head are not. The name armadillo lizard comes from the very peculiar defense posture that lizards may assume when threatened with a predator: They roll into a ball by seizing the tip of the tail firmly in their mouths. The posture not only exposes all of the spiny scales to maximum defensive advantage, it gives the lizard a shape that snakes cannot swallow.

Care: Armadillo lizards are possibly the most commonly encountered species of the genus *Cordylus* in the pet trade. They may live for more than 12 years and are extremely hardy as terrarium animals. They feed on small arthropods, flowers, seeds, and diced fruits. Terraria must have a thick layer of slightly moistened loose sandy soil, and air temperature should range from 80° to 104° F (26.5° to 40° C). Six to 14 hours of UV light per day is recommended.

Terrarium Suitability: 1

Cordylus giganteus Smith, 1844
Sungazer

Family: Cordylidae.
Length: SVL: 8.9 in. (226 mm). TL: 15.7 in. (400 mm).
Habitat and Range: Occurs in flat or hillside habitats in central South Africa.
Natural History: At 400 mm, the sungazer is larger than the next largest member of the genus *Cordylus* (usually called armadillo lizards) by about 25 percent and is more than twice as large as most of the remaining species. The name "sungazer" comes from the typical posture of sun-basking lizards, with back and neck arched and head pointing skyward. They live in large colonies among series of long, fairly deep burrows to avoid excessive heat. When basking, they may partially emerge from the shelter or take a prominent place on a rock or log. They are a threatened species because much of their range is being converted into farmland.
Care: Captives are very difficult to breed, and females may produce only one or two young in alternate years. Being long-lived—up to 20 years—they also mature slowly. They feed on any smaller creature they can overpower and may take flowers and diced fruits. Terraria must have a thick layer of soil for the tunnels, and air temperature should range from 80° to 104° F (26.5° to 40° C). Six to 14 hours of UV light per day is recommended.
Terrarium Suitability: 3

Eumeces schneiderii (Daudin, 1802)
Schneider's Skink

Family: Scincidae.
Length: SVL: 9.4 in. (240 mm). TL: 15.7 in. (400 mm)
Habitat and Range: Broadly distributed across North Africa and eastern Europe east to Pakistan, in sparsely planted grasslands and desert edges where soil is loose or sandy.
Natural History: North African populations may have thin orange stripes interspersed with tiny white spots, while eastern European populations have an unpatterned gray-bronze dorsum and white undersides. Schneider's skinks tend to stay concealed during the day, thus avoiding the intense desert heat. They will forage near sunset and into the early twilight in search of small arthropods, flowers, and sometimes small lizards. Recently assigned to the genus *Novoeumeces*.
Care: Though difficult to observe in the wild, they are commonly available in the animal trade. Terraria must have a thick sand layer, and the lizards require food daily. They will take any insects or other small animals they can overpower and will also eat canned cat food. Provide direct light and temperatures between 86° and 110° F (30° and 43° C). Spray the sand with a fine mist once weekly and provide a bowl of clean drinking water at all times.
Terrarium Suitability: 2

Gerrhosaurus major Duméril, 1851
Great Plated Lizard/ Sudan Plated Lizard

Family: Gerrhosauridae.
Length: SVL: 13 in. (330 mm). TL: 22.6 in. (550 mm).
Habitat and Range: East Africa, from Eritrea to South Africa.
Natural History: A large species that resembles the unrelated American alligator lizards (genera *Gerrhonotus* and *Elgaria*), conspicuous for its large, thick scales. Great plated lizards live in a variety of habitats, from near rivers and streams to coastal seashores to open grassland. They are expert burrowers and may excavate long tunnels in which they escape intense heat and have a humid microhabitat. They are diurnal and primarily ground-dwelling, but may be found on the lower branches of brush and shrubs. Plated lizards are omnivorous, taking small vertebrates, eggs, insects, spiders, centipedes, flowers, and leafy vegetation as part of their diet. Females lay two to six eggs.
Care: They need both a fairly deep substrate and a large enough water area to allow total immersion. They quickly acclimate to captivity and allow handling. Provide temperatures between 86° and 110° F (30° and 43° C). There should be eight to ten hours of UV light daily. Feed lizards a variety of invertebrates, small rodents, and vegetables. Include several large and roomy hiding places; lizards will take refuge in large groups with no ill effect.
Terrarium Suitability: 2

Hemitheconyx caudicinctus Dumeril, 1851
Fat-Tailed Gecko

Family: Eublepharidae.
Length: SVL: 6.1 in. (155 mm). TL: 8.2 in. (207.6 mm).
Habitat and Range: Semi-arid regions of western Africa north of the equator. Found near rocks and where other debris provides cover. The related *Hemitheconyx taylori* is found in northeastern Africa.
Natural History: The fat-tailed gecko has a short oval tail; regenerated tails are extremely robust and give the lizard its common name. This purplish-brown lizard as two very broad dark purple bands on the back, each bordered by very thin white or pale lavender scales. Some have a thin white stripe running down the spine. Fat-tailed geckos are active at night when temperatures drop. They feed almost exclusively on live arthropods.
Care: Their terrarium needs several inches of very slightly moist sand to help retain adequate humidity (30 to 60 percent) under cover. Use palm fronds, coconut husks, bark sheets, or flat rocks as cover. Provide a small dish of clean drinking water, and feed lizards dusted insects; be sure they are dusted with calcium powder at each feeding. Use low wattage light bulbs (red are fine), and keep terrarium temperatures between a daytime high of 90° F (32° C) and a nighttime low of 78° F (26° C). Fat-tailed geckos have lived for over 16 years in captivity.
Terrarium Suitability: 1

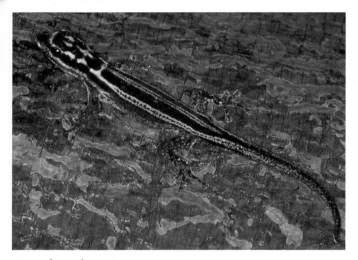

Lygodactylus picturatus (Peters, 1868)
African Yellow-Headed Gecko

Family: Gekkonidae.
Length: SVL: 1.6 in. (40.9 mm). TL; 3.5 in. (90 mm).
Habitat and Range: Lives in dry lowland forests and near villages from the Democratic Republic of the Congo east to Tanzania, and southern Ethiopia south to Zanzibar.
Natural History: Unlike most other geckos, this is a colorful diurnal species. While females are drab, with a gray and brown mottled pattern, males have a yellow head and forebody and a gray-green body and tail. There are two dark stripes along the dorsum, and the throat of males is black.
Care: These small insect eaters avoid direct sunlight and forage in crevices, under bark, and in other places near shelter. Nevertheless, they require high daytime temperatures of about 100°F (38°C). It is essential that there is also cooler shelter no warmer than about 82° F (28° C). Keep humidity between 70 and 90 percent, and lightly mist terrarium with water a few times weekly. There should only be one male per terrarium. Provide these geckos a variety of small insects such as fruit flies, wax worms, and small mealworms.
Terrarium Suitability: 2

Laudakia atricollis (Smith, 1849)
Blue-Throated Agama

Family: Agamidae.
Length: SVL: 5.7 in. (145 mm). TL: 13.4 in. (340 mm).
Habitat and Range: Forest-edged open savannah and dry open forest in East Africa, from southern Ethiopia south to Tanzania, and west to Democratic Republic of Congo.
Natural History: This is an active diurnal lizard that is often found in colonies of a dominant adult male plus several females and young. Males are olive or brown, and when warm, threatened, or mating, become black, with a blue head and forebody. The tail may be yellow or cream, sometimes with a blue tip. Females and young are mottled gray with square brown markings along the spine. These are among the few agamid species that will frequently climb into shrubs, trees, and on walls. Placed in the genus *Acanthocercus* by some authors.
Care: Captive animals need plenty of room and a pile of rocks or other suitable perching and basking sites. They like high temperatures between 86° and 110° F (30° and 43° C). There should be eight to ten hours of UV daily, with humidity between 50 and 75 percent. Blue-throated agamas are largely insect eaters but also take spiders, smaller lizards, baby rodents, flowers, and fruits. Females lay up to 15 eggs under large rocks, fallen logs, and in burrows. Young hatch after about 75 days.
Terrarium Suitability: 3

Mabuya striata (Peters, 1844)
Striped Skink

Family: Scincidae.
Length: SVL: 3.5 in (90 mm). TL: 9.4 in. (240 mm).
Habitat and Range: A wide-ranging skink found in most grassy and forest environments, and extending to sparsely vegetated arid areas. Found in eastern Africa, from northern Kenya south to South Africa.
Natural History: This is a broad-bodied species with a bronzy body and two conspicuous yellowish or tan stripes along the back. The iridescent scales may reflect bright flashes of color as the lizards dart among leaf litter and other low-lying cover. They tend to be most active during the midday, when they forage for the small insects, spiders, and fallen fruits upon which they feed. Skinks of the genus *Mabuya* are rather difficult to identify down to the species level, even for many herpetologists. Fortunately, most have similar lifestyles and ecological needs.
Care: Captives are very hardy and will take a variety of small live foods and diced pieces of fruit. They will drink from a dish but may also take water that is sprayed on vegetation. They are fairly easy to breed, producing up to ten live young per clutch. Keep terrarium temperature between 80° and 110° F (26.5° and 43° C). There should be eight to ten hours of UV daily, with humidity between 50 and 75 percent.
Terrarium Suitability: 1

Mochlus fernandi (Burton, 1836)
Fire Skink

Family: Scincidae.
Length: SVL: 7.9 in. (200 mm) TL: 13.7 in. (350 mm).
Habitat and Range: Coastal western Africa from Sierra Leone east to Uganda, and south into Angola. A resident of moist habitats, from stream sides to rainforests.
Natural History: These large skinks are brightly marked with a bronze back and alternating black and bright red lateral bars, with the females being less brightly colored than males. The tail of adults is bronze or brown, but in young it is banded with bright electric blue. Despite the flamboyant coloring, fire skinks are secretive, spending daylight hours foraging through forest cover—along fallen logs and rocks, and under leaf litter. Sometimes considered a member of *Lepidothyris* or *Riopa*.
Care: They are hardy terrarium animals that feed on all manner of small live foods, from insects to pink mice, along with fruits and some flowers. Keep terrarium between 80° and 110° F (26.5° and 43° C). There should be eight to ten hours of UV daily and humidity between 70 and 95 percent. Give lizards plenty of cover for hiding, including hardy live plants, and allow temperatures to vary from hot daytime to cooler (no lower than 68° F [20° C]) nights. They produce up to six eggs per clutch.
Terrarium Suitability: 3

Monopeltis leonhardi Werner, 1910
Kalahari Worm Lizard

Family: Amphisbaenidae.
Length: SVL: 11 in. (282 mm). TL: 11.8 in. (300 mm).
Habitat and Range: Almost completely fossorial, found in loose sandy soil of the Kalahari, southern Africa.
Natural History: Kalahari worm lizards represent the medium-sized members of the family Amphisbaenidae and are typical in color and appearance of many of the species. The pointed head is covered in large solid shields that are used to excavate tunnels. The nostrils are small and directed backwards, and the eyes are completely concealed by scales. There are no external ear openings or limbs. The pink to pale tan body is covered by small rectangular scales that are arranged in distinct rings, giving the creature a decidedly earthworm-like appearance. The tail is short, blunt, and not easily lost. Kalahari worm lizards' habits are reminiscent of the giant worms in Frank Herbert's *Dune* novels: they spend their time under the sand but strike to seize small animals that crawl near them. They seize prey animals—insects, centipedes, small lizards, and young rodents—and drag them beneath the sand to be consumed when they suffocate.
Care: There is essentially no available information on captive care of this species.
Terrarium Suitability: 4

Pachydactylus rangei (**Andersson, 1908**)
Web-Footed Gecko

Family: Geckkonidae.
Length: SVL: 2.3 in. (60 mm). TL: 5.5 in. (140 mm).
Habitat and Range: Restricted to sandy regions in the Namib Desert, from Angola to South Africa.
Natural History: A large-eyed nocturnal gecko that has a slender body, fine granular scales, and immense webbing between the digits that probably acts like snowshoes, distributing the lizard's weight to make walking on loose sand easier. The webbing also helps when the geckos excavate the comparatively deep tunnels they need in order to avoid the dangerous heat and dryness of the daytime desert. They forage from twilight and consume all small arthropods from scorpions to beetles. The Namib becomes quite fogbound at night, and the resulting early morning dew provides web-footed geckos with their water supply.
Care: This species has not done well in captivity, but captive breeding is increasing. Provide a terrarium with a deep layer of sandy substrate, formed into a series of low dunes; large flat rocks may also be added as shelter sites. The lower substrate levels should remain humid. Air temperatures should range between 80° and 95° F (26.5° and 35° C). Feed these lizards a variety of live gut-loaded insects daily. Mist as needed.
Terrarium Suitability: 4

Platysaurus capensis Smith, 1844
Cape Flat Lizard

Family: Cordylidae.
Length: SVL: 3.1 in. (80 mm). TL: 7 in. (176 mm).
Habitat and Range: Southern Africa, in arid rocky habitats. Look for these lizards along rocky walls, where they can take cover in extremely thin niches.
Natural History: Flat lizards are so named because of their greatly depressed bodies. Being so flat allows the lizards to find cover in tight recesses among rocks. Males are brightly colored blue or blue-green, with three very pale light stripes from the nape to the base of the tail; the tail may be maroon, orange, or brownish. Females and young are brown, with conspicuous stripes along the vertebrae and upper flanks; the tail is pale yellowish or tan. Cape flat lizards like high temperatures and may be seen basking in colonies of three to six individuals.
Care: Provide a roomy terrarium with one or two piles of flat rocks in which these lizards may take refuge. They will typically take refuge in large groups. There should be at least 2 in. (5 cm) of slightly moist sand or sand-soil mix substrate. Keep temperatures between 80° and 110° F (26.5° and 43° C), with a hotspot that may reach 135° F (57° C). Supply UV light daily. Feed these lizards a variety of gut-loaded insects daily. Spray the sand with a fine mist once weekly.
Terrarium Suitability: 2

Psammodromus algirus (Linnaeus, 1758)
Algerian Sand Lizard

Family: Lacertidae.
Length: SVL: 4.1 in. (104 mm). TL: 9.8 in. (250 mm)
Habitat and Range: Deserts and semi-desert habitats across northern Africa, from Morocco east to Tunisia, and in dry habitats in southern France.
Natural History: The Algerian sand lizard is the largest of the four similar species of the genus *Psammodromus*. The body is covered in shiny rectangular scales, and the tail is conspicuously long and cylindrical. The Algerian sand lizard is an active forager seen darting among tufts of vegetation in the early morning and late afternoon. It feeds on small invertebrates, including insects, spiders, and scorpions.
Care: Provide a roomy terrarium with one or two large flat rocks on which the lizards may bask. They should also have some branches or live potted plants in the enclosure. There should be at least 8 in. (20 cm) of very slightly moist sandy substrate. Keep temperatures between 80° and 110° F (26.5° and 43° C), with a hotspot that may reach 135° F (57° C). There should be eight to ten hours of UV daily. Feed these lizards a variety of gut-loaded insects daily. Spray the sand with a fine mist once weekly, and provide a bowl of clean drinking water at all times.
Terrarium Suitability: 2

Pseudocordylus melanotus (Cuvier, 1829)
Drakensberg Crag Lizard

Family: Cordylidae.
Length: SVL: 5.5 in. (140 mm). TL: 13 in. (334 mm).
Habitat and Range: Rocky areas in east-central South Africa.
Natural History: A large and conspicuous member of the armadillo lizard group, but lacking the large keeled body scales seen in true armadillo lizards (genus *Cordylus*). The back, head, and tail are chocolate brown, and the sides of males may be orange, pink, or yellow. In females and young the flanks are greenish or light brown. Look for Drakensberg Crag lizards basking in direct sunlight on large rocks. Diet includes a variety of small arthropods, small lizards, fruits, and some flowers.
Care: Provide a roomy terrarium with one or two piles of flat rocks in which the lizards may take refuge. There should be at least 8 in. (20 cm) of slightly moist sandy or sand-soil substrate. Keep temperatures between 86° and 110° F (26.5° and 43° C), with a hotspot that may reach 135° F (57° C). Supply UV light daily. Keep humidity between 55 and 75 percent. Feed these lizards a variety of gut-loaded insects daily and supplement with finely diced fresh fruits and vegetables two or three times weekly. Spray the sand with a fine mist twice weekly and provide a bowl of clean drinking water at all times. House only one male with up to three females per terrarium.
Terrarium Suitability: 2

Tarentola chazaliae (Mocquard, 1895)
Helmeted Gecko

Family: Gekkonidae.
Length: SVL: 8 in. (204 mm). TL: 4 in. (102 mm)
Habitat and Range: Coastal and near-coastal regions of Mauritania, Morocco, Senegal, and Western Sahara.
Natural History: This large-scaled gecko was long in a genus of its own, *Geckonia*. The enlarged scales are very obvious, and those along the rear margin of the skull form a slightly upturned frill—a bit like the dinosaur *Protoceratops*. Though they have the sticky toepads that would allow them to run along ceilings, helmeted geckos are largely ground dwellers that forage among stones, logs, and other ground debris. Movement is generally slow and deliberate, but can move quite rapidly in short bursts when alarmed or attacking an insect.
Care: The terrarium should be tall enough to provide some space for vertical branches for climbing. Provide several inches (10 cm or so) of fine sand substrate. Keep air temperature between 75° and 100° F (24° to 38° C) during summer, allow it to drop to 50° to 58° F (10° to 14.5° C) for three months of winter. Humidity may range from 60 to 90 percent. Feed daily; foods should include live insects treated with calcium and vitamin supplements. Females may lay two eggs in small excavated nests; incubate them at 84° F (29° C) and at 65 percent humidity.
Terrarium Suitability: 2

Tarentola mauritanica (Linnaeus, 1758)
Mediterranean Gecko/Crocodile Gecko/Moorish Gecko

Family: Gekkonidae.

Length: SVL: 3 in. (75 mm). TL: 6 in. (152 mm).

Habitat and Range: A native of the Mediterranean countries, where it favors arid and semi-arid habitats, including human homes and buildings. It has been introduced to several other locations around the world.

Natural History: This stout gecko has conspicuous enlarged scales that resemble small spikes, and the body scales are arranged in bands. Toes pads allow the bulky lizard to climb walls, windows, and ceilings, where they hunt insects, and they are easily observed around electric lights. Mediterranean geckos are brown to tan or pinkish, changing color depending on activity. They emit an audible chirp.

Care: The terrarium should be tall to provide ample placement of vertical branches for climbing. Keep air temperature between 80° and 112° F (26.5° to 44.5° C) during summer; you may allow it to drop to 50°F (10°C) for three months of winter. Humidity may range from 60 to 90 percent. Feed daily; foods should include live insects treated with calcium and vitamin supplements. These geckos will also accept earthworms. Females may lay two eggs in the substrate, on branches, or on terrarium walls. If possible, remove and incubate them at 82.5° F (28° C) and at 65 percent humidity. Young should hatch in five to seven weeks.

Terrarium Suitability: 1

Typhlosaurus lineatus Boulenger, 1887
Lined Legless Lizard

Family: Scincidae.
Length: SVL: 7 in. (180 mm). TL: 8.3 in. (210 mm).
Habitat and Range: A resident of the Kalahari Desert in South Africa and Namibia. Common in loose sand around the tufts of desert vegetation, especially in moist soils.
Natural History: Lined legless lizards are thin, smooth-scaled burrowers with no visible eyes or ear openings. The body is glossy black, and most individuals have bright yellow or orange-yellow bellies. Like many other legless lizard species, lined legless lizards spend all or the vast majority of their lives underground and may never expose themselves to sunlight. When rains soften soils, the lizards excavate new tunnels. These eventually harden as temperatures rise, giving the lizards a very secure set of "subway" tunnels. The tunnels, in turn, attract a variety of small invertebrates, in part because the prevailing humidity level stays fairly high and stable.
Care: A terrarium with a deep sandy substrate is essential. The lowest level of sand should be moist and the upper layers dry. Provide small live insects, especially mealworms, wax worms, and young crickets. Two to three large live young are produced.
Terrarium Suitability: 3

Uromastyx aegyptia (Forskal, 1775)
Egyptian Mastigure/Egyptian Uromastyx

Family: Agamidae

Length: SVL: 16.6 in. (423 mm). TL: 30 in. (765 mm).

Habitat and Range: The hottest desert habitats through much of northeastern Africa and the Arabian Peninsula, from Libya to Syria and Jordan south to lower eastern Egypt and east to Oman.

Natural History: This is the largest of the mastigures, and it is characterized by extremely small dorsal scales and rather dull gray coloring. Though these lizards are known to survive with a body temperature near 117° F (47° C), they do not routinely stay in situations that keep the body that hot for long. These mastigures escape the heat in burrows that are yards (meters) long and deep. Foods include a wide variety of vegetation, including grasses, seeds, flowers, and fruits, from which nearly all water is also obtained.

Care: Egyptian mastigures require large terraria. Provide a substrate of deep sand that will allow the lizards to excavate permanent burrows. Keep daytime air temperatures between 100° and 120° F (38° and 49° C), but allow drops to 65° to 70° F (18° to 21.5° C) at night. Keep humidity below 30 percent, but around 65 percent in the burrows. Provide UV light daily. Feed daily, offering collards, kale, grass, dandelions, bananas, melons, small birdseed, peas, beans, and berries.

Terrarium Suitability: 3

Uromastyx dispar maliensis Joger and Lambert 1996
Mali Uromastyx/Mali Spiny-Tailed Lizard

Family: Agamidae.
Length: SVL: 8.5 in. (216 mm). TL: 18 in. (457 mm).
Habitat and Range: The hottest desert habitats of northwest Mali and southwest Algeria.
Natural History: A stout-bodied lizard with small granular body scales, a blunt head that resembles a turtle's, a very spiny tail, and a dark dorsum with large yellow to orange patches on the back and sides. In males the yellow is bright, while in females it may be a lighter shade or orange. These lizards are active even during the hottest parts of the day. Like other mastigures, Mali uromastyx dig burrows that are at least 12 inches (300 mm) deep. Foods include a wide variety of vegetation, from which nearly all water is also obtained.
Care: Mali spiny-tails are popular beginners' lizards in the pet trade and are very hardy if given proper care. They require spacious terraria. Provide a substrate of deep sand that will allow the lizards to excavate permanent burrows. Keep daytime air temperatures between 90° and 105° F (32° and 40.5° C), but allow drops to 65° to 70° F (19° to 21° C) at night. Keep humidity below 30 percent, but about 65 percent in the burrows. Provide UV light daily. Feed daily, offering various greens, vegetables, fruits seeds, peas, and beans.
Terrarium Suitability: 2

A number of other *Uromastyx* occur in Africa. Although they tend to be found in inhospitable and rarely visited areas, several are present in the pet trade.

Uromastyx acanthinura
(Bell, 1825)

North African Uromastyx
SVL: 5.5in. (140 mm).

Uromastyx geyri
(Muller, 1922)

Saharan Uromastyx
SVL: 6 in. (153 mm).

Uromastyx ocellata
(Lichtenstein, 1823)

Ocellated Uromastyx/
Sudanese Uromastyx
SVL: 4.7 in. (120 mm)

Uromastyx ornata
(Heyden, 1827)

Ornate Uromastyx
SVL: 6.4 in. (163 mm).

Varanus albigularis Daudin, 1803
White-Throated Monitor/Cape Monitor/Black-Throated Monitor

Family: Varanidae.
Length: SVL: 30 in. (762 mm). TL: 65 in. (1,651 mm).
Habitat and Range: Sub-Saharan and eastern Africa, from southern Sudan to South Africa.
Natural History: White-throated monitors (which have a black-throated form) are widely distributed along Africa's eastern forests and savannas. They engineer long burrows into which they can retreat from the blistering sun. Prey and dentition alter radically as the lizards age. Juveniles have uniform long sharp teeth and feed on a variety of invertebrates and smaller reptiles. Adults have stouter teeth than the young, and the posterior teeth are broad and blunt. Diet then shifts predominantly to other vertebrates. Both cobras and vipers are included in the diet of white-throat monitors, and the lizards are immune to the effects of the snake's venom. They also consume snails.
Care: Care is very similar to that of the savanna monitor (*V. exanthematicus*), but white-throats generally need somewhat warmer and more humid conditions.Provide a hotspot of up to 140° F (60° C). Humidity should stay between 70 and 100 percent.
Terrarium Suitability: 3

Varanus exanthematicus (Bosc, 1792)
Savanna Monitor/Bosc's Monitor

Family: Varanidae.

Length: SVL: 23.8 in. (606 mm). TL: 53 in. (1,350 mm); generally much smaller.

Habitat and Range: Residents of grasslands and forests that border savannas in a broad band across central sub-Saharan Africa, from Senegal in the west to Sudan and Kenya in the east.

Natural History: The name describes the preferred habitat of these lizards: grasslands, fields, and forest-edge areas. It frequents places that experience intense seasonal rains followed by long dry periods. Juveniles are largely arboreal, becoming more terrestrial as they get larger. All ages eat a diet largely of live insects, but adults will also consume snails, centipedes, lizards, snakes, and rodents.

Care: Savanna monitors acan be hardy captives provided they are given an appropriate diet and temperatures, which need to range from 85° to 100° F (29.5 to 38° C). They can tolerate a wide range of humidity. Captives need clean drinking water in a large enough container to allow the lizards to completely soak. Though they dig in the wild state, captives do not require soil substrate if they are given adequate shelters in which to completely hide. Young will climb if given the opportunity, but this species is primarily terrestrial in habits.

Terrarium Suitability: 2

Varanus griseus (Daudin, 1803)
Desert Monitor/Gray Monitor

Family: Varanidae.
Length: SVL: 17 in. (432 mm). TL: 44.8 in. (1,140 mm).
Habitat and Range: Deserts from northeastern Africa east through the Arabian Peninsula to western India.
Natural History: Desert monitors have a wedge-shaped head with moderately broad temples and a narrow snout that is strongly constricted just in front of the eyes. The body is a sandy color, often highlighted with gray or reddish flecks, and there are several thin brown bands across the nape and back. The limbs and toes are comparatively short. The tail is round in cross section and slightly longer than the snout-vent length of the lizard. The tail also has dark rings its entire length. This species is adapted to life in some of the hottest deserts on earth, and may be active at an air temperature of 120° F (49° C). Their habitat makes desert monitors opportunistic feeders, taking any small live animals they can capture and overpower. They also feed on carrion.
Care: Specimens in terraria should be kept at temperatures above 80° F (26.5° C), but ideally in the 98° to 110° F (36.5° to 43° C) range. Like most other lizards, they need access to cooler areas away from the basking site so that they can regulate their own temperature.
Terrarium Suitability: 2

Varanus niloticus (Linnaeus, 1766)
Nile Monitor

Family: Varanidae.
Length: SVL: 49.2 in. (1,250 mm). TL: 108 in. (2,743 mm).
Habitat and Range: Found in and near watercourses across most of Africa excluding the Sahara and North Africa west of central Egypt.
Natural History: This is Africa's largest lizard, and it is a formidable predator that feeds on a variety of live foods—including crocodile eggs and young—and carrion. The teeth change from sharp and narrow in the young to broad and blunt in adults. Look for Nile monitors in habitats near standing water that include forest, tall grass, and seasonal grasslands. The snout tends to be more elongated than in other African monitors. Young are good climbers, while adults are mainly ground- and water-dwelling.
Care: Though extremely common in the pet trade, this is not a good species for any but advanced collectors and zoos. While a very few individuals will become quite tame in captivity, the overwhelming majority are tense, aggressive lizards. A pool of water must be present and cleaned frequently. Keep temperatures between 80° and 110° F (26.5° and 43° C), with a hotspot that may reach 135° F (57° C). Keep humidity between 70 and 95 percent. Feed these lizards a variety of gut-loaded prey.
Terrarium Suitability: 4

Xenagama taylori Parker, 1935
Club-Tailed Agama

Family: Agamidae.
Length: SVL: 3.5 in. (89 mm). TL: 4.3 in. (109 mm).
Habitat and Range: Arid and desert regions of central eastern Africa.
Natural History: These odd-looking lizards resemble the larger spiny-tailed agamas (genus *Uromastyx*), but the spiny tail has a leaf-like shape that terminates in short spiny tips. The spiny tail is used to plug up the burrow entrance to prevent predation. Males and females are similar in color, but males have large blue patches on the lower jaws. As residents of some of the hottest and driest habitats on Earth, club-tailed agamas are expert burrowers. They dig long, deep burrows where they can escape the most intense daytime heat and find refuge in the moist soil. The diet includes a broad variety of foods, including invertebrates, flowers, fruit, and leaves. Females lay up to five eggs per clutch and may lay four clutches per year.
Care: The terrarium should have a deep substrate of slightly moist sand for burrowing. Keep daytime air temperatures between 80°and 120° F (26.5° and 49° C), but allow drops to 65° to 70° F (19° to 21° C) at night. Keep humidity below 30 percent, but about 65 percent in the burrows. Provide UV light daily. Feed insects daily and a variety of greens, grasses, fruits, small birdseed, and peas twice weekly.
Terrarium Suitability: 3

Additional species that occur in Africa but are also found elsewhere are listed below. You may find species account for these lizards in the region section given in parentheses.

Acanthodactylus erythrurus (Region 10: Europe and Northern Asia)
Blanus cinereus (Region 10: Europe and Northern Asia)
Chamaeleo chameleon (Region 10: Europe and Northern Asia)
Lacerta lepida (Region 10: Europe and Northern Asia)
Scincus scincus (Region 8: Southern Asia and the Middle East)

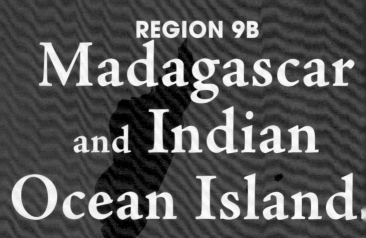

In zoological terms, Madagascar, the Seychelles, and other islands of the Indian Ocean are enigmas. Having separated from Africa some 150 million years ago, Madagascar has been largely on its own, little influenced by nearby continental faunas. About 90 percent of the wildlife of Madagascar, for example, is found nowhere else on Earth, though most Malagasy animals have distant relatives in Africa. Madagascar and its surrounding islands are home to the spectacular day geckos and the bizarre leaf-tailed geckos. Madagascar is also the place to see more types of chameleons than anywhere else, and these chameleons range from some of the Earth's smallest land vertebrates to much larger species capable of consuming small birds. Many of the region's reptiles have restricted ranges; the sad result of extensive logging and agriculture is that some species have become extinct because of habitat loss shortly after being discovered. On Mauritius, home of the extinct dodo, the lizards have fared better than the famed birds, but even so, some species have also gone into oblivion.

panther chameleon
(*Furcifer pardalis*)

Calumma parsonii (Cuvier, 1824)
Parson's Chameleon

Family: Chamaeleonidae.

Length: SVL: 15.8 in. (401 mm). TL: 27.7 in. (704 mm).

Range and Habitat: Primary rainforest in eastern and northern Madagascar; most common in montane forests from about 1,000 to 4,000 feet (305 to 1,219 m). Also found in suitable habitat on the islands of Nosy Boraha, Nosy Bé, and Ste. Marie.

Natural History: This is the second largest species of chameleon, and there are reports of individuals that surpass *Furcifer oustaleti* in length. Parson's chameleons stay high in the trees usually within dense foliage. These are extremely slow-moving and sedentary chameleons, sometimes staying in more or less the same spot for several days. They feed on a wide range of large insects, including stick insects, roaches, butterflies and their larva, locusts, and flies. They may also feed on small birds and lizards.

Care: This is one of the most challenging species of chameleon to keep; *C. parsonii* is prone to stress and dehydration. Care is much like that of *Chamaeleo jacksonii* (see Region 9a: Continental Africa), but *C. parsonii* requires much larger caging. Keep temperatures at the basking site no higher than 82°F (28°C). Provide plenty of cover in the form of live plants. Captive breeding of this species is rare. Parson's chameleon occasionally live more than 20 years.

Terrarium Suitability: 4

Chalarodon madagascariensis Peters, 1854
Malagasy Ground Iguana

Family: Opluridae.
Length: SVL: 4.7 in (120 mm). TL: 11.7 in. (298 mm).
Habitat and Range: Found in habitats with loose sandy soil in southern Madagascar.
Natural History: Unlike the other iguanas of Madagascar, this species has a long thin tail covered in small scales instead of large spines. Malagasy ground iguanas are active foragers, most likely to be seen as they rush across a flat area. They dig deep burrows into cooler soil for refuge and humidity. The diet is made mainly of insects and other invertebrates but will sometimes include flowers and fruits. Two to five eggs are laid under bark strips, rocks, other ground cover, or in holes dug by the females. They hatch after about 70 to 80 days.
Care: These are active lizards that need a spacious terrarium with at least 5 in. (13 cm) of sandy soil. Live plants may provide cover and climbing props. Provide temperatures between 70° and 82° F (21° to 28° C) with a warmer basking spot but allow a drop to near 68° F (20° C) for two to three months if you want to breed these lizards. Give them UV light daily. Feed C. *madagascariensis* gut-loaded live insects once or twice daily.
Terrarium Suitability: 2

Furcifer oustaleti (Moquard, 1894)
Oustalet's Chameleon

Family: Chamaeleonidae.
Length: SVL: 14 in. (350 mm). TL: 27.5 in. (700 mm).
Habitat and Range: The warmest regions of Madagascar in open areas such as grasslands and open woods.
Natural History: Oustalet's chameleon is the largest known species of chameleon. It is an are exceptionally slow-moving species, even within a family known for sluggishness. These chameleons may spend their entire lives on a single large tree, but they have also been observed on the ground. They are residents of the hottest and driest of the Malagasy environments. Unfortunately, not much else is known about their biology.
Care: Care is similar to that for other chameleons: These lizards need ventilated tall enclosures; provide plenty of climbing branches, high humidity, and full-spectrum lighting. An automatic misting system on a timer is recommended. The basking spot should reach 90° to 100°F (32° to 38°C). Feed a wide variety of invertebrate prey, along with the occasional pinky mouse, small bird, or small lizard. Females require moist cool substrate in which to deposit some 20 to 50 eggs. Incubate eggs in 1.5 parts perlite to 1 part water (by weight) at a temperature range of 82° to 88° F (28° to 31° C). Young should hatch in 210 to 280 days.
Terrarium Suitability: 3

Madagascar is home to the majority of the world's chameleons. Here are six more you might see there.

Calumma boettgeri
(Boulenger, 1888)
Blue-Nosed Chameleon
SVL: 2.8 in. (71.5 mm)

Calumma malthe
(Gunther, 1879)
Green-Eared Chameleon
SVL: 6in. (152 mm)

Furcifer campani
(Gunther, 1872)
Jeweled Chameleon
SVL: 3.3 in. (84.5 mm).

Furcifer labordi
(Grandidier, 1872)
Labord's Chamaleon
SVL: 6.1 in. (155 mm).

Furcifer lateralis
(Gray, 1831)
Carpet Chameleon
SVL: 4 in. (101 mm).

Furcifer rhinoceratus
(Boettgeri, 1893)
Rhinoceros Chameleon
SVL: 2.5 in. (63 mm).

Furcifer pardalis (Cuvier, 1829)
Panther Chameleon

Family: Chamaeleonidae.
Length: SVL: 10 in (260 mm). TL: 20.4 in. (520 mm)
Habitat and Range: An arboreal resident of sparsely vegetated areas in northeastern Madagascar (and offshore islands), Mauritius, and Réunion Islands.
Natural History: This giant chameleon is an aggressive inhabitant of bushes, shrubs, and trees throughout its range. Color and pattern vary considerably with locality. The dorsal crest is low, and there is always a light stripe along each side. The casque on the snout is especially well defined. Panther chamelons thrive in hot temperatures but tend to stay in the shade rather than direct sunlight. They can consume a variety of live prey, including arthropods, young lizards, and small mammals. Their size and ability to prey on many items allow panther chameleons to exploit new habitats and replace native species. Females lay up to 45 eggs per clutch.
Care: They are among the most hardy of chameleons in terraria, but there should be no more than one per enclosure. Keep humidity over 75 percent. Feed them live gut-loaded insects daily and provide baby rodents occasionally. Care is as for *F. oustaleti*.
Terrarium Suitability: 3

Furcifer verrucosus (Cuvier, 1829)
Giant Spiny Chameleon/Warty Chameleon

Family: Chamaeleonidae.

Length: SVL: 15.9 in. (403.9 mm). TL: 22.4 in. (570 mm)

Range and Habitat: Southern and southwestern Madagascar, mostly along the coasts. It is found in dry forests, thorn forests, and semi-deserts in the hottest parts of the island.

Natural History: The spiny chameleon takes its name for the serrated crest that runs along its dorsal surface; the crest is much more developed in males than in females. Although one of the longest chameleons, *F. verrucosus* is a very slender species. It adapts well to habitat alteration by humans, and its range seems to be increasing. It feeds on a wide variety of insects, other invertebrates, and small lizards. Females lay up to 50 eggs that hatch after about 200 days.

Care: Captive-bred *F. verrucosus* are sometimes available, but most of the specimens in the hobby are wild caught. If they are properly hydrated and rid of parasites, wild-caught specimens adapt quite well to captivity. Keep like *Chamaeleo calyptratus* (see Region 8: Southern Asia and the Middle East) only in a larger enclosure. Despite its size, *F. verrucosus* is a shy species and may not eat while being watched. They should be housed singly.

Terrarium Suitability: 3

Leiolopisma telfairi (Desjardins, 1831)
Telfair's Skink

Family: Scinicidae.
Length: SVL: 212 in. (8.3 mm). TL: 15.2 in. (385 mm).
Habitat and Range: Restricted to Round Island (east of Madagascar), where it occurs in all habitats from rocky slopes to fallen vegetation and leaf litter.
Natural History: Telfair's skinks are sleek animals, with an acute snout, thin but strong body, and long thin tail. The scales are glossy and smooth. The body may be gray or bronze, with tiny flecks of white and black. The belly is pale and unmarked. The limbs are well developed and strong. Most of the small vertebrates of Round Island are found nowhere else and are threatened or endangered. Among these are a species of boa (another is believed to have become extinct in the late 20th century) and a large drab day gecko.
Care: Though extremely rare in the wild—there are only about 5,000 Telfair's skinks left on Round Island—there are several captive colonies of these hardy lizards. They feed on small insects and other invertebrates but also take a variety of fruits, flowers, and nectar. They require moderate temperatures between 77° and 86°F (25° and 30° C), humidity at 80 to 100 percent, and plenty of low cover. They lay eggs.
Terrarium Suitability: 4

Oplurus cyclurus (Merrem, 1820)
Collared Ground Iguana

Family: Opluridae.
Length: SVL: 6.3 in (160 mm). TL: 9.8 in. (250 mm).
Habitat and Range: Grande Comore Island and southern Madagascar, where it lives in dry, open forests.
Natural History: A handsome and active lizard with a gray body covered in small white spots and tinier flecks. There is a thin black neck collar with a white posterior border; a second black and white band may be present across the shoulders. The tail is stocky and covered in large keeled scales that form distinct rings. Look for collared ground iguanas on tree trunks and roots, fairly close to the ground. They eat a variety of foods, taking insects, spiders, smaller lizards, and young rodents, fruits, nuts, and soft green leaves. In Madagascar, they may often be observed near an ant trail, eating the passing insects. They lay one to four eggs shortly after the cool season, and these hatch within 75 days.
Care: They require warm temperatures between 86° and 95°F (30° and 35° C), moderate humidity (70 to 85 percent), and cover. In captivity, this species has survived for more than nine years.
Terrarium Suitability: 1

Paroedura picta (Peters, 1854)
Panther Gecko/Ocelot Gecko/Malagasy Ground Gecko

Family: Gekkonidae.
Length: SVL: (mm). TL: 6 in. (150 mm).
Habitat and Range: Southern half of Madagascar in dry forests, thorn scrub, and savannas, usually near the coastline.
Natural History: Panther geckos are terrestrial geckos that lack adhesive toe-pads. However, they climb occasionally, especially as juveniles. The head is wide and appears too big for the body; males have proportionally larger heads than females. Most panther geckos have a pattern of irregular bands of light and dark brown and cream on the body and tail. There is a naturally occurring striped variety in which a white stripe runs down the spine from the back of the head to tip of the tail They are strictly nocturnal, hiding beneath leaves, stones, or bark or within small burrows during the day. They feed on any small invertebrates they can catch.
Care: Panther geckos are both hardy and prolific in captivity. Provide a terrarium with ample floor space and a substrate of soil or a sand/soil mix. Include numerous hiding places for the geckos. Temperatures can range from 78° to 88°F (25.5° to 31°C) during the day and can drop to 70°F (21°C) at night. Mist the enclosure regularly to maintain moderate humidity. Feed a variety of gut-loaded insects daily.
Terrarium Suitability: 1

Phelsuma cepediana Merrem, 1820
Blue-Tailed Day Gecko

Family: Gekkonidae.
Length: SVL: 2.3 in (58 mm). TL: 5.7 in (145 mm).
Habitat and Range: Moist forests of Mauritius.
Natural History: A beautiful member of the day gecko group, so named because active diurnally, as opposed to the nocturnal habits of most other geckos. The body is bright green, marked with reddish-orange spots. Large reddish stripes run from the nose to the hips. The tail is bright light blue. Females are less colorful than males. These geckos will most commonly be seen on vertical branches and on building walls. Diet includes small soft-bodied insects such as moths, ants, and flies. They also take nectar, pollen, and small fruits.
Care: They are more aggressive than most other day geckos, so males should be housed singly with females. Keep terrarium temperature around 77° to 82°F (25° to 28° C) and provide plenty of cover, preferably using live plants. Humidity must exceed 75 percent, and full-spectrum lighting is recommended. Give them a variety of foods daily: include small live gut-loaded insects, small worms, slugs, small berries and flowers, nectar, finely diced fruits, and baby foods. Mist the cage once or twice daily but do not let soil become wet. Females lay two eggs per clutch, and these hatch after 40 to 48 days.
Terrarium Suitability: 3

Phelsuma guentheri Boulenger, 1885
Round Island Day Gecko

Family: Gekkonidae.
Length: SVL: 5 in. (126 mm). TL: 11.8 in (300 mm).
Habitat and Range: Restricted to tiny Round Island east of Madagascar.
Natural History: Unlike most other day geckos, the Round Island day gecko is not bright green but a rather dull, dusky gray in coloration. Wild populations had been threatened by habitat destruction by introduced mammals, but subsequent elimination of the feral species has made reintroductions of captive-bred geckos possible. Cyclones have also devastated much of the large old trees on the island that once were the preferred habitat of the geckos. They now take refuge on smaller trees and among the island's rocky cliffs.
Care: Unlike other day geckos, this species requires both lower ambient air temperature (62° to 75° F [16.5° to 24°C) and lower humidity (65 to 78 percent) than other day geckos; they are very sensitive to higher temperatures and may quickly die when the temperature exceeds 80° F (26.5° C). They also require a few hours of UV lighting per day. Feed them gut-loaded insects. They also take seeds, flowers, finely diced fruits, and baby foods. They take most of their water from morning dew drops, so lightly mist the terrarium each morning. House only one male per enclosure.
Terrarium Suitability: 3

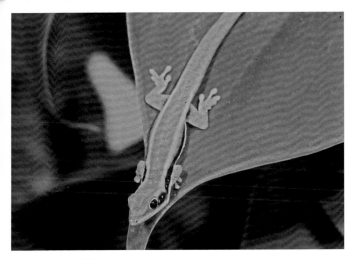

Phelsuma klemmeri Seipp, 1991
Neon Day Gecko

Family: Gekkonidae.
Length: SVL: 1.6 in. (40.6 mm). TL: 3.5 in. (90 mm)
Habitat and Range: Seasonal forests of northwestern Madagascar.
Natural History: Though tiny, the neon day gecko is one of the most brilliantly colored of lizards. The head and neck are yellow, and there are two neon blue stripes that extend from the neck and down much of the tail. There is a large black stripe on each flank, and the back is a mixture of dark blue and brown. Neon day geckos prefer living among live bamboos, which provide considerable climbing opportunities; when frightened and at night, they take refuge inside split bamboos.
Care: Though somewhat rare in the wild, several populations have been kept in captivity, largely in Europe. They require a thickly planted terrarium, a soft mossy substrate, and humidity over 75 percent. Air temperature should be 79° to 86° F (26° to 30° C), and a basking site heated to about 95° F (35°C) should be provided. They also require some access to full-spectrum light. They feed on nectar, mashed bananas, tiny crickets, and fruit flies. Foods should be dusted with calcium and vitamin supplements daily.
Terrarium Suitability: 3

Phelsuma laticauda (Boettger, 1880)
Gold-Dust Day Gecko

Family: Gekkonidae.
Length: SVL: 2 in. (51 mm). TL: 5 in. (130 mm).
Habitat and Range: Seasonal forests of northern Madagascar.
Natural History: This is a dull green day gecko with a few reddish dorsal markings and a characteristic pattern of numerous dust-like gold spots on the nape, shoulders, and most of the tail. The snout may have a blue triangle bordered by a pair of thin red chevrons. Gold-dust day geckos are common and widely distributed across northern Madagascar in a variety of habitats, including near human dwellings.
Care: They prefer some of the warmest temperatures of their genus, between 79° and 86° F (26° to 30° C) and can tolerate a range of humidity from 70 to 100 percent. Give them a basking site heated to about 95°F (35°C) and provide several hours of full-spectrum light daily. They feed on nectar, mashed soft fruits, tiny crickets, and fruit flies. Foods should be dusted with calcium and vitamin supplements daily. Females lay two eggs during the rainy season, and these hatch in about 45 days .
Terrarium Suitability: 3

Phelsuma madagascariensis (Gray, 1831)
Madagascar Day Gecko/Giant Day Gecko

Family: Gekkonidae.
Length: SVL: 4.2 in (106.8 mm). TL: 11.8 in. (300 mm).
Habitat and Range: Broadly distributed throughout Madagascar, in moist forest edges and near human habitation.
Natural History: Conspicuous bright green lizards with a maroon stripe that extends from the tip of the snout to the ear. There may be red, maroon, or orange spots distributed on the back and hips. As the common name implies, day geckos are active during the daytime. Madagascar day geckos and Round Island geckos tie as the largest members of their genus. They are usually residents of moist forests, where they spend considerable time high in the trees. However, in disturbed habitats they become common in and around houses and surrounding shrubs. Males are highly territorial and will not tolerate other males nearby. Interloping males are often seen being routed by the aggressive resident male. As with other day geckos, the skin of this species is easily sloughed if the lizard is seized, providing a quite unusual defense.
Care: Feeds on smaller animals from insects to young mice, flowers, and fruits. Care is as for *P. cepidiana* allowing for the difference in size.
Terrarium Suitability: 2

adult

hatchling

Phelsuma standingi Methuen and Hewitt, 1913
Standing's Day Gecko

Family: Gekkonidae.
Length: SVL: 5 in. (126 mm). TL: 11 in (280 mm).
Habitat and Range: Known only from moist forest and grassland habitats along the Onilahy River of southwest Madagascar.
Natural History: Large, pretty geckos that have a green body with gray-brown mottling. In young, the brown markings form distinct thin cross-bands. They dwell on trees that provide a variety of cover, including loose bark, leafy branches, and deep hollows. The southwest of Madagascar has seasonal temperature extremes that swing from a winter low of 57°F (14° C) to summer highs of 104°F (40° C), and humidity from 85 to 100 percent.
Care: Captives are hardy, but they require carefully controlled environments, including access to high intensity full-spectrum light. They also require plenty of cover and shaded spots. The use of several live plants in the terrarium is recommended, as is a constant drip system to provide water and maintain the high humidity geckos need. They feed on soft-bodied insects (crickets, wax worms), soft baby foods, and nectar. Care is as for *P. cepidiana* allowing for the difference in size.
Terrarium Suitability: 2

Tracheloptychus petersi (Grandidier, 1869)
Rainbow Plated Lizard

Family: Gerrhosauridae.
Length: SVL: 3.8 in (96.9 mm). TL: 8.3 in. (212 mm).
Habitat and Range: Most of south and central western Madagascar, in arid sandy and sparsely vegetated regions.
Natural History: Though much smaller than the African mainland plated lizards (genus *Gerrhosaurus*), the rainbow plated lizard is the most colorful of the group. The bronzy back and head are bordered by thin light dorsal stripes. The sides are lighter tan and bronze, with three rows of irregular white spots. The face and sides are light blue, more extensive and intense in males. The scales are large, rectangular, and arranged in symmetrical rows. Their preferred habitats are hot areas (95° to 106° F [35° to 41° C]) with loose and loamy soil. They forage around the bases of low plants and dig long, narrow burrows where they spend the nights.
Care: Terraria should have several inches of loose sandy substrate, lightly sprayed twice weekly; rainbow plated lizards tend to burrow and do best if they can do so. Provide intense direct lighting and several hours of UV daily. Provide daily feedings of gut-loaded live insects or small pink mice; supplement with finely diced fruits and vegetables twice weekly. They lay eggs, but little is known about their breeding needs.
Terrarium Suitability: 2

Uroplatus fimbriatus (Schneider, 1797)
Giant Leaf-Tailed Gecko

Family: Gekkonidae.
Length: SVL: 9.4 in. (237.6 mm). TL: 13 in. (330 mm).
Habitat and Range: Found in the moist rainforests of the eastern half of Madagascar.
Natural History: This is the largest of the peculiar leaf-tailed geckos of Madagascar. Though variable in color, with patterns that match tree bark on which they live, they are easily recognized by the huge eyes and short, spatula-shaped tail. The tail is very thin at the base. The head is very depressed and bears lateral fringes of skin along the lower jaw. When threatened, these geckos will hold the large jaws agape, revealing the bright red lining of the mouth. These nocturnal giants feed on any smaller creatures they can overpower.
Care: Terrarium animals require large tall enclosures containing several vertical branches of different diameters; branches with rough bark are preferred. Keep temperatures between 77° and 86° F (25° and 30° C). Humidity should range from 75 to 100 percent. The use of leafy live plants in the terrarium is recommended. Provide a dish of clean drinking water at all times. House males singly or with females. Feed lizards a variety of gut-loaded insects daily; supplement occasionally with pinky mice.
Terrarium Suitability: 3

Uroplatus henkeli Böhme and Ibisch, 1990
Fringed Leaf-Tailed Gecko/Henkel's Leaf-Tailed Gecko

Family: Gekkonidae.
Length: SVL: 5.6 in. (160 mm). TL: 10.2 in. (260 mm).
Habitat and Range: Found in the moist undisturbed rainforests of Nosy Be Island.
Natural History: The fact that this large gecko wasn't described by science until 1990 suggests two important facts: one, that there has only recently been any intense study of the zoology of Madagascar; and second, that these geckos are extremely difficult to see. Both sexes have a very pale gray to yellowish gray background color. Males have large dark brown spots and chevrons on the back, while females have gray-brown mottling. Though the short tail is spatula-shaped, it is not nearly so broad as that of the larger *Uroplatus fimbriatus*. They feed on any smaller creatures they can overpower.
Care: Captive animals require large tall enclosures and several vertical branches of different diameters. Care as for *Uroplatus fimbriatus*.
Terrarium Suitability: 4

Uroplatus phantasticus Boulenger, 1888
Satanic Leaf-tailed Gecko

Famliy: Gekkonidae.

Length: SVL: 2.2 in (55.8 mm). TL: 4 in (100 mm).

Habitat and Range: Known only from the forest east of Madagascar's capital, Antannarivo.

Natural History: Possibly the smallest of the Malagasy leaf-tailed geckos, this species also bears the most striking similarity to a dead leaf of all of the leaf-tailed geckos. The common name "satanic" refers to the spiny appearance of the head, not the lizard's disposition! The body is laterally compressed, with a distinct dorsal ridge, and there are ridges of skin along the lower flanks. The head has one or two small spiny projections over each eye, and the back of the head ends in a pair of dorsolateral points. The tail is long and acutely pointed, with deep scalloping along the edges. The overall shape and dead-leaf coloring of brown, red-brown, and yellowish give the animal excellent camouflage. Their activity is restricted to the lower parts of trees in wet rainforest. They reportedly may lay up to four eggs that females deposit in moist soil or inside rotting tree trunks. Eggs hatch in 70 to 90 days.

Care: Allowing for the difference in size, care as for *Uroplatus fimbriatus*, although *U. phantasticus* tends to do better at cooler temperatures (68° to 79°F [20° to26°C]).

Terrarium Suitability: 4

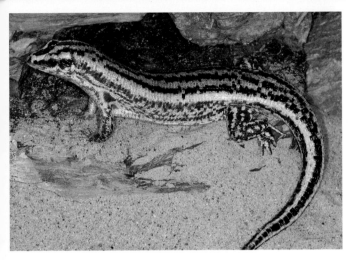

Zonosaurus maximus Boulenger, 1896
Giant Plated Lizard

Family: Gerrhosauridae.
Length: SVL: 9.4 in. (238 mm). TL: 27.6 in. (700 mm)
Habitat and Range: Madagascar, on the extreme southern coast.
Natural History: This large species closely resembles the unrelated American alligator lizards (genera *Gerrhonotus* and *Elgaria*) in having large thick scales, elongated body, and relatively short limbs. Giant plated lizards live near rivers and other fast-moving bodies of water, in which they forage for shoreline insects and escape from predators. Though most plated lizards are found in drier habitats, this species is a good swimmer. Giant plated lizards are diurnal, primarily ground-dwelling lizards but may be found on the lower branches of brush and shrubs. All members of the genus lay eggs. The tail can be dropped—the tail is easily lost—but a replacement does not grow in its place. Giant plated lizards feed on insects and worms, with an occasional small vertebrate—frogs in particular.
Care: They are adept burrowers that need both a fairly deep substrate and a water area that is large enough to allow total immersion. Keep the terrarium between 85° and 95° F (29.5° and 35° C), and do not house with smaller lizards.
Terrarium Suitability: 2

Europe and Northern Asia

eyed lizard (*Lacerta lepida*)

Greater Eurasia has a number of common and similar temperate lizard species, and the majority will only be active during the six or so warm months of the year. Both the number of species and their abundance is much sparser than in the other global regions (a bit more than half the family number of North America), but some places, such as Spain, Portugal, and Greece, have fairly conspicuous lizard faunas. Among the region's groups are amphisbaenids, chamaeleonids, agamids, geckonids, eublepharids, scincids, lacertids, anguids. There are no exclusively Eurasian families. Most species are small; the exceptions include Spain's eyed lizard and the widespread legless sheltopusik. Members of the family Lacertidae are the most widely distributed and likely to be observed, while several geckos are residents of the warmer Mediterranean areas.

Acanthodactylus erythrurus Schinz, 1933
Spiny-Footed Lizard

Family: Lacertidae.
Length: SVL: 2.9 in. (75 mm). TL: 9 in. (225 mm).
Habitat and Range: A resident of open sandy areas of the southern Iberian Peninsula and northern Africa east to northwestern India.
Natural History: This is an active diurnal species that moves across extremely hot desert sands in short bursts of speed interspersed by short pauses. It is very sensitive to temperature and is active when ambient air is 70° to 104° F (21° to 40° C). At other times, spiny-footed lizards will seek refuge in burrows under plants. They are possibly the fastest runners of the family Lacertidae. Young females lay four to six eggs in a single clutch, while older females may deposit two clutches per year. Young hatch after 70 days.
Care: Provide a terrarium with several inches of sandy soil and plenty of floor space. Both sexes are aggressive and will readily bite if handled. There should be no more than one male per terrarium. Feed lizards small insects, flowers, and diced fruits daily. Do not allow temperature to go below 68° F (20° C). Water is generally obtained from food, but these lizards may be misted once per week.
Terrarium Suitability: 2

Anguis fragilis Linnaeus, 1758
Slow Worm

Family: Anguidae.
Length: SVL: 5.7 in. (145 mm). TL: 15 in. (400 mm)
Habitat and Range: Open grassy areas across continental Europe and Great Britain, east into western Siberia.
Natural History: Despite the common name, the slow worm is neither slow nor a worm, but a member of a large family (Anguidae) that includes the sheltopusik and American alligator lizards. This is a shiny lizard with smooth silvery scales and a thin dark line running along the spine. There are no limbs or limb flaps. Moveable eyelids and external ear openings are present. Specimens from lower Greece, the Greek islands, and countries along the Aegean Sea may have tiny turquoise-blue spots on the dorsum and sides. This lizard is found under logs and boards and is active in fields, meadows, and lawns. It is primarily a slug eater but also consumes other small, soft-bodied arthropods.
Care: Slow worms are extremely hardy terrarium animals, and captives have survived in excess of 25 years. They need a simple terrarium setup, with soft soil (such as potting soil or peat), some live moss and grass, and some flat objects under which they can completely hide. Captives should be kept in the 68° to 75° F (21° to 24° C) range with a humidity of 60 to 85 percent.
Terrarium Suitability: 2

Blanus cinereus (**Vandelli, 1797**)
European Worm Lizard/Amphisbaenian

Family: Amphisbaenidae.
Length: SVL: 8 in. (200 mm). TL: 11.8 in. (300 mm).
Habitat and Range: Spain, Portugal, Algeria, and Morocco, in almost any type of soil. When rains soften substrate, worm lizards may make burrows that later bake into hard soil.
Natural History: This is Europe's only species of worm lizard; it is a light gray in color, with no markings. Young may be pink, and many adults retain a pale pink or tan head. Like other worm lizards, the body is ringed in scales, there are no visible eyes or ear openings, and the tail is extremely short. Theses lizards live almost entirely underground where they create their own tunnels and forage for worms, grubs, and ants. They are most likely encountered where soil is being turned over, such as in agricultural fields or gardens during plowing. Because they prefer fairly solid tunnels, they do most excavating (and hence are most likely to be encountered) during and after rains.
Care: Captives need a terrarium with at least 8 in. (20 cm) of soil with a clay base, and several flat pieces of bark or wood. They should always have a dish of clean drinking water and require a diet of earthworms, red worms, mealworms, and crickets.
Terrarium Suitability: 4

Chamaeleo chameleon Linnaeus, 1758
Mediterranean Chameleon/Common Chameleon

Family: Chamaeleonidae.
Length: SVL: 5.8 in. (147 mm). TL: 11.8 in. (300 mm).
Habitat and Range: A resident of low trees and bushes in dry habitats in southern Spain, Crete, Malta, the Canary Islands, across North Africa, and western Asia.
Natural History: This is one of only three chameleon species to occur naturally outside Africa and Madagascar. The Mediterranean chameleon lacks horns, crests, or other adornments that characterize many African species. Color change is modest, ranging from green to brown, but it is able to produce a variety of spotted, mottled, and banded patterns. These chameleons are primarily insect eaters, taking moths, crickets, and beetles, and will also sometimes feed on small flowers.
Care: They need warm temperatures (78° to 88°F [25.5° to 31°C]), plenty of air circulation, climbing branches, and full-spectrum lighting. They tolerate a wide range of humidity but usually will drink only from dripping water or misting. Care is similar to that of *Chamaeleo calyptratus* (see Region 8: Southern Asia and the Middle East).
Terrarium Suitability: 3

Gallotia galloti (Duméril and Bibron, 1839)
Western Canary Island Lizard

Famlily: Lacertidae.
Length: SVL: 5.7 in. (145 mm). TL: 14 in. (360 mm).
Habitat and Range: Rocky habitats protected from wind in the western Canary Islands. They can be seen at tourist sights such as Mount Teide National Park on Tenerife.
Natural History: These large members of the lacertid family are generally brown to olive, with light green markings. Males have distinct blue spots on the flanks; these spots are absent in young and females. Two similar species restricted to the Canary Islands are *Gallotia simonyi* and *G. stehlini*, but these grow to a much larger size (SVL: 200mm to 270 mm, respectively) and tend to be nearly uniformly dark brown or black. Introduced cats have decimated many populations and are the greatest threat to remaining lizards. They feed largely on soft vegetation and insects.
Care: Captive-bred specimens have become increasingly available, especially within the European herpetological community. Captives are hardy but need warm terraria with plenty of hiding places. A basking site should be heated to 91°F (33° C). Females lay up to seven eggs, and the young are large and can take crickets and small pieces of fruit and diced vegetables.
Terrarium Suitability: 2

364

Lacerta agilis Linnaeus, 1758
Sand Lizard

Family: Lacertidae.

Length: SVL: 3.8 in. (98 mm). TL: 9.6 in. (245 mm).

Habitat and Range: Most of Europe, from Britain east to central Asia, but absent from Spain and Italy. The disjunct distribution goes east to western Russia and far western Kazakhstan, and then continues with three population pockets in far eastern Kazakhstan.

Natural History: A handsome brown lizard with a central series of dashed light lines or spots down the back. Males have conspicuous green spots or blotches on the sides. Though common in sandy habitats, sand lizards are also found in fields, grasslands, near fences and walls, and in sunny valleys. Feeds on insects, slugs, worms, and flowers. Though their range covers a variety of climates, sand lizards tend to prefer warmth and tend to stay under cover on windy days. Sand lizards are legally protected in many places.

Care: Terrarium animals need a roomy enclosure with several inches (about 10 cm) of loamy sand with a layer of dry leaf litter. Keep the temperature between 70° and 90° F (21° and 32.5° C). in summer, and let it drop to 50° F (10°C) in winter. Provide UV lighting daily. Feed these lizards a variety of small live gut-loaded insects daily, and supplement with flowers, seeds, berries, and finely diced fruits.

Terrarium Suitability: 2

Lacerta lepida Daudin, 1802
Eyed Lizard

Family: Lacertidae.
Length: SVL: 8.3 in. (210 mm). TL: 24 in. (610 mm).
Habitat and Range: Dwells in dry forest areas from central France and northwestern Italy south through Iberia and northwestern Africa.
Natural History: This is the largest European lizard that has legs and is the largest member of its family. The body is green, with a series of irregular lateral blue spots and a dorsal network of tiny black markings. Juveniles are dull gray, with brown-ringed yellow or gray spots. The head scales are large and shiny, while body scales are small and granular. The eyed lizard is an active and formidable predator, taking any live food it can overpower—including lizards, small birds, and mammals— as well as flowers and fruit.
Care: Eyed lizards need a large terrarium and should be housed singly. They will attack other lizards, including their own species. They require an environment that provides warm dry summers and cool or cold winters. A heat lamp for one end of the terrarium is needed, and summer temperatures should be kept between 70° and 90° (22° and 32.5° C). Give these lizards UV lighting daily during the summer months and twice weekly in winter. Keep humidity between 45 and 70 percent, and make sure the terrarium is well ventilated.
Terrarium Suitability: 2

male

female

Lacerta viridis (Laurenti, 1768)
Green Lizard

Family: Lacertidae.
Length: SVL: 5.9 in (150 mm). TL: 15.7in. (400 mm).
Habitat and Range: Northern Spain and coastal France east to Turkey and Ukraine; north to Germany and Slovakia; mainly in steppes and grassy areas. Now extinct in Poland. This species has also been accidentally introduced to and still thrives in Shawnee County, Kansas, U.S.A.
Natural History: Only the eyed lizard is a larger European lacertid species. *L. viridis* is also bright green but lacks the large lateral spots of the eyed lizard. Males in breeding condition have a bright blue throat and lower jaws. However, coloration is highly variable, and may contain more brown on the back in some areas. Females usually have a pale yellowish stripe on each side that runs from between the eyes to at least the base of the tail. Green lizards are truly omnivorous, feeding on insects, spiders, small eggs, young mice, and other lizards, as well as flowers, seeds, berries, and soft green leaves. They are generally active from mid-April until early October. Look for them in open areas that have a fair amount of green grassy cover or other cover such as fallen logs, rocks, or other debris. Females lay 6 to 23 eggs in spring, and these hatch after 7 to 15 weeks.
Care: Care is similar to that for *Lacerta lepida*.
Terrarium Suitability: 2

Ophisaurus apodus (Pallas, 1775)
Sheltopusik

Family: Anguidae.
Length: SVL: 20.3 in. (515 mm). TL: 57.8 in. (1,470 mm).
Habitat and Range: Eurasia from central Europe east through the Urals and central Russia.
Natural History: The sheltopusik is a large-scaled lizard that looks like an armored snake. Though long known to Europeans and Asians, there has been relatively little fieldwork done on this species. Young sheltopusiks are mottled silver and black, but this coloring fades after about two years, when the lizards take on the ochre dorsal and pale yellow ventral coloration. Their natural diet consists primarily of snails, slugs, worms, small lizards, snakes (including vipers, whose fangs cannot penetrate the armored scales), and small rodents.
Care: The sheltopusik has a reputation for both extreme docility and a lifespan of 20 years or more. Provide a large terrarium filled with branches and rocks over which they may climb and bask. They can tolerate a wide range of humidity and temperatures, so keeping them at room temperatures with a basking spot is acceptable. In the wild they hibernate between October and March or April, so a cooling period is recommended. Feed them small rodents, lizards, snails, slugs, worms, and canned dog food three or four times per week.
Terrarium Suitability: 2

Podarcis lilfordi (Günther, 1874)
Lilford's Wall Lizard

Family: Lacertidae.
Length: SVL: 3.2 in. (80 mm). TL: 8.7 in. (220 mm).
Habitat and Range: Rocky and sparsely vegetated habitats on Majorca, Minorca, and nearby islands east of Spain.
Natural History: This beautiful species occurs in two distinct color varieties. One is black with deep blue spots on the sides and belly. The other has a broad green dorsal stripe, brown sides, and tiny dark spots. This is an elongated lean and lithe lizard that on sunny days seems never to stop its rapid exploring of rocks, logs, and other ground debris for insect foods. Lilford's wall lizards also readily consume spiders, flowers, and soft leaves during the day.
Care: The terrarium may be kept between 50° and 86° F (10° and 30° C), and provide several hours of UV light daily. Give the lizards some rocky mounds to climb on. Spray lightly with water every two or three days. They do best if they have two or three daily feedings of small live insects, such as one- to five-week old crickets, wingless fruit flies, and wax worms. Supplement with small flowers, small berries, and seeds.
Terrarium Suitability: 3

Podarcis muralis (Laurenti, 1768)
European Wall Lizard

Family: Lacertidae.
Length: SVL: 2.9 in. (75 mm). TL: 6.5 in. (165 mm).
Habitat and Range: Found in a wide variety of open habitats from villages to mountainsides across central continental Europe, from northern Spain and France east and south to Italy and Greece.
Natural History: The scientific name *muralis* is Latin for "wall" and refers to the most likely place to see these lizards. They sun and perch on walls, large rocks, and many manmade objects (trash cans, boxes, etc.). Color variation is extreme, from green-spotted black populations in west central Italy to brown and tan marbled specimens across much of the the rest of their range. Food consists mostly of insects and flowers.
Care: Requires the same care as *Pocarcis sicula*.
Terrarium Suitability: 2

Podarcis sicula (Rafinesque, 1810)
Italian Wall Lizard

Familyi: Lacertidae.
Length: SVL: 3.5 in. (90 mm). TL: 10 in. (260 mm).
Habitat and Range: Italy, Sicily, Corsica, and associated islands; the coast of the eastern Adriatic Sea and well into the continent and European Turkey; small isolated populations in southern France and in Spain also exist. Also established as accidental introductions in West Hempstead, New York; Philadelphia, Pennsylvania; and Topeka, Kansas in the U.S.A. Occurs in a wide variety of habitats, but prefers open or shrubby habitat to mountain or forest areas.
Natural History: This is an active and omnivorous lizard that is generally found on the ground or along low brick or stone walls. It is among the species most likely to be encountered around human habitations. Though very variable in color and pattern, Italian wall lizards are generally some shade of green—ranging from grass green to an olive drab.
Care: Captive animals need a roomy enclosure with several inches of loamy sand for digging. Provide a few mounds of flat rocks on which they can climb and find refuge. Keep temperatures between 70° and 90° F (22° and 32.5° C). year-round. Provide UV light daily. Feed them a variety of small live gut-loaded insects daily and supplement with weekly offerings of flowers and diced berries.
Terrarium Suitability: 2

Zootoca vivipara (Linnaeus, 1758)
Viviparous Lizard

Family: Lacertidae.
Length: SVL: 2.6 in. (65 mm). TL: 7.6 in (195 mm).
Habitat and Range: Broadly distributed across Europe, from Ireland north into Scandinavia, and east to Pacific coastal Russia and China.
Natural History: This lizard may have the greatest contiguous range of all lizards. It also has the most northerly distribution of all reptiles, well into the Arctic Circle in northern Scandinavia. Across most of its range, this cold-tolerant lizard gives birth to live young, but populations in some warm localities of the far southwest of its range lay eggs. The head shields are large, smooth, and shiny in the sunlight. Viviparous lizards are common in heath, grassland, and sandy areas with low scrub vegetation, where they hunt small invertebrates.
Care: Terrarium animals need a roomy enclosure with several inches (10 cm) of loamy sand for digging. Provide hollow branches, tree bark, or flat rocks. Keep temperatures between 70° and 90° F (22° and 32.5° C) in summer, and let them drop to 45° to 53° F (6.5° to 11.5° C) in winter. Provide several hours of UV lighting during the summer months. Feed these lizards a variety of small live gut-loaded insects daily and supplement with weekly offerings of flowers, seeds, berries, and finely diced fruits.
Terrarium Suitability: 2

Additional species that occur in Europe and northern Asia but are also found elsewhere are listed below. You may find a species account for these lizards in the region section given in parentheses.

Eumeces schneiderii (Region 9a: Continental Africa)
Laudakia stellio (Region 8: Southern Asia and the Middle East)
Psammodromus algirus (Region 9a: Continental Africa)
Tarentola mauritanica (Region 9a: Continental Africa)

Professional Academic Resources

American Society of Ichthyologists and Herpetologists
(publishers of *Copeia*)
Maureen Donnelly, Secretary
Grice Marine Laboratory
Florida International University
Biological Sciences
11200 SW 8th St.
Miami, FL 33199
Telephone: (305) 348-1235
E-mail: asih@fiu.edu
www.asih.org

Association of Reptile and Amphibian Veterinarians (ARAV)
P.O. Box 605
Chester Heights, PA 19017
Phone: 610-358-9530
Fax: 610-892-4813
E-mail: ARAVETS@aol.com
www.arav.org

Association of Zoos and Aquariums
8403 Colesville Rd.
Suite 710
Silver Spring, MD 20910
Telephone: (301) 562-0777
Fax: (301) 562-0888
www.aza.org

Australian Herpetological Society
(publisher of *Herpetofauna*)
www.ahs.org.au

Australian Society of Herpetologists
John Wombey, Secretary
c/o CSIRO Wildlife and Ecology
PO Box 84, Lyneham, ACT 2602

Australia
Email: J.Wombey@dwe.csiro.au

The Herpetologists' League
(publisher of *Herpetologica*)
/www.herpetologistsleague.org/en/

Society for the Study of Amphibians and Reptiles (SSAR)
(publisher of *Journal of Herpetology* and *Herpetological Review*)
Marion Preest, Secretary
The Claremont Colleges
925 N. Mills Ave.
Claremont, CA 91711
Telephone: 909-607-8014
E-mail: mpreest@jsd.claremont.edu
www.ssarherps.org

Deutsche Gesellschaft für Herpetologie und Terrarientiere
(publishers of *Salamandra*, *Mertensiella*, and *Elaphe*)
www.dght.de/ag/schlangen/index.html

Herpetological Societies
Amphibian, Reptile, and Insect Association
23 Windmill Rd.
Irthlingsborough
Wellingborough NN9 5RJ
England
www.arianorthampton.com/page2.htm

British Herpetological Society
11 Strathmore Place
Montrose, Angus
DD10 8LQ
United Kingdom
www.thebhs.org

Center for North American Herpetology
www.cnah.org

Chicago Herpetological Society
Phone: (312) 409-4456
www.chicagoherp.org

Herpetological Association of Africa
web.wits.ac.za/Academic/Science/APES/
Research/MWLab/HAA/

International Herpetological Society
8 Buxton Lane
Frizinghall, Bradford
W. Yorks, BD9 4LP
England
Telephone: 01-274-548342
E-mail: ihsnewsletter@yahoo.co.uk

Kansas Herpetological Society
Phone: (785) 272-1076)
www.ukans.edu/~khs

League of Florida Herpetological Societies
www.jaxherp.tripod.com/league.htm

Nebraska Herpetological Society
www.nebherp.org

Northern Ohio Association of Herpetologists (N.O.A.H.)
NOAH, Department of Biology
Case Western Reserve University
Cleveland, OH 44106-7080
www.noahonline.info/site_down

San Diego Herpetological Society
PO Box 503835
San Diego CA 92150
E-mail: sdhs@sdherpsociety.org
www.sdherpsociety.org

Western New York Herpetological Society
www.wnyherp.org/index.php

Information sources

General Herp Information
Convention on International Trade in Endangered Species (CITES)
www.cites.org

Field Museum of Natural History
request article reprints at:
www.fmnh.org/research_collections/zoology/aandr_reprints.htm

International Reptile Conservation Foundation
www.IRCF.org

The Lizard Wizard
www.thelizardwizard.co.uk/care_guides.htm

The Reptile Forums
www.reptileforums.com

Virtual Museum of Natural History
www.curator.org

Agamids
BeardedDragon.org
www.beardeddragon.org

Dragon Attack (sailfin dragons)
www.sailfindragon.com

Melissa Kaplan's Herp Care Collection: Water Dragons
http://www.anapsid.org/waterdragons.html

UK Bearded Dragons
www.ukbeardeddragons.co.uk

The Uromastyx Home Page
www.kingsnake.com/uromastyx

Anoles

Anolis Contact Group
www.acg.saumfinger.de

Todd Jackman's Anole Page
www87.homepage.villanova.edu/todd.jackman/anolis/anolis.html

Chameleons

AdCham
www.adcham.com

Chameleons Online
www.chameleonsonline.com

Geckos

Gecko Network
www.geckonetwork.com

GeckoForums.net
www.geckoforums.net

The Gex Files
www.the-gex-files.nl/

Global Gecko Association
www.gekkota.com

Leopard Gecko Guide
www.leopardgeckoguide.com

Iguanids

Cyclura.com
www.cyclura.com

Green Iguana Society
http://www.greenigsociety.org

Iguana Specialist Group
www.IUCN-ISG.org

International Iguana Foundation
http://www.iguanafoundation.org/index.php

Jen Swofford's Iguana Pages
www.baskingspot.com/iguanas/

Utila Iguana Recovery Program
www.utila-iguana.de

West Coast Iguana research (ctenosaur information)
www.westcoastiguana.com

Skinks
BlueTongueSkinks.net
www.bluetongueskinks.net/

Corucia.myfreeforum.org
corucia.myfreeforum.org/

Tegus
The Tegu Community Forums
www.thetegu.com/

Varanids
International Varanid Interest Group, (publishers of *Biawak*)
www.varanidae.org

Monitor-Lizards.net
www.monitor-lizards.net

References

There are some excellent books about lizards in different parts of the globe, but many are not in English. Nevertheless, all the books listed have excellent illustrations and photos, so even if the text is difficult to read, the pictures should aid in proper identification of species.

Lizards in General

Badger, David. 2002. *Lizards: A Natural History of Some Uncommon Creatures*. Voyageur Press, Stillwater, MN.

Pianka, Eric, and Laurie Vitt. 2003. *Lizards: Windows to the Evolution of Diversity*. University of California Press, Berkeley.

Sprackland, Robert. 2009. *Giant Lizards. Second Edition*. TFH Publications, Neptune, NJ.

Sprackland, Robert. 1977. *All About Lizards*. TFH Publications, Neptune, NJ.

North America

Conant, Roger, and Joseph Collins. 1998. *Reptiles and Amphibians: Eastern/Central North America. Third Edition*. Houghton Mifflin, Boston.

Smith, Hobart. 1946. *Handbook of Lizards*. Comstock/Cornell University Press, Ithaca, NY.

Stebbins, Robert. 2003. *Western Reptiles and Amphibians. Third Edition*. Houghton Mifflin, Boston.

Caribbean Islands

Maclean, William. 1982. *Reptiles and Amphibians of the Virgin Islands*. Macmillan, London.

Malhotra, Anita, and Roger Thorpe. 1999. *Reptiles and Amphibians of the Eastern Caribbean*. Macmillan, London.

Schettino, Lourdes. 2003. *Anfibios y Reptiles de Cuba*. Instituto de Ecología y Systemática, Habana.

Mexico and Central America

Beletsky, Les. 1999. *The Ecotravellers' Wildlife Guide: Tropical Mexico*. Academic Press, San Diego.

Espinal, Julio, Hobart Smith, and David Chiszar. 2004. *Introduction to the Amphibians and Reptiles of the State of Chihuahua, Mexico*.

Universidad Nacional Autónoma México.

Grismer, Lee. 2002. *Amphibians and Reptiles of Baja California*. University of California Press, Berkeley.

Köhler, Gunther. 2000. *Reptilien und Amphibien Mittelamerikas. Band 1: Krokodile, Schildkröten, Echsen*. Herpeton Verlag, Offenbach, Germany.

Leenders, Twan. 2001. *A Guide to Amphibians and Reptiles of Costa Rica*. Zona Tropical, Miami.

Savage, Jay. 2002. *The Amphibians and Reptiles of Costa Rica: A Herpetofauna between Two Continents, between Two Seas*. University of Chicago.

South America and the Galapagos

Avila-Pires, T. 1995. *Lizards of Brazilian Amazonia*. Zoologische Verhandelingen Leiden, 299.

Bartlett, Richard, and Patricia Bartlett. 2003. *Reptiles and Amphibians of the Amazon*. University Press of Florida, Gainesville.

Cei, J. 1993. *Reptiles del noroeste, nordeste y este de la Argentina. Herpetofauna de las selvas subtropicales, Puna y Pampas*. Monografia XIV. Museo Regionale di Scienze Naturali, Torino.

Cei, J. 1986. *Reptiles del noroeste, nordeste y este de la Argentina. Herpetofauna de las zonas áridas y semi áridas*. Monografia IV. Museo Regionale de Scienze Naturali, Torino.

Coloma, Luis, and Santiago Ron. 2001. *Megadiverse Ecuador*. Centro de Biodiversidad y Ambiente, Quito.

Donoso-Barros, Roberto. 1966. *Reptiles de Chile*. Universidad de Chile, Santiago.

Gasc, Jean-Pierre. 1990. *Les Lezards de Guyane*. Editions Raymond Chabaud, Paris.

Hoogmoed, Marinus. 1973. *Notes on the Herpetofauna of Surinam IV*. Dr. W. Junk, The Hague.

Murphy, John. 1997. *Amphibians and Reptiles of Trinidad and Tobago*. Krieger, Malabar, FL.

New Guinea, New Zealand, and Oceania

Bauer, Aaron, and Ross Sadlier. 2000. *The Herpetofauna of New Caledonia.* Society for the Study of Amphibians and Reptiles.

McCoy, Michael. 1999. *Reptiles of the Solomon Islands.* (CD-ROM); Zoographics, Kuranda, Australia.

McKeown, Sean. 1980. *Hawaiian Reptiles and Amphibians.* Oriental Publishing, Honolulu.

Morrison, Clare. 2003. *A Field Guide to the Herpetofauna of Fiji.* Institute of Applied Sciences, University of the South Pacific.

Robb, Joan. 1986. *New Zealand Amphibians & Reptiles.* Collins, Auckland.

Ryan, Paddy. 2000. *Fiji's Natural Heritage.* Exisle, Auckland.

Australia

Cogger, Harold. 2000. *Reptiles & Amphibians of Australia. Sixth Edition.* Ralph Curtis Books, Sanibel Island, Florida.

Wilson, Steve, and Gerry Swan. 2003. *Reptiles of Australia.* Princeton Field Guides, Princeton, NJ.

Southeast and Eastern Asia

Chan-Ard, Tanya, Wolfgang Grossman, Andreas Gumprecht, and Klaus-Dieter Schulz. 1999. *Amphibians and Reptiles of Peninsular Malaysia and Thailand.* Bushmaster Publications, Wuersalen.

Daniel, J. 2002. *The Book of Indian Reptiles and Amphibians.* Oxford University Press, Mumbai.

Das, Indraneil. 2007. *Amphibians and Reptiles of Brunei.* Natural History Publications (Borneo), Kota Kinabalu.

Das, Indraneil. 2004. *Lizards of Borneo; a Pocket Guide.* Natural History Publications (Borneo), Kota Kinabalu.

Das, Indraneil. 2002. *Snakes and other Reptiles of India.* Ralph Curtis Books, Sanibel Island, FL.

Goris, Richard. 2004. *Guide to the Amphibians and Reptiles of Japan.* Krieger, Malabar, FL.

Inger, Robert, and Tan Fui Lian. 1996. *The Natural History of Amphibians and Reptiles in Sabah.* Natural History Publications (Borneo), Kota Kinabalu.

Manthey, Ulrich. 2008. *Agamid Lizards of Southern Asia.* Edition Chimaira, Frankfurt.

Manthey, Ulrich, and Wolfgang Grossman. 1997. *Amphibien & Reptilien Südostasiens*. Natur und Tier Verlag, Münster.

McKay, J. L. 2006. *A Field Guide to the Amphibians and Reptiles of Bali*. Krieger, Malabar, FL.

Zhao, Er-Mi, and Kraig Adler. 1993. *Herpetology of China*. Society for the Study of Amphibians and Reptiles.

Ziegler, Thomas. 2002. *Die Amphibien und Reptilien eines Tieflandfeuchtwald Schutzgebietes in Vietnam*. Natur und Tier Verlag, Münster.

Southern Asia and the Middle East

Leviton, Alan, Steven Anderson, Kraig Adler, and Sherman Minton. 1992. *Handbook to Middle East Amphibians and Reptiles*. Society for the Study of Amphibians and Reptiles.

Continental Africa

Auerbach, R. 1985. *The Reptiles of Gaborone*. Botswana Book Centre, Gaborone.

Branch, Bill. 1998. *Field Guide to Snakes and other Reptiles of Southern Africa*. Ralph Curtis Books, Sanibel Island, FL.

Spawls, Stephen, Kim Howell, Robert Drewes, and James Ashe. 2002. *A Field Guide to Reptiles of East Africa*. Academic Press, San Diego.

Madagascar and Indian Ocean Islands

Glaw, Frank, and Miguel Vences. 2006. *Field Guide to the Amphibians and Reptiles of Madagascar. Third Edition*. Vences and Glaw Verlags GbR.

Henkel, Friedrich-Wilhelm, and Wolfgang Schmidt. 2000. *Amphibians and Reptiles of Madagascar and the Mascarene, Seychelles, and Comoro Islands*. Krieger, Malabar, FL.

Europe and Northern Asia

Arnold, E., J. Burton, and D. Ovenden. 1992. *Collins Field Guide: Reptiles & Amphibians of Britain & Europe*. Collins, London.

Bruno, Silvio. 1986. *Tartarughe e Sauri d'Italia*. Giunti, Firenze.

Szczerbak, Nikolai. 2003. *Guide to the Reptiles of the Eastern Palearctic*. Krieger, Malabar, FL.

Subject Index

Index

Common Name Index

Index

GUIDE TO LIZARDS

Index

Index

Scientific Name Index

Index

Acknowledgements

I extend my sincere thanks to the many friends and colleagues who have contributed information for this book. To my publisher, Christopher Reggio, and editor, Tom Mazorlig, I extend my thanks for their considerable interest and help in this project. Many people and institutions kindly made specimens and literature available to me for my studies. In reference to this book I extend my thanks to my friends and colleagues for their unselfish help: Ben Aller, E.N. Arnold, Walter Auffenberg, Michael Balsai, Jelena Basta, the late Mark Bayless, Ilaiah Bigilale, Wolfgang Böhme, Harold Cogger, Patrick Couper, Tim Criswell, Neil Davie, Daniel Diessner, Michael Dlooglach, Giuliano Doria, Bernd Eidenmüller, Kelsey Engel, Susan Evans, Danté Fenolio, Samuel Gabriel, Maren Gaulke, Anthea Gentry, Tupolam Gire, Harry Greene, Ulrich Gruber, Rainer Günther, Marinus Hoogmoed, Hans-Georg Horn, Raymond Hoser, Grant Husband, the late Steve Irwin, the late Dennis King, Max King, Konrad Klemmer, Günther Kohler, the late Bert Langerwerf, Bill Love, Robyn Markland, Colin McCarthy, Rob McInnes, the late Sean McKeown, Joe McMahon, the late Robert Mertens, Mark O'Shea, the late H.G. Petzold, Barry and Pat Pomfret, Paul Rodriquez, Ron Roper, José Rosado, Andy and Jane Rowell, Ross Sadlier, Glenn Shea, Ben Siegel, Frank Slavens, Becky Speer, Peter Strimple, Gerry Swan, Geoffrey Swinney, Anne Sylph, Michel Thireau, Rainer Thissen, Stella Thissen, the late Garth Underwood, Jens Vindum, Klaus Wesiak, Sandy Whyte, Rudolf Wicker, and the late Eric Worrell. Institutions that provided access to specimens were: Alexander Koenig Museum (Bonn), American Museum of Natural History, Australia Zoo, Australian Museum, Australian Reptile Park, California Academy of Sciences (San Francisco), California Zoological Supply (Santa Ana), The Field Museum of Natural History, Florida State Museum, Frankfurt Zoo, Glades Herp (Ft. Meyers), House of Reptiles, Jungle Larry's (Naples, FL), LLL Reptile, London Zoo, The Museum of Comparative Zoology (Harvard), The Museum of Vertebrate Zoology (Berkeley, CA), The Natural History Museum (London), the National Museum of Natural History (Leiden, the Netherlands), The National Museum of Natural History of Paris, The National Museum of Papua New Guinea, The National Museums of Scotland (Edinburgh), The Natural History Museum of Vienna, ProExotics, Queensland Museum, San Diego Zoo, Senckenberg

Museum (Frankfurt), University College London, Woodland Park Zoo (Seattle), the Zoological Museum of Amsterdam, the Zoological Museum at Munich, and the Zoological Museum at Berlin. Financial assistance to conduct much of my research and travel was generously provided by The Linnean Society of London, The San Diego Herpetological Society, The Shoestring Foundation, and The University of London. As ever, my most special thanks go to my wife, Teri, for her three decades of unstinting encouragement and companionship from the bush of Australia to the Great Basements of Europe. I also want to acknowledge the contributions of my dear companion of nearly 11 years, King (1998-2009). He kept me company and made sure I took necessary breaks during most of the writing and photography work that went into this book. He is, and ever will be, sorely missed.

About The Author

Robert George Sprackland, Ph.D., has studied reptiles for more than 50 years. He is the Director of Science for The Virtual Museum of Natural History at www.curator.org, a non-profit scientific and educational organization that provides species accounts and conducts tropical biodiversity surveys, principally in Australia and New Guinea. He studied herpetology at the University of Kansas (BA), San José State University (MA), University College London (Ph.D.), and the National Museums of Scotland (postdoctoral). His published books include *All About Lizards*, *Giant Lizards*, *Aquaterrariums*, *Care of Savannah and Grasslands Monitors*, and the CD-ROM *Key to the Sharks and Rays of the World*. He has also published articles in periodicals including *Natural History*, *Reptiles*, *American School Board Journal*, *Nikkei Electronics Asia*, *Herpetological Review*, *Military History Quarterly*, *Tropical Fish Hobbyist*, *High Tech Careers*, and others.

Photo Credits

Alle (courtesy of Shutterstock): 378; Ben Aller and Michaela Manago: 276; Randall D. Babb: 25, 28 (inset), 31, 37, 45, 50, 90, 102, 108, 320; Marian Bacon: 82, 85, 93, 118, 132, 236, 255, 287, 308, 336, 341 (bottom left), 342, 351; Joan Balzarini: 289; R. D. Bartlett: 4, 17, 18, 19, 32, 20, 38, 39, 48, 53, 60, 62, 66, 68, 69, 71, 73, 76, 78, 79, 81, 88, 101, 104, 113, 120, 122, 127 (inset), 131, 133, 139, 157, 173, 201, 220, 226, 240 (bottom right), 246, 247, 249, 250, 256, 264, 286, 290, 291, 295, 304, 314, 328, 334, 341 (center left and right), 343, 355, 364, 365, 368; John Bell (courtesy of Shutterstock): 3, 64, 144, 375; Horst Bielfeld: 369; Adam Black: 12, 146; Wolfgang Boehme: 259; Ryan M Bolton: 98; Allen Both: 219, 277, 331; Jon Boxall: 44; Walter J. Brown: 67, 74; Marius Burger: 302, 310 (inset), 341 (top right), 352 (inset); John Coburn: 180; Suzanne L. Collins: 40, 43, 46, 70, 77; Scott Corning: 260, 261; Mike Cota: 266; Steve Cukrov (courtesy of Shutterstock): 96; Eco Print (courtesy of Shutterstock): 309; Steve Estvanik (courtesy of Shutterstock): 275; Five Spots (courtesy of Shutterstock): 376; Carl J. Franklin: 92; Paul Freed: 41, 84, 123, 134, 138, 143, 148, 149, 152, 154, 167, 169, 176, 182, 187, 189, 202, 206, 210, 232, 233, 234, 252, 273, 284, 315, 341 (top left), 344, 357; S.R.Ganeshand and S.R. Chandramouli: 268 ; James E. Gerholdt: 28 (large), 30, 21 (top left, bottom right), 324, 353; Raymond Hoser: 240 (top right); Ray Hunziker: 21 (bottom left), 174; Eric Isselée (courtesy of Shutterstock): 8 (top); Pieter Janssen (courtesy of Shutterstock): 340; V. T. Jirousek: 166, 170, 205, 363; Mike Knight: 87; Wayne Labenda: 171; Anna Lafrentz (courtesy of Shutterstock): 313; Bert Langerwerf: 142; Michael Ledray (courtesy of Shutterstock): 307; Patrick LeFebvre: 329 (top left and right, bottom right); Mario Lopes (courtesy of Shutterstock): 358; M. Lorentz (courtesy of Shutterstock): 377; Erik Loza: 221; Anthony Mahadevan (courtesy of Shutterstock): 285; Shawn Mallan: 126; Michaela Manago: 274; Barry Mansell: 45, 103 (inset), 106; Morgan Mansour (courtesy of Shutterstock): 379; Peter J. Mayne: 21 (center left); Sean McKeown: 6, 16, 111, 112, 151, 345, 347, 348, 350; G. and C. Merker: 11, 33, 56, 100, 110, 282, 288, 294, 318, 349, 356; Jan Messersmith: 161; Sherman Minton: 181; L.A. Mitchell: 178; Byron W. Moore: 305; John C. Murphy: 253, 278; Kenneth T. Nemuras: 75; Aaron Norman: 21 (top right), 22, 55, 59, 127 (large), 245, 248, 262, 265, 338; Mella Panzella: 293; Matt Paschke (courtesy of Shutterstock): 333; Jonathan Plant: 322, 360, 362, 366, 367, 370, 372; Carol Polich: 13, 29, 51, 52, 339, 341 (bottom right), 346; Robert Porter: 240 (top left); R. Powell: 80; Dr. Morley Read (courtesy of Shutterstock): 136; Soo Jen Ric (courtesy of Shutterstock): spine; Dinal Samarasinghe: 292; Mark Smith: 97, 107, 137, 141, 244, 270, 280, 352 (large); Robert G. Sprackland: 36, 72, 124, 125, 129, 140, 150, 153, 156, 160, 168, 175, 186, 188, 190, 191, 204, 211, 227, 235, 237, 238, 239, 240 (center right), 251, 254, 258, 263, 272, 279, 298, 332, 371; Karl H. Switak: 21 (center right), 23, 24, 26, 27, 34, 42, 47, 49, 54, 57, 58, 61, 83, 99, 103 (large), 114, 121, 128, 130, 155, 172, 184, 185, 200, 208, 209, 218, 228, 240 (center left, bottom left), 267, 303, 306, 310 (large), 311, 312, 316, 317, 319, 321, 323, 325, 326, 327, 329 (bottom left), 330, 354, 361; Nikita Tiunov (courtesy of Shutterstock): back cover; John Tyson: 8 (bottom); U.S. Geological Survey: 105; R. W. Van Devender: 95, 109, 115, 135, 183, 203, 207, 269, 271; Jeremy Wee (courtesy of Shutterstock): 242; Arnaud Weisser (courtesy of Shutterstock): 1; Ashley Whitworth (courtesy of Shutterstock): cover